TRANSITION IN THE BALTIC STATES

Transition in the Baltic States

Micro-Level Studies

Edited by

Neil Hood

Robert Kilis

and

Jan-Erik Vahlne

HC 243 .T72 1997

First published in Great Britain 1997 by
MACMILLAN PRESS LTD
Houndmills, Basingstoke, Hampshire RG21 6XS and London
Companies and representatives throughout the world

A catalogue record for this book is available from the British Library.

ISBN 0–333–67733–1

First published in the United States of America 1997 by
ST. MARTIN'S PRESS, INC.,
Scholarly and Reference Division,
175 Fifth Avenue, New York, N.Y. 10010

ISBN 0–312–17235–4

Library of Congress Cataloging-in-Publication Data
Transition in the Baltic states : microlevel studies / edited by Neil
Hood, Jan-Erik Vahlne and Robert Kilis.
p.   cm.
"This book is based on the proceedings of an interdisciplinary
conference entitled 'Microlevel Studies of the Transition in the
Baltic States' held from 16 to 18 August 1995 in Riga, Latvia, and
organised by the Stockholm School of Economics in Riga"—CIP galley.
Includes bibliographical references (p.   ) and index.
ISBN 0–312–17235–4 (cloth)
1. Baltic states—Economic conditions—Congresses.   2. Post
-communism—Economic aspects—Baltic States—Congresses.
3. Business enterprises—Baltic States—Congresses.   I. Hood, Neil.
II. Vahlne, Jan-Erik, 1941–   III. Kilis, Robert.   IV. Microlevel
Studies of the Transition in the Baltic States (1995 : Riga, Latvia)
HC243.T72   1997
338.5'0947'409049—dc20   96–38948
                                                                            CIP

This book is printed on paper suitable for recycling and made from fully managed and sustained
forest sources.

10   9   8   7   6   5   4   3   2   1
06   05   04   03   02   01   00   99   98   97

Printed and bound in Great Britain by
Antony Rowe Ltd, Chippenham, Wiltshire

Contents

SECTION THREE: SECTORAL EXAMPLES

SECTION FOUR: CONCEPTUAL CONSIDERATIONS

List of Figures

List of Tables

Preface and Acknowledgements

This book is based on the proceedings of an interdisciplinary conference entitled *Micro-level Studies of the Transition in the Baltic States* held from 16 to 18 August 1995 in Riga, Latvia, and organised by the Stockholm School of Economics (SSE) in Riga.

The topic of the conference emerged as a reaction to a prolonged debate on the issues concerning the transition in Central and Eastern Europe. This debate has been predominantly conducted from a macro-level perspective, and it is evident that merely confining it to an economic approach can give only partial answers to many of the key questions. Transformation processes are clearly multiplex, and interlinks between social, political, psychological, cultural, and economic factors must be tackled properly and deeply.

In order to contribute to the debate and approach the transformation process from both a micro and an interdisciplinary approach, it seemed desirable to combine the expertise of forty-three Baltic and Western scholars who were invited to take part in the conference. The selection of papers published here reflect the wide spectrum of views, disciplines and perspectives represented at the conference.

The editors would like to acknowledge the assistance of staff at SSE Riga who organised the conference, and in particular would like to recognise the distinctive role which Robert Kilis played in identifying and bringing the participants together. They would also like to record their sincere thanks to Irene Hood of the University of Strathclyde for her heroic efforts in assisting the editorial process and her extensive liaison with all the contributors. Finally the editors record their gratitude to the Marcus Wallenberg and Prince Bertil Foundations, and to the British Council, for their sponsorship of the conference.

List of Contributors

Danute Budreikate   Lithuanian Academy of Sciences, Vilnius, Lithuania

Anthony F. Buono   Bentley College, Waltham, Mass., USA

Alex Fleming   World Bank, Washington, USA

Jaroslaw Górniak   Jagiellonian University, Cracow, Poland

Neil Hood   SIBU, University of Strathclyde, Glasgow, UK

Gregory Jedrzejczak   World Bank, Washington, USA

Jan Jerschina   Market and Public Opinion Research Institute, CEM, Cracow, Poland

Robert Kilis   Stockholm School of Economics in Riga, Latvia

Gundar J. King   Pacific Lutheran University, Tacoma, USA, and the Riga Business School, Latvia

Kari Liuhto   Institute for East–West Trade, Turku School of Economics and Business Administration, Turku, Finland

Igors Ludborzs   Coopers & Lybrand, Riga, Latvia

Niels Mygind   Centre for East European Studies, Copenhagen Business School, Copenhagen, Denmark

Garri Raagmaa   Estonian Institute for Future Studies, Tallinn, Estonia

Slavo Radosevic   Science Policy Research Unit, University of Sussex, Brighton, UK

Gediminas Rainys   Economic Research Centre, Vilnius, Lithunia

Richard Rose   Centre for the Study of Public Policy, University of Strathclyde, Glasgow, UK

Laimonis Rumpis   Latvian Academy of Sciences, Riga, Latvia

George Schöpflin   London School of Economics, London, UK

David Smallbone   Centre for Enterprise and Economic Development Research, Middlesex University, Enfield, UK

Maaja Vadi Tartu University, Tartu, Estonia

Jan-Erik Vahlne Gothenberg Business School, Gothenberg, Sweden

Urve Venesaar Estonian Academy of Sciences, Tallinn, Estonia

Hans-Joachim Zilcken Stockholm School of Economics in Riga, Latvia

1 Introduction
Neil Hood, Jan-Erik Vahlne and Robert Kilis

AGENDA

'Transition' has become a key word in contemporary thinking about the series of complex changes taking place in the post-socialist world. While theorists and policy-makers are still debating the questions concerning the depth and future direction of these changes, it is clear by now that a turbulent period of transformation has involved almost everybody within these countries from leading businessmen, politicians, entrepreneurs, and bureaucrats to small shopkeepers, farmers, housewives. Although a 'quantum jump' has not yet happened and there are still numerous strains and stresses, it is unlikely that East European people will turn back to their communist past. Emerging market mechanisms increasingly pervade the economy and society, and it is time to carefully consider how economic actors and social groups not just adapt to a new economic environment, but also struggle to form the new rules of the game.

H.J. Wagener distinguishes three types of transitional change among which the transformation of the economic system is the most important. It entails both a change of the economic order, namely the constitutionally or otherwise imposed rules and institutions of economic life, and a change of economic behaviour which, unfortunately has not been given due attention by the research community. Without an adequate knowledge of this element, we can not hope, stresses Wagener, to build a general theory of transition (Wagener, in Saunders, 1992, p. 390). Further, to understand the behavioural patterns of the people and the workings of the social system in transitional countries is even more important, because the transition is not an automatic and predestined process. It is a time of choices, serious decisions and radical uncertainty.

In pursuing their individual goals, the actors draw upon their historical and social experience. Each choice and move in its turn acts as a 'catalyst' for the formation of other acts and decisions, and is irre-

versible. A person cannot do for him or herself what is done for others.
Given the inherited variety of experience and current interests, the
enactment of individual goals in aggregate result in different organisational forms and principles. These supplement the total repository of the
contending strategies and ideologies out of which new institutional
structures and business culture emerge. The agents, be they individuals
or social groupings, learn from each other and adapt to new trajectories
open to them, actively searching for new ideas and exemplars to follow.
Even the most conservative strategies require a huge input of imagina-
tion and effort. To know which scenario is likely to be dominant and
what kind of rules of the game will finally be formed is to know what
decisions have been and are possible, and which have been made by
whom and why. These trajectories of individual decisions, however
close or distant they might be from the power centre, will in aggregate
shape the paths of this passage to a market economy. The focus of the
research presented within this volume is on the microlevel not only in
the sense of how macro-economic and political factors and policies
work though the actions of individuals and groups, but also as to how
the problems and successes in the microlevel niches structure the environment for political decisions and influence the subsequent efficiency
of the implemented policies.

Transition is a complex change. It is not only that the constituent elements of a market are interdependent, and several transformative
processes are happening simultaneously but with different speed, but
equally because of the intricate links between micro- and macro-level
activity patterns. The link between macro-economic reforms and the
actual growth process is not a direct one but it is mediated through a
complex texture of social relations. As is mentioned several times by
contributors to this book, one cannot hope to deduce the essential characteristics of individual units from macro-economic statistics, such as
GDP or productivity levels in industry, or income distribution per
household. This is not just because of the viciousness of averaging, but
more because relevant causal links between the two halves are left
unpacked in a single though multiplex indicator. The changes in the
behaviour of household members or of managers of enterprises are
neither a single numerical expression of a general tendency in a statistical yearbook, nor an inevitable complication of the initial structural set-
up of the political design. No single academic approach alone could
possibly accommodate the complexity of intertwining causal chains in a
unified model – so there is a visible need for an inter-disciplinary
approach, such as that offered in this volume.

REGION

The focus of the chapters is on the Baltic States – Estonia, Latvia and Lithuania. In contrast to Central and East European (CEE) countries, which maintained their sovereignty over the past fifty years, the Baltic States, as part of the USSR, were fully integrated into the Soviet economic and political system. After the collapse of the command economy, they had an additional task to those faced by CEE countries, namely to build autonomous and viable economic systems. To make the task more difficult, the Baltic States had to enter the world of the so-called post-industrial economy that itself is rapidly changing. Coupled with the advent of flexible specialisation, capital decentralisation and increasing globalisation (Harvey, 1989), is the challenge of possible future political and economic integration into the European Union. By and large, it is a radically different environment from that of the 1920s when, for the first time, they gained independent nationhood.

During the past six years, in contrast to the rest of the former USSR, the three states have made vigorous moves towards breaking ties with the Soviet system, joining the international community, establishing both a market economy and a parliamentary democracy. As noted by many observers, they have made considerable progress on the way.[1] Having successfully implemented the liberalisation stage, established well functioning and stable national currencies, the three states are speeding up the privatisation process, restructuring legal frameworks and attracting foreign investment. The overall picture seems to suggest a steady recovery from the post-independence crisis.[2] In fact, some analysts (*Business Eastern Europe*) put Estonia in the leading group of CEEC, with Latvia and Lithuania in the second. In the political sphere, all three governments have expressed a strong wish to join the EU and NATO, despite the strong warnings issued by the Russian side. At the time of putting this volume together, they are the only remaining republics of the former USSR which have not rejoined the CIS.

There are perhaps several reasons why the Baltics have done surprisingly well in comparison to the other Soviet republics and some CEE countries. They had certain historical advantages which made them more flexible in adopting radical transitional strategies and embarking upon the building of a market economy. Those worth mentioning include the shortest period of Soviet rule, a skilful workforce and developed infrastructure, relative sophistication of the economies, the presence of high-tech industries, advanced agriculture (especially dairy and meat production), plus the remains of a historical tradition of private enterprise, and a strong national consensus with regard to the goals of the transition. At the same time, the inheritance from belonging to the USSR is a heavy one. One particular remnant is a relatively high proportion of large state-owned industrial enterprises for which neither the resources nor the market for their output are present at local level. After regaining independence, the supply of material inputs and energy from the FSU ceased to be cheap, and traditional Eastern markets disappeared. However, the incurred social costs of supplementing low wages to masses of predominantly Russian-speaking workers (especially in Estonia and Latvia) in these enterprises are quite often seen as a political time bomb. It should also be noted that during Soviet rule, the Baltic republics had very limited trading connections with the rest of the world, which meant that the practices of international trade had to be learned simultaneously with the struggle to enter new export markets. The other, cultural, residue is that the loss of property rights, which was reinforced by a lack of individual incentives, might have transformed the previously motivated and dynamic Baltic people into more passive objects in the service of distorted societal interests. In many ways this background has impacted upon their way of thinking.

The uniqueness of the Baltic States goes deeper in history, however, especially if the differences between the three countries are taken into account. Early and rapid industrialisation and the presence of a large Russian-speaking minority, as well as a somewhat different historical trajectory under the influence of German culture and Lutheran religion, have made Estonia and Latvia different from Lithuania. The latter has Catholic traditions with an absolute national majority, closer ties to Poland and longer history of the predominance of agriculture. In addition, cultural and geographic proximity to Finland made it easier for Estonia to embark upon a path of more radical reforms and do so earlier than its neighbours. It should also not be forgotten that due to various historical and social reasons, the image of peasant lifestyle and values and those of the countryside in general as a source of national values, is a powerful popular disposition which still informs the ideological life of the Baltic nations. These factors result in a distinctive work ethic and outlook on the part of the majority of the middle and older generations of Estonians, Latvians, and Lithuanians. Finally, as aptly pointed out by Graham Smith (Smith, 1994, p. 5), both elites and populations draw heavily on the image of the golden age of the interwar republics, and these references play a significant legitimising role in the forming of new social institutions. This is most visible in the field of citizenship rights. Given all this, it seems fruitful to look upon the historical and cultural uniqueness of the region, its history and differences between the three countries as a good test case for a comparative analysis of the successes and failures of the reforms which are being undertaken on the route towards a market economy.

ISSUES

The transition in the Baltic States, as with any other major social change, constitutes a difficult task for researchers, not the least because complex contemporary developments are still too close to be able to provide a basis from which to read off the pattern of the trends that will undoubtedly dominate the future. The principal purpose of this volume has been to try to identify some of the basic constituents and catalysts of the transformation as seen from a bottom-up perspective. In addition, in order to comprehend the links between the many antecedents and consequences of the process and its context, an interdisciplinary approach has been adopted to relate economic changes to political, social and cultural domains. The contributors have tried to provide answers to some *key questions*, such as: What kinds of reforms have been successful? Which failed? What difficulties have owners, managers, employees and households encountered and how have these problems been dealt with? What are the main cultural and psychological barriers of the reform process? Where are the main obstacles likely to be in the future? What lessons can be drawn from the countries which started the transition process earlier? The chapters have focused on certain of the key issues, weaving around them a discussion of a broader range of other topics.

In the words of Winiecki, the list of developments in the transition period that had been expected to happen and did actually happen is rather short (Winiecki, 1993, p. 107). It is now a generally shared view that the progress of East European economies towards a market economy has not been as smooth as initially expected (Buckley and Ghauri, 1994, p. 6). One of the reasons for that is the role of what George Schopflin (Chapter 15) calls the intangibles of transition – values, attitudes, behavioural dispositions from the past. If western economies are based on institutions and infrastructural support systems developed over centuries, including predictable administrative policies, educated customers, experienced entrepreneurs, then in the transitional economies, such as the Baltic States, they are yet to be firmly established. The three countries are anxious to sweep away the cluster of institutions based on the premises of command economy, and the advent of market forces on a step-by-step basis brings new forms of socio-economic organisation. Historically, however, any such form has been sustained and reproduced by certain beliefs and values, and modes of thinking. The culture comprising these forms of collective representation, by definition, possesses a considerable degree of resistance to change and inertia. The crucial question then is: does the dismantling of the Soviet enterprise model, the controlled price system, state monopolistic ownership of the means of production, create effective incentives for investment and lead to a wholesale change in the culture? If the answer is yes, is the free play of market forces enough to channel the values change in the required direction? As poignantly challenged by Shen (Shen, 1994) in his analysis of the Baltic post-independence economies, it is merely market language and symbols, not their essence, that have been imposed on an institutional structure, which is still Soviet in its effects. The first set of the issues, then, rotate around the emergence of new business, organisational and societal culture, and the strategies adopted by individual actors and groups to cope with a new dynamic economic environment.

At the heart of the regeneration of the Baltic economies are changes happening in *organisational culture* within companies, and the development of new organisational forms and capabilities within post-soviet Baltic enterprises. It is well known that in a typical socialist enterprise workers were accustomed not to see a relationship between productivity and income; managers were concerned almost exclusively with production and supply, and while being quite competent in engineering and the technical side of production, they were short of any serious consideration of marketing, quality of goods produced, and the satisfaction of customers. In general, the prevailing organisational culture was characterised by rigid hierarchies and explicit risk and responsibility avoidance.

It is equally important to acknowledge that firms and enterprises, both under socialism and in transitional economies, have a relevant *social dimension*. It is here that the productive activities link with the characteristics of national culture, promoting definite patterns of behaviour. As the imposed ideology of collectivism and false egalitarianism in the wider society resulted in reduced individual responsibility, so the workers were not used to self-monitoring and acquiesced to the moral dimension of the firm as a social unit. Managers in turn, through the deployment of various inside benefit schemes were able to control the lives of the workers and even members of their families. All parties concerned tended to view a workplace as a pool of resources. Currently, since the managers hold key positions and in fact implement transition, their practices still shape the cultural identity of the wider society (Liuhto, Chapter 3). Therefore, it is clear that the relationship between the culture in economic units and in the wider society deserves special attention. These are empirical questions as to how to depict current trends, situate the locus of changes, and assess their relative weight.

One way of managing the task is simply to ask the people themselves and find out what are the current attitudes and values of individuals and social groups along the relevant scales pertaining to economic performance, such as collectivism/individualism, leftism/rightism, passivity/activity, achievement/status quo, economic optimism/hopelessness and so on. Some findings (see Vadi and Buono, Chapter 4) suggest that those groups who are likely to play a key role in the transformation of the business sector – students, managers, directors, teachers – are more individualistic than other social groups. However, despite the acknowledgement that the emerging pattern leads to the prediction that the culture of Baltic organisations is going to resemble that of Western Europe, especially in terms of decision-making, responsibility and communication, a warning signal should be sounded. It must be acknowledged that in work organisations people tend to be so individualistic in their orientations that collectivistic norms and dispositions are unlikely to develop in an appropriate motivational system for a new Estonian economy.

The other warning signal from the study of social consciousness is that in the Baltic States there is an increasing gap and tension between the vision and attitudes of the 'conductors of change', namely the elites, and those of ordinary people (Jerschina and Górniak, Chapter 5). It is even more serious in the light of a customary distrust of state institutions and the tendency to ignore formal societal rules, relying instead on established personal networks. Such a tendency in the long run might result in a cycle of institutional weakness. The breaking of ties with the collectivist ethos and the movement towards a highly individualised society might have negative outcomes in the form of generating the low-trust business culture of a highly atomised society (Casson, 1995, p. 175). This is surely a fragile basis for a continuing communal consensus regarding the goals of the chosen social development, and for collective morality in general.

Nevertheless, to merely focus on the current situation will not suffice, as the complexity of the cultural set-up in the Baltic region reflects the existence of several *historical layers of values and dispositions*. As noted, the transition can be viewed as the emergence of a new pattern out of this historical diversity. Not all of the historical components are productive in generating adequate responses on the part of economic actors to the demands of an increasingly globalised and competitive world economy. For example, the development of 'family farm values' which can be traced back at least as far as the nineteenth century (King, Chapter 14), although efficient in sustaining a work ethic and commitment to personal endeavour, lacks the necessary emphasis on performance, competition and flexible co-operation.

One important remnant of the Soviet period is a sophistication in operating in the *second economy*. At the time people were able to set themselves up to a limited extent by circumventing the rigid rules of the establishment. They could work outside the direct control of the state, and in doing this, develop skills and methods as to how to get along in times of hardship and constant shortage of goods and services. To a significant degree, they could also develop their entrepreneurial potential. From the early 1990s onwards these skill have proven to be very useful in coping with the effects of recession (Rose, Chapter 6). At the same time, the drive to establish one's own business shows itself in the rapid increase in the number of newly-established SMEs (Smallbone *et al.*, Chapter 12). But the accompanying habit of reacting against irrational state regulation, facilitates an anti-state ideology and unconscious resistance to the government's control. Even now both entrepreneurs and ordinary citizens are not sure that the state is using their tax revenues sensibly, and therefore try to avoid tax payments, hide their profits, and invent sophisticated strategies to circumvent governmental regulations which are themselves in constant flux.

One of the most remarkable historical legacies of the past in the Baltics is the question of *nationality*. In recent years important political battles have been fought over the issues of citizenship, especially in Estonia and Latvia (see Smith and Aaslund, in Smith, 1994). It is not surprising then that the national dimension also shows up in the economic field. Ethnic boundary making has a notable property of being able to absorb many unrelated issues under the same umbrella and expand far beyond the political and cultural domains. Nevertheless, as the studies in this book show, although the ethnic divisions can in principle work against the establishment of a rounded civil society in the future, it is less clear that the national dimension matters at the level of micro-economic conditions of Baltic households. From the perspective of earnings, national differences may not be as big as is often assumed (Rose, Chapter 6).

Almost all the chapters in one way or another speak about a *lack of experience* and understanding of the functioning of a market economy among farmers, workers and managers. This shows up in many contexts. For example, in officials presenting poor business plans (Smallbone *et al.*, Chapter 12), in the mistakes of general managers (Rainys, Chapter 11), and the lack of awareness of employees about the consequences of their ownership thereby inhibiting the development of employee ownership (Mygind, Chapter 7). In the same vein, as Ludborzs (Chapter 9) shows, the incompetence of official authorities in controlling accounting practices makes the introduction of new practices of financial control much harder. A recurrent theme is that of learning and acquiring skills and expertise to exercise sound and pragmatic judgement. Authors suggest a number of ways to increase the level of the economic knowledge of economic actors. These range from the claim that market institutions are well-designed and selective devices that pressure people either to change and acquire new values or retreat, to the suggestion that there is a need for a clear and comprehensive plan as to how to educate and train people (King, Chapter 14). This latter claim emphasises the development of small groups and organisations, especially SMEs and entrepreneurs, and calls for a comprehensive scheme of social and consultancy support.

The other major set of issues is related to the question of which *policy options* are most suitable in the Baltic context for achieving stability in a macro-economic environment, and what major implications the study of micro-economic units has for government. The questions are discussed thoroughly in the concluding chapter, and only major points are raised here. First, the bulk of the chapters suggest that, although the Baltic governments have been quite successful in dismantling the socio-economic relations of the Soviet past, and have taken vigorous steps to develop a viable private sector by simultaneous diminishing the direct presence of the state in the market, they must be neither 'laissez faire', nor 'lazy fair' in the future. Nor can they simply wait for the explosion of private business activities without any involvement on their part. At the same time, this involvement should be directed and precise. First, it should attempt to close the gap between the ambition to set up the new rules of the market game, and the failure to sustain their enforceability and consistency. The lack of sufficient co-ordination among various government institutions with regard to general principles that regulate taxation procedures (even supposing the proper tax system were in the place), unclear policies in relation to property rights, constant changes in the legal system, and non-transparent implementation of legislation create an atmosphere of uncertainty for active and committed entrepreneurs and foreign investors and are all factors which inhibit long-term growth-oriented projects. In addition, this uncertainty gives much space for certain officials to exercise their position for making arbitrary decisions, thus further breeding corruption.[3]

Secondly, the governments sometimes over-stress the importance of a particular sector at the expense of others which are equally important for the development of a market economy. For example, the development of SMEs has been slowed down by sometimes being regarded as secondary to the more fundamental task in the eyes of the government, namely privatisation (Smallbone, Chapter 12). Finally, governments should make clear their intentions regarding future economic policies. A constant lack of explicit commitment on the part of the government is sometimes translated by the representatives of business communities as an indication of a more fundamental ambivalence and indecisiveness to extricate itself from the ownership and control of the productive assets. One of the best ways to convince the public about the true intentions of government would be to speed up privatisation and at the same time favour honest enterprises, facilitate credit resources for small enterprises, streamline insolvency resolution procedures, stabilise taxation and develop the state security system.

THE ORGANISATION OF THE BOOK

The chapters in the book are grouped into four broad sections. Those in Section One (Chapters 2 to 6) examine the theme of attitudes and values, both within organisations and as relating to surveys of individuals and societal groupings. Liuhto (Chapter 3) applies theoretical perspectives drawn from management studies of transition processes in organisations to generate a series of questions about the emergence of a new distinct Estonian style of management in the course of the twentieth century. He asserts that the structure of the Estonian entrepreneurship in the 1990s is very similar to that of the 1920s, which leads him to hypothesise about typical characteristics of Estonian enterprise culture as reflected in the small size of companies and in trade orientation, with the majority of the enterprises being located in Tallinn. He questions whether the current socio-cultural changes are leading towards this hypothetical form-model. Closely related to the theme of how changes in the Estonian economy and culture are linked to the management orientation and organisational behaviour of Estonian firms is the paper by Vadi and Buono (Chapter 4). Drawing on extensive literature, the authors (following Hofstede) carve out the dimension of individualism/collectivism, and then scrutinise it along the three sub-dimensions of the social content of the self, life values, and attitudes towards different kinds of social behaviour.

In a somewhat different paper, Radosevic (Chapter 2) dissects the characteristics of what he calls 'latecomers', namely the Baltic post-socialist enterprises, by looking at how management closes three organisational gaps: product development, market development and managerial quality.

The author develops a model which hypothesises that the organisational capability gaps in domestic enterprises are a function of the sectoral, market and of the technological context in which enterprises operate. Also relevant are: management's expectations and actions, the privatisation context, foreign strategic investors and partners, and the macro-economic climate. The predictions of the model are then tested through statistical data and illustrated by case studies of Estonian and Latvian enterprises. Radosevic rounds up his discussion with a theoretical argument that the prospects of growth in enterprises, although significantly influenced by management behaviour (micro variables), is ultimately determined by meso variables (privatisation, sectoral context) and the macro-economic environment.

Two last papers in Section One are based on comparative studies. The focus of the chapter by Jerschina and Górniak (Chapter 5) is on the socio-economic attitudes of people across ten Central and Eastern Europe (CEE) countries. He asks two sets of questions, namely, what is the relationship between social stratification, the attitudes and orientations of people, and the main collective political actors (active/silent citizens, passive experts and conductors of change)? and what level of support might be expected for the process of reforms? A substantial element of the survey and analysis is the examination of the position of national minorities in the respective countries, which of course, is highly relevant in relation to the Baltic States.

The section ends with the paper by Richard Rose (Chapter 6). He critically addresses two commonly held ideas about the Baltics. These are that the macro-economic transformations appear to be extremely negative for everyone because the fall in living standards is so dramatic, and that there are increasing differences of micro-economic conditions among the nationalities in the three countries. His work is supported by the data from a 1995 survey and by theoretical considerations. Although Rose states that the official macro-economic statistics are not a good guide to micro-economic conditions in post-command economy in that they do not take due account of the three dimensionality of the economy and the informal sector, he also stresses that while the economy and society can be analysed at more than one level, it can only be understood by bringing the micro and macro perspectives together.

The majority of the participants in the Riga Conference agreed that there has been limited awareness of the distinction between the desired goals of policy-making and actual situation on the ground. In addition, policy implications should be designed not only for the government officials, but also for economic units themselves. The papers in Section

Two (Chapters 7 to 11) reflect the need for more thorough research of a series of factors and developments pertaining to the policy imperatives as the process of economic restructuring in the Baltic economies develops.

Two of the papers in the section deal with finance at the enterprise level. Ludborzs (Chapter 9) discusses the development of the current accounting system in Latvia and meticulously charts the way ahead as the country moves from Soviet-style accounting to the Western model. This is shown to involve the gradual adoption of laws, the implementation of accounting procedures and the indirect presence of good practice through the well-known Western auditing firms. In the second of these papers, Rainys (Chapter 11) contrasts the characteristics of formal and informal exit of enterprises in the Lithuanian context. A core issue in his study is why the non-judicial procedure of business exit is so prominent. One of the factors responsible for that is that the judicial exit route requires a high degree of competence and efficiency from the courts which is currently lacking. The other factor is that it is difficult to sell enterprises as production units since there are few growing industries and little need for new production facilities, while the amount of foreign investment remains small. So, although the majority of enterprises utilise less than 20 per cent of their production facilities, there is no clear movement towards radical restructuring. An interesting part of the study is the case studies through which the author tries to show how bankruptcy, caused by both subjective mistakes and external factors, did not result in formal exit, and why enterprises were not using bank services. Even if they applied for credits, the banks themselves did not welcome the bankruptcy process because they were not interested in acquiring assets for which there was no market.

Echoing the theme of the chapter by Richard Rose, Raagmaa (Chapter 8) discusses the importance of the informal sector and the hidden economy in Estonia. He investigates how changes in the social context of entrepreneurship, in economic structure and enterprise culture shapes and reshapes the workings of the informal economy in different sectors. He highlights the fact that it is of the utmost political significance to understand whether the practices developed in the second economy which flourished under socialism, will go to into legal or illegal businesses. The author also dissects certain habits that have accompanied the growth of the second economy and which most probably still inform behaviour. He concludes that Estonia has currently reached a period where the official economy is not yet growing sufficiently, but where the hidden sector continues to grow rapidly and is beginning to legalise its activities through investment.

The chapter by Mygind (Chapter 7) take a closer look at one of the key issues of the transitional economies, namely privatisation. He discusses the developments in employee ownership during the privatisation process in all three Baltic States. The discussion is based on four-factor model of the conditions favouring or disfavouring employee ownership, the institutional system, the social system, the value system and the production system. The importance of new institutional arrangements is demonstrated by the links between the type of privatisation, political tendencies and legislative changes. Mygind interestingly contrasts the strategies of privatisation adopted in each of the countries, and attempts to relate the differences with the specific social and historical conditions present in each country.

This section contains an interesting contribution by Jedrzejczak and Fleming (Chapter 10) on the emergence of capital markets in Latvia. The critical driving forces which will have an impact on the development of these markets are identified. These include the supply of securities emerging from the privatisation process and from the new funding requirements of governments and enterprises. On the demand side are the investment needs of individuals and institutions, as well as the growth of business opportunities. Each of these issues are examined in detail in the current Latvian context. Thereafter the main policy options are evaluated and specific advice proffered to the government.

Section Three (Chapters 12 and 13) looks at the development of two sectors in the Baltic countries. These are small- and medium-size manufacturing enterprises and farming which, due to various historical reasons, have a relevance that reaches beyond the economic into the social and cultural domain. The changes in these two sectors are analysed in the papers by Smallbone *et al.* (Chapter 12) and Zilcken (Chapter 13). Both give a valuable diagnosis of problems and constraints encountered by 'small commercial agents'. David Smallbone and colleagues examine the constraints on the development of manufacturing SMEs in all of the Baltic States. These include low domestic purchasing power, the negligence of governments, weak financial and legal control, high interest rates and an underdeveloped financial infrastructure. The authors demonstrate the links between these constraints and the existence of a large number of weak and non-operating firms, the disproportionate presence of short-term commercial activities with high revenues and relatively high profit margins, and the lack of managerial and business skills.

The agro-food sector is one that has undergone dramatic changes in the past few years and it has an imprint of additional political and ideological sensitivities. The land reforms have led to a decreasing number of state and collective farms, and the emergence of a new class of private farmers. At the same time there has been no radical improvement in agricultural output, which would require substantial investment in new equipment and machinery. Although some banks, including the World Bank, have made credits available, there has been an unexpectedly low response on the part of the farmers in taking them up. The paper by Zilcken (Chapter 13) addresses the question of the investment behaviour of private farmers based on a survey undertaken in Latvia.

Section Four has two broader thematic chapters, plus a brief concluding chapter by the editors. King (Chapter 14) addresses the issues of how agents adapt to a new societal system of a market economy through changing values. He asserts the need for a clear plan on how to introduce new values in the Baltic societies, and puts an emphasis on the small groups and organisations which are true generators of sustainable market-oriented attitudes and values, the most critical being personal achievement and organisational performance, and the propensity to change. The chapter by Schöpflin (Chapter 15) takes a reflective look at some of the intangibles of transition, exploring some of the underlying patterns which have been resistant to change throughout the post-communist societies.

It will be evident that the majority of the chapters draw on the results of very recent empirical studies conducted in the Baltic countries and deploy a mixture of methodologies – from surveys and interviews to case studies and psychological questionnaires. The concluding chapter by the editors attempts to translate some of the findings in the papers into terms which would inform both managers and policy-makers as to the priority areas for the implementation of the transition in the Baltic States.

Notes

1. For a detailed analysis of the recent developments in political, economic and social spheres, see Lieven (1993), Van Arkadie and Karlsson (1992), Smith (1994), Lainela and Suttela (1994) and Shen (1994).
2. According to recent statistics (*Business Eastern Europe*, 18 September, 2 October), inflation in Estonia on a year on basis in 1995 was 25.9 per cent, in Latvia 23.7 per cent and in Lithuania 35.7 per cent. Average gross monthly wages rose by 37.6 per cent in nominal terms over the same period of 1994 in Estonia, and is now $209 per month ($199 in Latvia and $128 in Lithuania). By the end of September 1995, direct foreign investment per head in Estonia was $154. The Lithuanian government predicted GDP growth of 5 per cent for 1995.
3. According to recent reports from the survey done by the World Bank (*Business Eastern Europe*, 9 October 1995) 90 per cent of the responding foreign investors said they were giving bribes to officials.

REFERENCES

Buckley, P. and Ghauri, P. (eds) (1994) *The Economics of Change in East and Central Europe: Its Impact on International Business* (London: Academic Press).

Casson, M. (1995) *Entrepreneurship and Business Culture* (Aldershot, Hants: Edward Elgar).

Harvey, D. (1989) *The Condition of Postmodernity* (Oxford: Blackwell).

Hofstede, G. (1984) *Culture's Consequences: International Differences in Work-related Values* (London: Sage).

Lainela, S. and Suttela, P. (1994) *Transition in the Baltic States* (Helsinki: Bank of Finland).

Lieven, A. (1993) *The Baltic Revolution: Estonia, Latvia and Lithuania and the Path to Independence* (New Haven: Yale University Press).

Saunders, C.T. (ed.) (1992) *Economics and Politics of Transition* (London: Macmillan in association with the Vienna Institute for Comparative Economic Studies).

Shen, R. (1994) *Restructuring the Baltic Economies: Disengaging Fifty Years of Integration with the USSR* (Westport, Conn.: Praeger).

Smith, G. (ed.) (1994) *The Baltic States: The National Self-Determination of Estonia, Latvia and Lithuania* (London: Macmillan).

Van Arkadie, B. and Karlsson, M. (eds) (1992) *Economic Survey of the Baltic States: The Reform Process in Estonia, Latvia and Lithuania* (London: Pinter).

Winiecki, J. (1993) *Post-Soviet-type Economies in Transition* (Aldershot, Hants: Avebury).

SECTION ONE

VALUES, ATTITUDES AND PERSPECTIVES

2 The Baltic Post-Socialist Enterprises and the Development of Organisational Capabilities
Slavo Radosevic

INTRODUCTION[1]

A crucial mechanism through which successful post-socialist economies will grow is the learning effort and development of organisational capabilities of their local firms combined with the acquisition of foreign technology. Their growth and techno-economic profile are determined by the way they will manage to develop their organisational capabilities, which are analysed here from a functional perspective as a problem of closing three gaps: product development, market development and management. A descriptive model of the growth of organisational capabilities is then developed which assumes that it is to be strongly determined by the sector and technology characteristics in which the enterprise finds itself. However, the development of organisational capabilities of post-socialist enterprises is modified by the specific enterprise characteristics (top management), privatisation context, the role of strategic partners and by the country's macro-economic climate.

This conceptual framework is applied here to examples of several enterprises in post-socialist Baltic States. In the last part we discuss the main industrial restructuring issues in the Baltic States using the previously developed conceptual framework. The conclusion summarises the main arguments.

FROM THE SOVIET TO POST-SOCIALIST ENTERPRISE

Enterprises in the Western sense did not exist under socialism (Hirschausen, 1995). Basically production rather than business units existed and they were

19

part of a hierarchy. Business functions like marketing, finance and R&D were rudimentarily developed 'in house' or, using today's terminology, were outsourced either to ministries or to other organisations, whether in the form of foreign trade organisations, branch institutes, ministries or industry directorates. Innovation tasks were located in branch institutes and design bureaux with very little technological effort being practised at the shop-floor level. The Soviet system was characterised by vertical segmentation of the linear model and by horizontal segmentation into branches of industry (Hanson and Pavitt, 1987; Tunzelmann, 1995).

R&D was not organised as an 'in-house' activity or R&D *in* industry, but as R&D *for* industry (Radosevic, 1994). This meant that much technological activity was oriented towards the needs of industry and yet was outside enterprises. This encouraged pseudo-innovation as design bureaux fulfilled planned tasks, and produced piles of technical documentation that then lay unused on the shelf. There was a proliferation of 'knowledge products' of low quality and trivial design (Amman and Cooper, 1982). The absence of a direct relationship with the customer was the dominant characteristic of the Soviet system. This system proved inadequate for generating new technologies because of the lack of interactive learning between research and production (Tunzelmann, 1995).

The internalisation of business functions which were previously dispersed throughout a hierarchy leads to changes in the techno-economic profile of post-socialist enterprises. A new environment requires firms to make the shift towards non-tangible and non-technological assets, away from a focus on mastery of production know-how, especially technically complex projects and the neglect of user needs and cost aspects.

Enterprises in post-socialism now have to work up neglected business functions (marketing, finance, operations management) and develop new activities (integration at product level and network-building at firm level, downstream integration). The challenge is to take imported Western hard-

Table 2.1   Changing techno-economic profile of post-socialist enterprises

Centrally planned system	*Economy in transition*
Production know-how, technical complexity, cost-and user-insensitive	Marketing, finance, organisation, system integration at product level, network building at firm level, cost-driven

Source: Radosevic (1996).

ware from a range of domestic suppliers, network them together, add their own software applications and install them at a customer site with consultancy and support services. As they emerge from a situation where all distribution was in state hands, the biggest weaknesses of post-socialist enterprises are in downstream capabilities and distribution networks.[2] In practical terms, this means a shift from the supply department to the sales department. Those able to acquire strategic assets such as distribution systems, supplier networks and a local brand name will basically shape industry structures in the future.

Post-socialist enterprises cannot be described simply as followers. They have distinctive characteristics which style them as latecomers. The term 'follower' implies an enterprise which is strategically positioned behind the world competitive frontier because of factors located *within* the enterprise. A latecomer enterprise is one that lags behind because of strong structural constraints in the business and economic environment, making its strategic position distinctively different from the one of the follower.[3] A latecomer firm must overcome these 'negative externalities' through a dynamic capability-building process.

Post-socialist latecomers must compensate for systemic defects that are comparatively much stronger than in other middle-income economies. These defects come from high uncertainties in the economic environment caused by slow and undefined privatisation, high transaction costs due to under-developed financial and other markets and macro-economic imbalances. The industrial structure in which a firm operates is fluid and firms are continuously faced with strategic choices. Distinctively post-socialist 'negative externalities' include the absence of a well functioning banking system and of satisfactory mechanisms of contract enforcement.

THE DEVELOPMENT OF ORGANISATIONAL CAPABILITIES OF POST-SOCIALIST LATECOMERS: A DESCRIPTIVE MODEL

Here we develop a descriptive model of factors which determine the development of organisational capabilities of post-socialist enterprises. The fundamental building blocks in our framework are:

(a) sectoral, technological and market characteristics in which enterprises operate;
(b) individual behaviour of top management;
(c) privatisation context which creates a specific agent–principal relationship;

(d) behaviour of foreign strategic partners (principals, foreign investors and partners, importers);
(e) macro-economic climate (price and trade liberalisation, price stability).

(a) Sectoral characteristics (micro-economic environment)

Sectoral, technological and market characteristics are the dominant factors in determining the development of organisational capabilities in our model. The assumption is that in some sectors there are *a priori* higher and in others lower chances for turn-around of enterprises, given other unchangeable factors. The problem for analysis is how to discern sectors which might represent coherent groupings and where enterprises share similar technological and market problems. Taking into account that any classification is imperfect, we distinguish three groups of sectors: production know-how-based, engineering-based and R&D-based. There are two underlying criteria: first, the type of technological capability, and, second, its location (within an enterprise, within the network of enterprises, within the external R&D institutions).

Production know-how-dominated sectors are those where technological capability is confined basically in a factory. These are mainly traditional, light industries like footwear, garments but also commodities (like fertilisers, other petrochemicals, steel). The production networks on which they are based are relatively simple, in that the suppliers of inputs come from the region or country, and production is highly localised. In the case of commodity producers, process design combined with production know-how is the main element of technological capability.

Engineering-based are those industries where technological capability is dislocated among several enterprises since products are often made of several components. Process engineering is the dominant factor of competitiveness. Product is usually the system or complex compound.

R&D-based sectors are those where the key to competitiveness is development work which is done either independently in an R&D institute or in the R&D unit of enterprises. Production itself is not the main problem, which is instead the ability to configure sophisticated, usually imported, components for customer-designed applications. In terms of networking, these sectors lie between the two previous sectors.

The sectoral, market and technological context in which enterprises operate are the dominant factors in our model. The assumption is that in engineering-based sectors it is *a priori* more difficult for enterprises to develop their organisational capabilities than in production know-how or

R&D. Trade data also seem to confirm this assumption. Eastern European trade was, and continues to be, dominated by scale-intensive and traditional products (Guerrieri, 1994; Rosati, 1994). More detailed evidence (country, and industry) shows that Eastern Europe is strongest in traditional products and simple scale-intensive products. In our taxonomy these are sectors grouped within production know-how based sectors. Complex scale-intensive and specialised suppliers are areas where competitive development is very much network-based and is not confined to one enterprise with possibly modern equipment. The opening of post-socialist economies is likely to reinforce advantages in traditional and simple scale-intensive groups.

However, by taking sectors as determining factors we do not undermine the differences between different enterprises in the same sector. Many enterprise differences cannot be explained by differences in sectors but they are discretionary or the result of attitudes of top management.[4] In addition to this, restructuring is determined by other factors, which we will discuss below.

(b) Top management behaviour

The decision whether to wait or experiment, whether to engage in productive restructuring or rent-seeking behaviour, are determined in the early phases of transition by top managers and have crucial effects on restructuring opportunities.

In a fluid industrial structure with high environmental uncertainties, routine management is not of much use. Pressures from within (lower management, key specialists, workers) and from outside (privatisation, agency, ministry, potential investors, the local community) have created a situation where the usual distinction between strategic, tactical and operational management is breaking down. Many seemingly tactical and operational decisions are implicit strategic decisions.[5] Also, in order to become flexible and cost-competitive, explicit strategic decisions are taken more often, like debt/equity swaps with banks, 'lay offs', constant reshuffling and downsizing. Faced with such uncertainties, 'wait and see' seems to be a rational response of managers, especially where management is unable to declare many strategic decisions as its own position and room for manoeuvre is constrained by strong stakeholders (privatisation agency, workers, ministries, the local community).

Strategic myopia is a pervasive characteristic of the latecomer's decision-making. The managers have difficulty in comprehending the full scale and scope of changes and the strategic choices before them.

'Transformative management' is squeezed by 'crisis management'. Overwhelming strategic confusion and lack of focus are general characteristics (Radosevic, 1996). In such situations the top managements' expectations play a crucial role (Kuznetsov, 1995). As Swaan (1994, p. 11) put it: 'behavioural change is not a direct result of changes in ownership and governance structures: the main incentive for successful managers is their anticipation of future rewards once privatisation would make headway.'

It is more likely in countries where a change of expectations was clearly signalled through macro-economic and privatisation policy, that managerial behaviour in consequence becomes more focussed on productive adjustment. On the other hand if the shock was too big it might have created a paralysis or induced only rather short term, rent-seeking, behaviour.

(c) Privatisation and agent–principal problems

In centrally planned systems enterprise managers were agents, while government agencies and ministries were principals. Such enterprises are now undergoing the privatisation process which often results in the specific corporate governance structure under the control of investment funds or insiders. In the case of enterprises waiting to be privatised, the result is an ownership interregnum. A specific corporate governance structure implies that the temporary principal–agent conundrum significantly slows the restructuring of enterprises.

This explains why many state-owned enterprise (SOEs), which have spared themselves the governance mess, have managed to restructure themselves and to acquire much needed capabilities, without entering into foreign take-overs. An unchanged governance structure, with the state becoming resistant to attempts to give 'soft' finance, forced managers to actively restructure enterprises.

Privatisation modifies, but does not solve, the restructuring problem. It is an indispensable condition for restructuring but it does not by itself restructure. If pursued as the only government objective ('privatisation at any price'), it may neglect the production potential within state-owned enterprises. It is not clear that the static welfare effects and long-term consequences of such a stance are always positive. Whichever method of privatisation is adopted, the trade-off between numbers of privatised and restructured enterprises is left unresolved.

In summary, the style and pace of privatisation significantly determines the prospects of enterprise restructuring. However, the convergence in privatisation methods, in terms of their multiplication in all post-socialist economies, means that it becomes more difficult to generalise on specific national prospects for restructuring resulting from privatisation.

(d) Foreign strategic partners and latecomers' growth

Foreign strategic investors and partners play an important role in closing specific functional gaps (in product development, market development, and management). There is some evidence that the most active adjustment responses come from firms that have been privatised through foreign investment (Carlin *et al.*, 1994). While domestic enterprises lack direction and have significant management and financial gaps, these drawbacks are overcome through foreign affiliates. Only foreign management and the insertion of affiliates into an international structure can transform the internal culture and add value to existing production competencies.

Different channels play different roles in closing product, market development and management gaps of enterprises in post-socialist economies. Foreign direct investments (FDI) are probably the most effective channel for compensating for the external and internal disadvantages which the latecomer faces. Subcontracting is a mechanism where weaknesses in marketing and finance functions can be compensated for through a foreign principal – who takes care of marketing as products are often sold under his brand name. A good example of this is Baltika, Estonia's largest clothing factory, which made a breakthrough with its own-label contracts, starting with upgraded jobbing and integrating Baltika designs (ODM) (Percival and Straunik, 1995). Also, there is scattered evidence that within post-socialist economies there is an emerging hierarchical inclusion in production networks in industries such as clothing.[6] Alliances and licenses still seem to be a relatively rare mechanism for the 'catching up' of post-socialist enterprises (see Hagedoorn and Sadowski, 1995).

(e) Macro-economic climate

The macro-economic climate plays an important role in the development of organisational capabilities through shaping management's expectations. The more the macro-economic situation seems to be unstable the more enterprises are likely to turn towards rent-seeking behaviour through different forms of financial management and to neglect active adjustment. The decisive factors here are price and trade liberalisation and price stability. The first enables the necessary freedom for business while the latter ensures rational economic behaviour.

In conditions of strong uncertainty, induced by inflationary waves, enterprises postpone adjustment. The same behaviour occurs if different forms of 'soft' finance are available (arrears, non-payments, soft loans).

In this respect a divergent situation is developing among post-socialist economies. At one extreme are those countries where stabilisation remains the overwhelming concern (Bulgaria, Romania, Russia), at the other is the Czech Republic with full employment and low inflation. In between are Hungary, Poland and Slovakia. The Baltic States also belong to this intermediate group.

The degree of financial stability and the capacity of domestic financial systems to operate in an open environment seems to be a crucial supportive element for enterprise growth. In most post-socialist economies the financial system is shallow, representing a significant factor in slowing down the growth of enterprises. Although the level of aggregate savings is slowly rising, very different national patterns of their allocation will have diverging effects on enterprise growth.

In summary, very tentatively our model implies that the organisational capability gaps of domestic enterprises are a function of the sectoral, market and technology context in which enterprises operate; management's expectations and actions; the privatisation context; the role of foreign strategic investors and partners; and, the macro-economic climate. From this it follows that, for example, a country with the highest share of engineering-based industries has the biggest organisational capability gap. Alternatively, a country with the highest share of production know-how-based sectors (traditional industries and commodities) should have the least trouble in closing the organisational gap. Also, we would expect that the countries which have the highest share of FDI, subcontracting links or exports are in a more favourable position. A legally clear and effectively implemented privatisation procedure is also conducive to enterprise restructuring. Stable macro-economic performance changes management expectations and orients them more towards active adjustment than towards rent-seeking behaviour.

THE BALTIC POST-SOCIALIST LATECOMER ENTERPRISES: EXAMPLES OF (NON-)ADJUSTMENT

In this section we will try to apply the above model to examples of several Baltic enterprises. However, before that we shall look at some environmental factors which limit production and thus inhibit the growth of the Baltic enterprises.

Latecomer enterprise environment in the Baltic States

The most significant deterrent factors for enterprise growth in the Baltic States are insufficient domestic demand and financial problems (see Table 2.2). A lack of domestic demand is the result of the tight macro-economic situation, which on the one hand, through macro-economic stability,

Table 2.2   Limits to production in the Baltic States (balance)*

Limits to production	Baltic States	
None	Estonia	4
	Latvia	1
	Lithuania	1
Insufficient demand	Estonia	57
– Domestic	Latvia	72
– Domestic	Lithuania	59
– Foreign	Latvia	35
– Foreign	Lithuania	34
Skilled labour shortages	Estonia	6
	Latvia	8
	Lithuania	2
Lack of appropriate equipment	Estonia	6
	Latvia	35
	Lithuania	4
Shortage of raw materials	Estonia	17
	Latvia	23
	Lithuania	23
Financial problems	Estonia	34
	Latvia	59
	Lithuania	44
Competitive imports	Latvia	28
	Lithuania	14
Uncertainty in the EC environment	Latvia	35
	Lithuania	27
Unclear economic laws	Latvia	34
	Lithuania	3

Source: OECD short-term economic indicators: transition economies, 1995/2.
* Based on business surveys where respondents assess the current business situations compared with the 'normal' state. 'Normal' and 'same' answers are ignored and the balance is obtained by taking the difference between the weighted percentage of respondents giving favourable and unfavourable answers. Balance is the difference between the per cent of respondents giving positive and negative replies.

induces rational behaviour, but on the other hand, inhibits economic growth. A tight monetary policy has stripped cash out of enterprises while the surrounding financial system is not yet geared to or is unable to finance restructuring. The second group of factors which deter growth are low foreign demand and uncertainty in the economic environment. Uncertainty gives rise to a very specific, post-socialist, 'negative externality' for enterprise growth.

The significance of these factors has changed in 1994/5, although very often it is not clear in which direction. Nevertheless, there are some tendencies which seem to represent a recognisable pattern. In Estonia demand is ceasing to be a critical bottleneck for business. In Latvia this is the case only with domestic demand. In Lithuania foreign demand is becoming difficult to meet and there is a similar tendency in Latvia where financial problems have somewhat eased (at least that was the situation until the beginning of 1995). The same is the case with the decreasing uncertainty in the economic environment and with a more transparent legal framework.

Overall, this indicates that there are significant 'negative externalities' in the Baltic economies influencing the growth of their enterprises. While many of these factors might seem to be of a cyclical character, like lack of demand, in the post-socialist context they are basically the problem of the structural competitiveness of these economies.

Issues of organisational growth of Baltic enterprises

In this part we will apply our descriptive model of organisational development to the examples of several enterprises in the Baltic States. The idea is to show how factors in our model might illuminate some aspects of their behaviour. What follows are short descriptions of seven Latvian and Estonian enterprises visited by the author before 1995. These sketches should reflect the main problems these enterprises are facing in building their organisational capabilities.

Latvijas Finieris

Latvijas Finieris is a producer of plywood and furniture based in Riga. Plywood is exported while furniture is so far sold only on the domestic market. It has successfully shifted from Eastern to UK and other western markets. The best indication of this is the rise in the number of employees from 1400 (1992) to 1700 (1994). The shift to western markets did not require much restructuring. The product range is the same as before, except that they are trying to develop office or home furniture sets for the domestic market. Possibilities for export of their products, other than plywood, are not likely in the short term. The plywood export is through a foreign agent who works on commission. It is only in the case of a large order that foreign buyers come to check for quality.

This is a joint stock company where the State now has less than 50 per cent of shares. The rest is distributed among 210 employees. Such a situation has enabled management to have full control over the business. However, the producer is very sensitive to the relationships between domestic prices of the wood and gas which come from Russia, and the exchange rate. This means that the temporarily favourable position of the producer might easily be endangered by external factors. While feeling quite secure in low value-added activities, strong barriers to entry into higher value-added activities (such as furniture export) would face the enterprise with many more adjustment problems.

Pioneer (Tallinn)

Pioneer is a toolmaker producing a wide range of injection moulds of different design and size for various areas of industry (engine parts, consumer goods), different types of sheet steel stamping dies as well as manufacturing parts made of metal powders. Based in Tallinn, it produces basically the same type of products although the range has expanded significantly. They now design 450 products annually and the output mix is very diversified.

It is a joint venture under foreign majority ownership (52 per cent) with two Estonian banks holding the rest of the equity and 30 per cent of production going to export. The original idea was to expand exports to Russia but now they have to penetrate more western markets as well as serve the domestic market. The key to change was the foreign owner who managed to make the enterprise flexible and able to react quickly to new orders. Due to an experienced and skilled workforce the output quality seems not to be their problem but rather the throughput and design time.

The organisation structure has been simplified, the number of workers has been reduced by half (to 230), and management seems to be in full control of the restructuring process. They could export much more to western markets but are not stimulated to do so with the prevailing exchange rate.

Railway Carriage Works

Founded in 1852 this enterprise, based in Riga, has since 1974 produced only electric carriages, mainly for Russia. The enterprise is still 100 per cent state owned although there are plans to try to sell it through a public sales and employee stock ownership plan (ESOP).

The production dropped from 650 to 164 carriages and the number of workers has been reduced from 4800 (1990) to 3085 (1994). Their product is quite suitable for the Russian market but it would be quite difficult to sell it to the western markets. They see the only solution as continuing to export to the Russian market which they still do through complex barter schemes. Their design is outdated, construction periods are too long, and the carriages are of low quality, which is why they can give only a two-year guarantee.

Many problems arise from the complexity of the product which is still produced almost all 'in house' including metal sheets and seats. The external purchases include the electronics, and all plastic and electric installations. The enterprise is faced with many problems, including shrinking markets, constant liquidity problems and outdated technology. One possible solution would be for it to find foreign strategic partners who would turn it into a specialised producer or into an assembler. The investment for its restructuring is far beyond its financial capacity and much is needed in improving both management and organisation. Management does 'business as usual' and it is difficult to see how they can 'turn around' the enterprise.

Eesti Kivioli

Eesti Kivioli is the state joint-stock company which was founded in Estonia with the aim of processing the local oil shale into chemical products. Processing of oil-shale is still going on (oil shale retorting produces shale oil and oil shale-based chemicals) as well as the non shale oil based products (formaline, etc.) and applied chemistry goods production (detergent powders, shampoos, soaps, etc.). The market is mainly domestic, except in the case of commodity chemicals.

This conglomerate is facing serious problems in adapting to new market conditions. The competitiveness of many of their products is very questionable and this is to a great extent masked by the state controlled prices of some oil shale-based products as well as through taxation policy, which is the reflection of the strategic importance of this resource for Estonia.

Restructuring requires a clear distinction in terms of restructuring for consumer goods, commodity chemicals and specialised chemicals. It is our impression that management does not have clear ideas about the market opportunities in these different areas. In addition, the erosion of the Oil Shale Institute indicates that there is no clear adjustment strategy for product development. Uncertainties regarding privatisation are high and management is not in full control of the process as the stakes and political importance of the resource is high. All this shapes the current strategy which lies between fragile real adjustment and rent seeking through state support. It is unlikely that a foreign or domestic strategic partner could be found.

VEF

VEF is a telecommunication equipment producer based in Riga and is still in 100 per cent state ownership. However, plans for transformation into a joint-stock company (JSC) are underway as are privatisation plans. It consists of 18 different producers (factories) and is organised as a 'quasi holding' company. It produces switching (60 per cent of sales) and telephone equipment (20 per cent), offers telecom services and still has ownership of some social infrastructure (hotel, hospital, etc.).

This ex-Soviet electronic combinate has shrunk significantly from 15 000 employees (1990) to 5000 (1994) and plans further downsizing. They had developed a distribution system in Russia with 28 small firms and 240 distributors which had to be replaced temporarily by a cash and carry system. However, they hope to rebuild some of this network.

The enterprise is pursuing a strategy of sustainable real adjustment. Top management reacted rightly to new circumstances by putting much effort into product development. Management is in search of foreign partners understanding that in their business they must rely on strategic partners to overcome R&D and market barriers. In order to keep the momentum in technology development, VEF is inviting and supporting small electronic firms as well as other small firms as subcontractors.

VEF is also trying to build a strategy in relation to Eastern markets which would give them advantages in quality and cheap engineering work. Currently, the biggest obstacle in market development is the lack of a liberal trade regime with Russia and other CIS countries.

Alfa

Alfa is an electronics components producer and is today a remnant of ex-Soviet electronics combinate in Riga which was unable to restructure and adjust to new conditions. Once it employed 10 000 but it is reduced to a level of 1700 of which only 50 per cent are actually working. They are producing electronic components for watches for an East Asian customer. The enterprise is under privatisation, with the state currently holding 75 per cent and employees 25 per cent of the shares. Once 95 per cent of its former production was distributed to the ex-USSR. However, the enterprise was unable to keep these markets as well as shift towards the West. Key specialists, most of whom were Russian, also left and the enterprise is left without a core workforce.

The enterprise is searching for new business opportunities, such as selling transistors and integrated circuits in the West, Western electronic components in the Baltic States and Russia, and for a joint venture in manufacturing electronic and radio technical components. However, the biggest asset of today's Alfa, as perceived by management, is unused production space of 150 000 square metres (80 per cent). Today, renting of premises makes 30 per cent of their income and is going to rise as they find new tenants. It is our impression that management sees a better future in rent-seeking through leasing out premises than in active adjustment.

EKTA

EKTA is a small electronics firms association and is a part of Tallinn electronics centre representing a partnership of 33 small companies. Some of these are very small (2–3 employees) while the others have with 30–50 employees. The companies joining into the partnership are R&D and manufacturing companies in electronics, trade, supplying and service companies and a computer R&D Division *EKTA* which functions as the basic infrastructural support and services for the other companies.

EKTA was established in 1976 as part of the Institute of Cybernetics and was producing electronic components which USSR enterprises were unable to purchase directly from abroad. Since then it has grown into an enterprise with 415 employees of which 40 are PhDs. At the beginning of the 1990s, with the break-up of demand from the USSR, they realised that they were too large for the new conditions and were lacking any support from industry and decided to break up into smaller firms. This gave them more initiative and flexibility and attracted foreign partners. This important reorganisation enabled them to save many skilled engineers who would otherwise have fled abroad.

The first joint venture was set up in 1989 and now there are several of them. One third of their production goes to the West, mostly to Sweden, Germany and Finland. Infrastructural support of EKTA in terms of lower renting fees, technical support and close contacts with other firms represents a strong support for small firms. EKTA is an example of sustainable real adjustment pursued with vigour and knowledge.

Conclusions

The characteristics of the analysed enterprises can be summarised and compared, as shown in Table 2.3. Our sample of enterprises shows some interesting features from the perspective of our model. First, structural

Table 2.3   A summary of organisational gap issues in the sample of enterprises

Enterprise	Product development	Market development	Management (strategy)	Privatisation context	Strategic partner
Latvijas Finieris (Plywood and furniture)	Basically the same commodity type products	Successful re-orientation towards West.	Sustainable real adjustment. Problems in the long term.	Management in control of situation.	Not present.
Pioneer Tallinn (Toolmaker)	Much wider range of products based on the old production know-how.	Export is taken care of by the foreign co-owner.	Sustainable real adjustment strategy.	Foreign co-owner. No principal–agent problems.	Strong stakes of foreign partner.
Railway Carriage Works, Riga	Requires improvement. No capital available.	Barter trade with East. Entry barriers to West too high.	Survival strategy. Need for strong turn-around management.	Still 100% SOE.	Not present.
Eesti Tivoli (Oil shale and non-oil shale chemicals)	Requires clearer product portfolio. Product development neglected.	Domestic market only/ In export only commodity chemicals.	Not real adjustment yet. Rent-seeking through state support.	Unclear and inhibits active adjustment.	Not present.
VEF Riga (Telecommunication equipment)	A whole set of new imitative products.	In process of finding an appropriate market position between East and West.	Strategy of sustainable real adjustment.	Awaiting privatisation. Management has developed strategy.	In active search for foreign strategic partners.
Alfa Riga (Electronic components)	Radically reduced product range. Product development neglected.	In search of modalities to open western markets.	Waiting. Rent-seeking dominant over restructuring.	In the process of privatisation. Restructuring inhibited.	Not present.
EKTA Tallinn (Electronics association)	New range of custom-made products. R&D driven.	Active opening of foreign markets.	Successful turn-around management.	Privatised.	EKTA is highly instrumental in small firms growth.

conditions for active restructuring are more favourable in enterprises where production know-how (Latvijas Finieris, Pioneer) or R&D (VEF, EKTA) is the basis for growth than in capital intensive and engineering based, like Eesti Kivioli and Railway Carriage Works. In the latter group financial and management requirements are too high to be overcome in the short term. However, the most important market barriers are too high except for commodity chemicals in the case of Eesti Kivioli. Also, the chances of finding a strategic partner (domestic or foreign) are less likely. One solution is common to both these enterprises, namely to split the enterprise into viable units which can then be restructured and where these barriers are supposed to be lower.

Second, although sustainable real adjustment is more likely in production know-how based (Latvijas Finieris, Pioneer) and R&D based sectors (VEF, EKTA) than in engineering based sectors (Railway Carriages Works, Eesti Kivioli) there is nothing deterministic about the sectoral factors due to the interplay of these with other factors in the enterprise environment. As a result two enterprises in the same sector might resolve their restructuring problem entirely differently. For example, two ex-Soviet electronics combinates in Riga (VEF, Alfa) have turned to very different strategies (one towards sustainable real adjustment, the other towards sophisticated rent seeking). This shows that the role of top management and the area within which they search for new opportunities is important, sometimes crucial.

Third, strategic partners make the process of restructuring much faster as the case of Pioneer confirms. The VEF restructuring would have proceeded more smoothly had they found a suitable strategic investor. Sometimes a domestic strategic partner like EKTA can give a push to the development of new small firms. Also, strong foreign buyers may provide this push and maintain a momentum of restructuring as was possible in the case of several EKTA small firms.

Fourth, the privatisation context plays an important role as it shapes management expectations and activities. Where management is firmly in control of the privatisation process or where conflicts among stakeholders are not high, progress moves easily as the cases of Pioneer and Latvijas Finieris confirm.

Fifth, enterprises are in different restructuring phases; from the waiting phase (Eesti Kivioli, Riga Railway Carriage Works, Alfa), experimentation (VEF) to active shake up (Pioneer, EKTA). This seems to be determined by the top management attitudes and expectations and the privatisation context.

PATTERNS OF INDUSTRIAL ADJUSTMENT IN POST-SOCIALIST
BALTIC STATES: DISCUSSION

In this part we will discuss the specific elements of our descriptive model
of development of organisational capabilities in the post-socialist Baltic
States. These patterns are largely rooted in micro-strategies and reflect an
inherited sectoral structure from the Soviet period.

Sectors and organisational capability gaps in the Baltic States

Based on our descriptive model we should expect that in industries where
technological problems are confined to one factory, as in many traditional
industries or commodities, adjustment prospects are already reflected in
relatively lower output decreases in relation to average decrease.

Tables 2.4 and 2.5 and 2.6 partially confirm our predictions. In Table
2.4 we show two groups of industries – traditional and engineering and
machinery sectors.[7] They very imperfectly represent production know-
how- and engineering-based sectors. Estonian figures on engineering and
metal industries do not conform to our predictions which is mainly due to
their high aggregation levels. However, our prediction is fully confirmed
by the Estonian sample of products (Table 2.6). Also, the Lithuanian and
Latvian trends do show, to some extent, the divergence between production know-how-based sectors (light industry, commodities, wood, furniture) versus machinery and metal industries.

More specific data on the physical production of some principal products in the case of Latvia (Table 2.4) shows that there is some ground for
our prediction that the more complex the production network, the less
likely are the possibilities for survival or 'catching up'.

Our field research and other case studies produced within the project on
industrial restructuring in the Baltic States (see Hirschausen, 1995) allow a
few qualitative generalisations regarding restructuring prospects in three
sectors in the Baltic States along these lines.[8]

In *production know-how based sectors* the main technological problems
are in quality control and operational management. Low quality of production, high costs, long production time, are problems caused by organisational weaknesses. Products are basically commodities for which
customers do not need intensive interaction with producers, as long as
specifications correspond to those accepted as market standards. A typical
example is plywood production in Latvia or garments in Estonia.

Table 2.4   Output trends in specific industrial sectors in relation to industry
average (1990 = 100; industry = 100)

Lithuania	1994
	%
Light industry	153.11
Timber, timber processing, paper, cellulose, furniture	137.19
Machinery and equipment	112.64

Latvia	1994
	%
Footwear	158.00
Wood manufacture	196.00
Furniture	165.00
Fabricated metal	96.00
Machinery and equipment	86.00

Estonia	1994
	%
Light industry	66.33
Forest industry	119.40
Engineering and metal industry	120.08

Source: Gulans (1995), Rainys (1995), Kilvits (1995).

Here upgrading is a process of gradual shift from lower to higher value-added activities. In the Baltic States, this often takes the form of a shift from commodities, like wooden boards or clothes made according to wholesaler's specifications, towards products like originally designed furniture or clothes targeted at specific markets. Development essentially means the involvement of non-tangible elements like marketing, design, and user specifications. This is only partly a problem of equipment. Baltic producers are still on a very low rung of this ladder. It is our feeling that business communities in the Baltic States have not yet grasped when main bottlenecks inhibit their shift into higher value-added activities. However, production know-how-based networks have adjusted relatively easily to the new context.

In the ex-Soviet republics *engineering-based sectors* used to be Union-based, and had very weak links with local enterprises. They were oriented entirely towards the Soviet market, and can be considered as export

Table 2.5 Production of some principal products in Latvia
(1989 = 100, in physical units)

	1993
Commodities	%
Timber cut, mn m3	114
Sawn-wood, thsd, m3	54
Plywood, thsd, m3*	67
Fibreboard, thsd, m3*	50
Paperboard, t.	9
Complex products	
Automatic telephone exchanges, nm	36
Buses, units	63
Railway passenger carriages, units	22
Mopeds, units	12
Washing machines, units	3

Note: * Figures are for 1994.
Source: Based on Gulans (1995).

enclaves within the Baltic economies. Good examples of such industries are the chemicals industry in Estonia, railway carriage production (Riga Carriage Works) and minibus assembler RAF (Riga).

In these sectors the technological bottlenecks are more complex. They are related to the state of the capital stock as well as to the much bigger problem of re-orientation from Eastern to Western markets. Here organisational restructuring is very costly, and almost impossible to implement with the current level of demand and management competencies. A good example is the electric train and railway carriage production in Riga, where the existing 'flow' (line) type of production process is very unsuitable in terms of current levels of demand, and of plans to diversify into other production lines, like trams. The advantage of the 'flow' system is high volume with a limited range of products. Its limitation is that it is sensitive to bottlenecks, and is especially unsuitable for low levels of capacity utilisation. At full capacity the factory was producing 2–3 units a day, while today it produces one in two days. Its current system creates huge slack, and is very wasteful of working capital. Reorganisation would require an almost total turn-around in factory lay-out.

The distribution problem in this sector is more complex as products are designed according to users' specifications. A lack of constant pressure

Table 2.6   Production of some principal products in Estonia
(1990 = 100, in physical units)

	1993
Commodities	%
Footwear, thousand pairs	14.36
Sawn-wood, thsd, m3	31.40
Plywood, thsd, m3	27.83
Fibreboard, thsd, m3	40.61
Knitwear, thousand units	27.26
Complex products	
Concrete mixers, units	2.40
Converters	5.27
Excavators	1.01
Automation for sootblower	18.86

Source: *Statistical Yearbook*, Statistical Office of Estonia (1994).

from users in the Soviet period has left big problems on the technological side. Even if they produce higher quality products, producers cannot get an appropriate price for the higher quality in western markets as they do not have image and market credibility. The options are either to continue to under-price products for quite some time, and thus endure losses, or to shift back to lower value-added categories, for which an adequate price is received. By contrast, when they export to Russia, the market is undemanding and there is no pressure to improve performance or quality. This duality of market situations, in the case of plants which have the greatest difficulties to re-orient towards the West, cannot be overcome without some sort of external pressure or incentives.

The survival of the engineering-based sectors is entirely dependent on barter. This is, however, an inconvenient method of payment when shipments are small. In other words, entry barriers to this trade are not marginal. Those Baltic governments which are more helpful in setting up barter schemes (usually gas and oil for Baltic products) directly support the survival of these production lines. However, for many smaller-scale plants the only solution is cash-based trade, which reduces the already low level of effective demand.

In *R&D-based sectors* the problems are to a degree similar to those found in engineering-based sectors in terms of equipment and organisation. However, the fact that here the know-how is embodied in human resources makes the problems more tractable. Accumulated skills, primarily the skills of design engineers, can be employed in developments appropriate for a new market context.

Here both a good knowledge of users' needs and close interaction in all phases of product development are essential. In this respect the Soviet system was a poor school to learn in. Entry barriers against R&D-based products on foreign markets are too high for small Baltic firms. Large-scale growth cannot occur without infrastructural support. A case in point is the Tallinn electronics association (grouping of 17 small firms), which assists its members to access foreign markets and establish technical co-operation. The point is that it is often marketing, rather than technology barriers, which form the key bottleneck.

The main problem is finance for product development. Even though their new products are based on assembling and minor software-based reconfigurations, they still find it difficult to finance even a few months of engineering development. There is a lack of 'soft' finance or schemes for product development finance. Institutional sources of such finance, like the Estonian Innovation Foundation, are few in number and significantly underfunded.

In R&D-based sectors the only way out of the crisis is the development of new products. For example, VEF, the Latvian telephone producer, renewed 50 per cent of its product range in 1993/1994 period. Mostly these are small developments of 3–4 months duration, using on average five engineers. Design is mainly adaptive, with heavy use (40 per cent) of Western components. The main problem here is how to get rid of old debts, and at the same time introduce new products. A sort of 'soft' finance for R&D would improve the situation. Even so, the 'screwdriver innovation' pattern that has predominated seriously limits the scope for independent, commercially viable developments. The only solution is to stimulate joint ventures with other similar Baltic producers, or, even better, become an R&D subcontractor to Western firms. However, these involve short production runs which can hardly be the basis for the redevelopment of an entire sector.

Privatisation context in the Baltic States

Privatisation and restructuring in the Baltic States has so far taken the pattern shown in Table 2.7.

Mass privatisation in Lithuania has created a new structure, namely private investment funds, which might develop into restructuring and capitalising agents. The problem for the state is how to assist them, how to

Table 2.7   Privatisation and restructuring in the Baltic States

Type of restructuring	Estonia	Latvia	Lithuania
Pre-privatisation restructuring	None	None	None
(De)centralised	Centralised	Centralised	?
Dominant type of privatisation	Public sales	Lease plus purchase option	Mass privatisation
Future path of privatisation	Convergence through diversification of methods of privatisation		

force them to export, while at the same time avoiding the danger of 'government capture'.

In Latvia the leasing method of privatisation has been applied, among others. This has allowed organisational and operational restructuring to proceed through leases, pending full financial and legal restructuring. This method may be administratively the least demanding, and may minimise the danger of 'government capture'.

In Estonia direct sale imposes a heavy burden on the capacity of the state properly to handle privatisation procedures and maximise long-term benefits for the country. With several big enterprises having zero chances of privatisation without a change in production profile, this burden will not ease in the immediate future.

Will the Baltic economies be inhabited by small firms or dominated by few big firms? If we extrapolate current, short-term trends, we may hypothesise that Lithuania will be dominated by several big holding companies, while Estonia might be dominated by small firms. In the first case, the crucial problem is the relationship between the big holding companies and the state. In the latter case, it is vital to develop a public/private infrastructure to support small firms. In Lithuania big holding companies may internalise infrastructural activity, but they may also capture government.

In all three countries, and indeed in the other post-socialist economies, there is convergence through diversification of privatisation methods, as all countries adopt a variety of methods. This might lead to much more similar industrial structures than it is possible to envisage today. However, the convergence is occurring within very specific national patterns. In Lithuania, investment funds are already a reality, and a factor strongly shaping the future pattern of privatisation. In Estonia and Latvia they will also play an important role, with the introduction of some form of mass privatisation.

Strategic partners and investors

The integration of the Baltic economies into international production networks might significantly compensate for the disadvantages in their business environment and might serve as a mechanism to overcome numerous financial, marketing and technological barriers. FDI and subcontracting links serve as approximations of these processes which are primarily micro-based. With regard to this it seems that the situation is diverging among individual Baltic States. According to our model this might have significant implications for the development of organisational capabilities in individual Baltic economies. In terms of per capita FDI Estonia ranks very high. It is third among post-socialist economies, after Hungary and Czech Republic. On the other side is Lithuania with only $20 of FDI per capita which is below the very low CIS level (see UN ECE, 1995). A stronger involvement of foreign enterprises means that the probability for enterprise restructuring, not only through direct ownership, but through different forms of spillovers in terms of knowledge transfer, increased competition, and so on, is much higher.

Integration of the Baltic enterprises into foreign production networks is much stronger through different forms of subcontracting. However, quantification of these forms of trade is more difficult. The most common form of subcontracting is probably outward processing trade. According to Estonian statistics, imports for inward processing already makes 12 per cent of the total while export of processed goods account for 15 per cent of total exports between January and September 1994 (UN ECE, 1995, p. 133). Much thorough research is, however, required into the forms of integration of the Baltic enterprises into global production networks. In Radosevic (1996) several examples of the Baltic sectors were illustrated, pinpointing the role they play in these networks.

Macro-economic climate and top management's expectations

A favourable macroeconomic climate should be conducive to enterprise restructuring in the Baltic States. In all three countries the new domestic currencies were stable and freely convertible, and public finances were under control (UN ECE, 1995). This clearly plays a positive role in enterprise restructuring as it strongly shapes management expectations away from rent-seeking behaviour and towards active adjustment. However, the relatively stable macro-economic situation in the Baltic economies has not yet been turned into economic growth as is the case in some of the other post-socialist economies, as Table 2.8 indicates.

Table 2.8   GDP and gross industrial output, 1994/1989 (1989 = 100)

	GDP	IND
Estonia	64.9	38.7
Latvia	49.9	37.6
Lithuania	33.3	31.3
Baltic States	45.5	34.8
CETE-4*	87.2	78.4
SETE-8**	69.0	47.9
CIS	52.1	54.3

Notes:
* Hungary, Poland, Czech Republic and Slovakia.
**Romania, Bulgaria, Slovenia, Albania, Croatia, FYR Macedonia,
   FR Yugoslavia.
Source: UN ECE (1995).

This indicates that the link between macro-economic reform and the actual growth process is not a direct and automatic one. It is inevitably mediated through a complex social fabric where enterprise restructuring is one of the key elements. A vision of post-socialist transformation which is reduced to macro-economic stabilisation and privatisation seems to be very simplistic (Hirschausen, 1995, p. 5). A stronger decrease of GDP and industry in the post-socialist Baltic States, above the average for post-socialist economies, explains much of the lack of demand problem which inhibits enterprise restructuring in these economies. In addition to that, in spite of very restrictive monetary policies in all three Baltic countries, average price levels were still significantly above the level in four Central European post-socialist economies and Slovenia (see UN ECE, 1995, p. 97). This indicates that the sustainability of macro-economic stability might become a problem. However, whether it will be directly reflected in enterprise restructuring is difficult to say. From our perspective the Baltic States show that the macro-economic situation, if taken as an isolated element, does not *per se* guarantee enterprise restructuring and growth in the economy.

CONCLUSIONS

In this paper it is argued that the development of organisational capabilities of post-socialist enterprises lies at the heart of the regeneration of these economies. Our conclusion is that the development of organisational capabilities, which ultimately means enterprise growth, is a complex process. It is determined not only by micro- or enterprise variables. Although our evidence is far from conclusive we think that the mezzo variables (sectoral, market and technological characteristics; privatisation context) in interaction with micro (top management behaviour; strategic partners) and macro factors (macro-economic variables) ultimately shape the prospects for the development of organisational capabilities and enterprise growth.

With the opening-up of the economy it is mainly the simple production networks, like those in woodworking and the garment industry, that have re-oriented themselves easily to world markets. Their speedy integration into subcontracting networks, and rudimentary clustering at a local level, are possible where there is available know-how. In the cases of more complex production networks, like those in machinery sectors, where inputs have to be supplied from several enterprises, and where costs per unit are much higher, such networks are deteriorating on account of cash-flow problems, or (barely) surviving through barter. As partial proof of this, the share of engineering goods exported to the West from Baltic countries was only 3 per cent in 1992, by far the lowest product group (UN ECE, 1995). The R&D-based sector is in-between these two extremes, with some parts being completely destroyed, while new net-works are simultaneously being created.

There seem to be three types of network transformation which, at a very preliminary level of research for the Baltic and eastern Europe, are dominant:

(a) Reorientation of simple networks (for example, the woodworking industry, light machinery);
(b) Destruction of old knowledge-intensive production networks and the creation in their place of new networks (for example, the IT industry)
(c) Collapse or preservation or 'lock-in' of old networks (for example, heavy machinery; petrochemicals).

The sectoral characteristics of enterprises seem to dominate or determine the probability and the scope of restructuring effort. However, the operation of other factors of our model makes the restructuring prospects of specific enterprises, especially within specific sectors, less determinate. Although, sectoral characteristics seems to be dominant, that is, equally present in all three countries, their interaction with other factors produces distinct national patterns of industrial restructuring. However, we have focused mainly on enterprise and sector levels where these patterns emerge but where they are still difficult to discern. In order to understand better the mutual interaction of suggested factors it would be necessary to try to quantify or approximate variables of the model.

Notes

1. I am highly indebted to Nick von Tunzelmann, Neil Hood and to participants of the Riga conference for valuable comments.
2. Even when the system departed from a strictly centrally planned organisation towards an organisation based on combinates or associations of several enterprises these were not permitted to move into distribution. In order to insure themselves against disruptions in supply, combinates often integrated backward, rarely forward.
3. For a similar approach along these lines, see Hobday (1994).
4. For an example of this in the case of a Russian defence complex see Kuznetsov (1995).
5. Whether to buy from a traditional partner or from a top manager's newly formed company, which serves as a mechanism to liquidate his 'nominal' enterprise, is implicitly a strategic decision ('wild', 'spontaneous' or 'nomenclature' privatisation) as well as many other forms of private–public enterprises links.
6. Czech firms, usually German subcontractors, are subcontracting Romanian, Ukrainian and Belarussian enterprises to play the role of second-tier suppliers.
7. However, we have to bear in mind that the statistical classification of industries do not correspond to our sectors, which are technological groupings based on the location of technological capabilities.
8. This part is based on Radosevic (1995).

REFERENCES

Amman, A. and Cooper, J. (1982) *Industrial Innovation in the Soviet Union* (New Haven and London: Yale University Press).

Bomsel, O. (1994) *Enjeux Industriels du Post-Socialisme*, Cahier de Recherche 94-C-2, CERNA, Ecole des Mines, paper given to Association Française de Science Economique, Paris.

Carlin, W., Reenen, J. van and Wolfe, T. (1994) *Enterprise Restructuring in the Transition: An Analytical Survey of the Case Study Evidence from Central and Eastern Europe*, EBRD Working Paper No 14.

Guerrieri, P. (1994) *'Technology, Structural Change and Trade Patterns of Eastern Europe'*, paper presented at workshop on 'Research Co-operation with Countries in Transition', Six Countries Programme Conference, Vienna, 2 December.

Gulans, P. (1995) 'Industrial Restructuring in Latvia: Analyses by Branch and Case Studies', in C. Hirschausen, *et al.* (eds) (1995b).

Hagedoorn, J. and Sadowski, B. (1995) 'General Trends in International Technology Partnering: The Prospects for Transition Economies', MERIT, Maastricht (mimeo).

Hanson, P. and Pavitt, K. (1987) *The Comparative Economics of Research, Development and Innovation in East and West: A Survey* (London, Harwood Academic Publishers).

Hirschausen, C. (1995a) 'Industrial Restructuring in the Baltic States: An Introduction', in C. Hirschausen *et al.* (eds) (1995b).

Hirschausen, C. (1995b) *Industrial Restructuring in the Baltic States: Achievements, Obstacles and Perspective of Post-Socialist Reform*, Final Report EU-Phare-ACE, May.

Hobday, M. (1994) 'Export-Led Technology Development in the Four Dragons: The Case of Electronics', *Development and Change*, 25(2), pp. 333–361.

Kilvits, K. (1995) 'Industrial Restructuring in Estonia: Analyses by Branch and Case Studies', in C. Hirschausen *et al.* (1995b).

Kuznetsov, Y. (1995) 'Learning to Learn: Emerging Patterns of Enterprise Behaviour in the Russian Defence Sector, 1992–1995', The Brookings Institute, Foreign Policy Studies Program (mimeo).

Percival, L. and Straunik, A. (1995) 'Baltika: against the odds', *Business Central Europe*, April.

Radosevic, S. (1994a) 'Strategic Technology Policy for Eastern Europe', *Economic Systems*, 18(2). pp. 87–116.

Radosevic, S. (1994b) *'National Systems of Innovation in Eastern Europe: Between Restructuring and Erosion'*, paper presented at workshop on 'Research Co-operation with Countries in Transition', Six Countries Programme Conference, Vienna, 2 December.

Radosevic, S. (1996) 'The Eastern European Latecomer Firm and Technology Transfer: From "Muddling Through" to "Catching Up"', in G. Bugliarelo *et al.* (eds) East-West Technology Transfer: New Perspectives and Human Resources, NATO ASI Series 4, S&T Policy, Vol. 3, Dordrecht, Kluwer, pp. 129–154

Rainys, G. (1995) 'Industrial Restructuring in Lithuania: Analyses by Branch and Case Studies', in C. Hirschausen *et al.* (eds) (1995b).

Rosati, K.D. (1994) *'Changes in the Structure of Manufacturing Trade Between Poland and the European Community'*, Working Paper No. 49, Foreign Trade Research Institute, Warsaw, February.

Swaan, W. (1994) *'Behavioural Constraints and the Creation of Markets in Post-Socialist Economies'*, paper presented at the Fourth Trento Workshop, 'Centralisation and Decentralisation of Economic Institutions: Their Role in the Transformation of Economic Systems', Institute of Economics, Hungarian Academy of Sciences, Budapest (mimeo).

Tunzelmann, N. von (1995) *Technology and Industrial Progress* (Aldershot, Hants: Edward Elgar).

UN ECE (1995) *Economic Survey of Europe 1994–1995* (Geneva: UN).

3 Organisation and Management Transition in Estonia: A Cultural Approach
Kari Liuhto

'When we were in Estonia, we were astonished by the high standard of living, order and economic activity, which was quite contrary to the conditions in the European parts of Russia. We drove our own car from Moscow to Estonia and were caught by surprise already where the roads that were in poor condition and without repairs for years suddenly changed for better right after Pihkova. We saw small, but well-tended, farms quite far apart from one another, and farmers cutting the hay with their own mowers for their own cows, usually a few in each farm, and we saw the farmers ploughing their fields with their own tractors. Milk churns waited by the roads in small sheds for the cars to pick them up to the dairy.

We often heard the Estonians say that they lived better than elsewhere because they worked harder and better. Surely this was only half of the truth. The real reason was the fact that the socialism had walked over their fields later than elsewhere and with a weaker and more inconsistent force, so there was simply less time for it to do damage. The active farming communities were destroyed in a much more thorough manner, often even physically, in the republics that had belonged to the Soviet Union right from the beginning. These communities had been divided into castes more clearly, amongst which a parasite-like layer of party bureaucrats could be detected. It is not by coincidence that the economic forms based on lease, co-operatives and particularly private ownership developed more slowly in the "old" republics because they were met with almost an open resistance on the behalf of the local party and state organs.'

Thus wrote Andrei Sakharov of his visit to Estonia in July–August 1987. A free translation of Andrei Sakharov (1991) *Muistelmat*, vol. 2, pp. 724–5.

INTRODUCTION

For the most part, research on the economic transition of the former Soviet Union has been carried out from the macro-economic perspective, even though it is most probable that macro-economic programmes will not be realised if their accomplishers, namely companies, are unable to implement them (Kozminski, 1993, p. 145). Moreover, enterprises cannot meet these new challenges unless they have a motive, will and skills to change. The outcome of the entire economic transition is largely dependent on the ability of the organisational and managerial culture to adjust according to the new requirements. The objective of this research is to contribute as one component to a larger whole which aims at outlining what the significance of business cultural transition is when the former socialist economies are striving toward a market economy.

This chapter is based on empirical research carried out in 114 Estonian enterprises at the beginning of 1995. These enterprises were chosen so that they represented the Estonian enterprise sector by industry, location, size and ownership. Due to the broadness of this approach, detailed empirical results are not reported here. The chapter is divided into this introduction and three major sections. The first attempts to examine how other studies have viewed cultural change in organisations, the next analyses the development of Estonian enterprises from the beginning of the twentieth century until the present, while the last section attempts to combine the theoretical perspective with a developmental perspective. At the end of the chapter, the observations made on Estonian management culture are employed to contribute to the discussion of organisation cultural transition in other former Soviet republics.

CULTURAL CHANGE IN ORGANISATIONS: A THEORETICAL PERSPECTIVE

The starting point of this study is that cultural change in organisations operating within the same industry forms the cultural transition in that entire industry. Similarly, the cultural transformation in all the industries of a nation forms the cultural transition of the whole nation. This means in effect that the nation's business cultural transition can (and should) be studied by looking into the ways the culture of organisations has changed.

The basis for the transition of culture within an organisation can stem from the inability of those forces that maintain its stability to manage to control the transformative pressure with which it is confronted (Lewin, in

Thompson, 1990, p. 595). The stability of the organisation's culture can be shaped both by internal and external factors (Schein, 1985, p. 299). According to Lundberg (1985, p. 182), change of organisational culture begins with external forces which enable the change. This is in turn reflected within the organisation by the generation of forces which allow the change. Finally, the emergence of external or internal transformative pressure triggers off the events that begin the change. All in all, these transition events result in an attempt to create new visions of a new culture. Strategies and operational plans are later constructed so that these visions can be realised.

Dyer (1985, p. 211) points out that the management of the organisation will confront a crisis which challenges the abilities and practices of managers. The process of change advances by breaking down the symbols, beliefs or structures that maintain the old patterns. For instance, if a new leadership emerges in some management microculture of the organisation, the result will be a conflict between the old and new management culture. If the new management culture 'wins' over the old one in the conflict, the new managers will form the foundation for the new management culture. They begin to shape new pattern-maintenance of symbols, beliefs, and structures, which gradually form the new management culture.

These two models presented above are in agreement in one important issue; they both regard the transition of management culture occurring as a result of the collapse of the old and the creation of the new management culture. In effect, the old management culture does not necessarily change *per se* but the transformation may be explained by the creation of the new management culture.

If the transition process in the organisation is started, it does not necessarily result in a cultural change in the organisation. This is simply due to the strong tendency of organisational culture to return to the old practices if the forces that support cultural change disappear, or if the forces that accomplish cultural change become exhausted. In fact, Gagliardi (1986, p. 119) points out that 'as soon as the pressure is released, however, it [culture] will tend to return to its original state and attitude'.

Organisational cultural change is very rarely comprehensive (Feldman, 1986, p. 603). This means that a cultural transition will never occur suddenly but certain parts of culture will transform more rapidly than the others. According to a commonly accepted principle, deep cultural layers, such as sets of values, will change more slowly than the visible cultural features (Juuti, 1992, p. 156). On the whole, the change of organisational culture confronts a dilemma: partial changes are usually suppressed by resistance to change, but, on the other hand, a comprehensive change is extremely difficult to accomplish (Laurent, 1989, pp. 88–9; Gersick, 1991, p. 34; Hendry and Hope, 1994, p. 403).

The change is complicated by its tendency to introduce new and surprising features, thus creating 'side-effects' (Aaltio-Marjosola, 1991, p. 195) or to release 'bottled-up energy', which cannot be predicted or controlled in advance by a manager (Juuti, 1992, p. 157). Besides being a complex process, organisational cultural change is expensive and may produce uncertain or even cosmetic results (Gagliardi, 1986, p. 119; Hendry and Hope, 1994, p. 402).

One important factor concerning cultural change within an organisation is whether a new culture can be constructed more easily than the old culture changed. The answer to this question can be approached from two different perspectives. For instance, Wilkins and Patterson (1985, p. 280) consider the changing of the old culture more rapid than the creation of a new cultural structure. A contrasting view has been advanced by those researchers who emphasise the unchangeability of culture and insist on the creation of a new culture as the basis of cultural transition (for example, Dyer, 1985, p. 217). Finally, it is important to pay attention to the fact that the change of management culture in an organisation can simply emerge through the normal development of the organisation.

The above theoretical discussion is perhaps best concluded by summarising a few questions that arise from the study of cultural transition:

1. Does a cultural transition result from a natural evolution?
2. Does a transition result from the destruction of the companies representing the old business culture and the birth of companies representing a new culture?
3. Is the transition taking place in the organisational culture real, and how has the transition occurred?

These questions introduced here will be commented upon in the latter part of this chapter, which studies the cultural change taking place in Estonian entrepreneurship. Before so doing, however, the development of Estonian entrepreneurship during the twentieth century needs to be briefly summarised.

THE TRANSITION OF ESTONIAN ENTREPRENEURSHIP IN THE TWENTIETH CENTURY: A DEVELOPMENTAL PERSPECTIVE

In this section Estonian entrepreneurship is viewed from a developmental perspective, namely by examining how entrepreneurship has formed during this century. The century has been divided into four periods: 1) the Russian Empire (1900–19); 2) independent Estonia (1920–39); 3) Soviet Estonia (1940–91); 4) and independent Estonia (1992 and onwards). This commentary concentrates only on the major characteristics of each period. These are, for example, the expansion of entrepreneurship, the ownership of enterprises, the structure of enterprise sector, the size and location of companies, foreign trade intensity, and the role of foreign companies.

The pre-birth of the Estonian organisation and management culture (1900–19)

At the beginning of this century Estonia belonged to the Russian Empire. Being a part of this supranational country had a significant impact on entrepreneurship and management culture in the country. First of all, the companies operating within Estonia were not as concentrated on their own region as they would have been had Estonia been a nation state. The most important area outside Estonia was the present St Petersburg, which was a major market and a financial centre, as well as Russia's window to the West (Kavass-Sprudzs, 1972, p. 137).

The non-independent position of Estonia as a part of the Russian Empire naturally implied that Estonia had no right to shape its own economic policy. This was reflected, for instance, in the existence of 'closed industries', namely those industries that were the monopoly of a few 'multinational' Russian companies. The metal industry was one of the sectors in the hands of one Russian company (Torpan, 1984, p. 45). In practice this Russia-centred economic policy meant that the economy and entrepreneurship of Estonia were controlled from St Petersburg.

The development of national business culture was also slowed down by Estonia's foreign elite, which controlled the majority of the Estonian economy. An example of the foreign domination is illustrated by the fact that 600 German-Baltic families owned over half of the Estonian land before Estonian independence (Hinkkanen-Lievonen, 1984, p. 179). Furthermore, the share which foreign investors held in the total industrial capital of the country was about 12 per cent in 1914. The share of German companies within the total foreign investment was approximately 50 per cent (Torpan, 1984, p. 206).

Another typical characteristic of Estonian industry was the small number of enterprises. In 1900, there were only 235 large industrial enterprises registered in Estonia (Torpan, 1984, p. 187). This was not exceptional in a society which was still largely agrarian at the beginning of this century.[1] Besides having a small number of industrial enterprises, Estonian entrepreneurship typically consisted of very small companies. In 1900 over 90 per cent of the industrial enterprises in Estonia employed less than 50 workers. In addition, Estonian industry was one-sided (Torpan, 1984, p. 186–7) and the entrepreneurial activity was centralised in a few cities. The majority of industrial activities were located in the northern parts of Estonia: Tallinn and Narva (Liuhto, 1995b).

The First World War, the October Revolution and the national unrest following the socialist revolution led to the collapse of the entire Estonian economy and entrepreneurship within it. As a result of the economic collapse, most of the industrial capacity of Estonia was destroyed. According to Hinkkanen-Lievonen (1984, p. 251), only one fifth of the capacity of the metallurgic industry was operating in 1920. In addition to the industrial losses, the economic infrastructure as a whole suffered enormous damage. The greatest loss, however, must have been the complete closing down of the Russian market (Raun, 1987, p. 125).

The birth and the first transition of Estonian organisation and management culture (1920–39)

The beginning of the 1920s was a period of a surprisingly rapid reconstruction of Estonia and of considerable economic growth. The economy continued to grow until the world recession, during which economic activity in Estonia declined. However, Estonia was also able to rapidly recover from the world recession, and already in 1934 the net industrial production exceeded that of all the previous years (*Eesti 1920–1930*, 1931, p. 143; *Eesti Statistika*, 1935, p. 84; Pihlamägi, 1992, p. 19; Liuhto, 1995a).

The structure of the Estonian enterprise sector remained surprisingly homogeneous. Structural stability was maintained despite the enormous reconstruction challenge and the world recession. The most important changes between 1920 and 1937 were that the food, textile and clothing industries managed to raise their shares of national output by 5 per cent, whereas the metal and wood processing industries both lost 5 per cent from their shares. Over 70 per cent of the large industrial enterprises operated in these four sectors (*Eesti Statistika*, 1935, p. 85).

From a regional perspective, independence introduced no significant changes in Estonian entrepreneurship and Tallinn accounted for over half of all industrial output in 1936. Other important towns were Narva and Tartu, whose total share accounted for about one sixth. An interesting feature concerning the ownership of Estonian enterprises was that 87 per cent of them were in private hands, whereas only 2 per cent were under state or communal ownership. The rest, about one tenth, were in foreign hands (Tööstus, 1939, pp. 10–17). However, the seeds of the first transition in Estonian entrepreneurship were destroyed by the arrival of the Soviet army, which covered the Estonian economy with a red flag for the following five decades.

The invasion of Soviet-style entrepreneurship and management Sovieticus in Estonia (1940–91)

At the beginning of the Soviet rule in the 1940s, socialist doctrines were quickly forced on Estonia. Banks, large industries and foreign enterprises were nationalised almost immediately, after which the nationalisation wave flooded over all the other forms of private entrepreneurship. The last element to be nationalised at the end of the 1940s were private farms, which were incorporated into large state farms (Raud, 1987, pp. 91–4; Raun, 1987, p. 151). The speed with which Soviet ideology invaded Estonia is indicated by Van Arkadie and Karlson (1992, p. 117) who claimed that 'by 1950 the three [Baltic republics] were barely distinguishable in their economic organisation, and their political system, from the other Soviet republics'.

Although some considerable economic reforms were accomplished in the Soviet Union, the description of the official Soviet entrepreneurship is very monotonous because all the enterprises were under the state monopoly (Nove, 1989). In fact, the entire Soviet entrepreneurship could be described as one large factory (Kozminsky, 1993, p. 7). If it is necessary to chop the Soviet system into smaller components, it could be done by dividing the state enterprises into three major groups: all-union, mixed all-union-republican, and republican (Tiusanen, 1991, p. 29).

The first two of these enterprises operated in practice under the direct control of the ministries in Moscow, whereas only republican enterprises were controlled by the local authorities, although even they were indirectly within the reach of the co-ordination of the Moscow super-ministries. It could be simply stated that in reality Estonian national business culture did not exist. The republican enterprises in Estonian hands during the Soviet era could be compared to communal enterprises closely tied to the state machinery.

Although private entrepreneurship was no more evident in Soviet Estonia than it was in the Soviet Union, the parasite of socialism, or the seed of capitalism, was growing in the black and grey markets. These markets were particularly important in providing private individuals with supply channels for consumer goods. Besides this street entrepreneurship, the Soviet Union had even some non-legal private enterprise activities

(Grancelli, 1988). Non-legal entrepreneurial activities expanded especially during the Brezhnev era, when several illegalities in state enterprises were ignored so long as the state goals were met (Millar, 1988, pp. 3–19; Liuhto, 1993).

The economic problems of the 1980s resulted in the Soviet authorities being forced to adopt some of the methods of the market mechanism to prevent the socialist ship from sinking. Soviet economic reformers turned to the archives of the NEP (*New Economic Policy, 1921–8*), which was probably the only successful market economy experiment ever carried out in the Soviet Union (Liuhto, 1994). The following reforms at the microeconomic level were implemented in the middle of the 1980s: allowing individual labour (1985), producers' co-operatives (1987), and foreign-owned companies in the Soviet territory (1987).

These reforms shed the first light for Estonian entrepreneurship, but only at the turn of the 1990s, when the Joint Stock Company Law was decreed, did major, concrete changes begin to take place. This legal reform triggered off a massive boom in the registration of organisations. As a result, during less than a year, the total number of the Estonian organisations expanded from a few thousand to approximately 30 000 organisations on the eve of Estonian independence (Liuhto, 1992).

The rebirth of Estonian entrepreneurship and management culture (1992 onwards)

Since Estonian independence, the annual registration rate of new organisations has settled of 15 000, and due to this, over 83 000 new organisations were registered in Estonia by the beginning of 1995. Although the number of registered organisations in relation to the Estonian population is relatively high, the number of the operating companies is only 25 000–30 000 (Liuhto, 1996).

At present Estonian organisations are typically very small in size, with 97 per cent of them having less than 50 employees. The small size does not come as a surprise, indeed it is more or less a rule in all the transition economies. In addition to the small size, typical for Estonian entrepreneurship is the enormous growth of private entrepreneurship. As a matter of fact, the number of the state and municipal organisations has fallen from 25 per cent at the beginning of 1992 to less than 2 per cent at the beginning of 1995. Although Estonia, in common with the other transition economies, has experienced active 'privatisation', it must be remembered that the state enterprises still represent a significant share of total production and employment (Liuhto, 1996).

When studying the transition of Estonian entrepreneurship, one should not neglect the large number of foreign companies, which increased to over 8000 in 1995. Thus foreign companies represent about 10 per cent of the total number of the organisations in Estonia. Moreover, in terms of population, foreign investment in Estonia is significantly higher than in any other former Soviet republic. From the Eastern bloc, only Hungary and the Czech Republic have been able to attract more foreign investment per capita than Estonia.

The majority of organisations are registered in trade, whereas the share of industrial enterprises accounts for only one tenth of the total. Every second Estonian organisation is registered in the capital, Tallinn (Liuhto, 1996). Interestingly, the structure of Estonian entrepreneurship is very similar to what it was 60–70 years earlier. In other words, typical characteristics of Estonian entrepreneurship are the small size of companies and trade orientation. Furthermore, Estonian entrepreneurship can be characterised as very open, which is manifested in the large number of foreign-owned enterprises.

THE ORGANISATIONAL AND MANAGERIAL TRANSITION IN ESTONIA

The aim of this chapter is to study the experiences of Estonian entrepreneurship in the context of questions arising from the literature dealing with organisational culture and against the historic background as outlined. Referring back to the three questions posed earlier, they would be answered in summary as follows:

(i)   Does a cultural transition result from a natural evolution?
      Yes.
(ii) Does a transition result from the destruction of the companies representing the old business culture and the birth of companies representing a new culture?
      The cause of cultural transition is, first and foremost, the creation of companies representing a new management culture.
(iii) Is the transition taking place in the organisational culture real, and how has transition occurred?
      Changes have occurred even in companies representing the old organisational culture. However, they continue to reflect more of the old culture than the new organisations do.

The first answer could be argued from the tendency of organisational culture to return to its normal state after the unnatural transition forces have disappeared. One of these could be the dismantling of a state monopoly, for instance, which in Estonia has released a private entrepreneurial spirit comparable to that from Aladdin's lamp. The answers to questions (ii) and (iii) are so closely connected to one another that they can be explained at the same time. The background to the cultural transition has been the establishment of a vast number of new organisations during the first five years of the 1990s. Even though these new companies still bear some of the characteristics of the Soviet managerial style, this is less so than in the organisations which already operated in Soviet Estonia. In Table 3.1, some empirical findings of Soviet influence on Estonian management culture are summarised from the author's empirical research.

Table 3.1   The impact of the Soviet era on the Estonian management culture and its transformation

Statements	1	2	3	4	5	Ave	Standard
			per cent				*deviation*
National cultural features are manifested more strongly in management than previously, because it was not useful to display national features in the management of Soviet companies operating in Estonia.	17	40	14	13	06	2.60	1.19
The Soviet management philosophy had no effect on enterprise management in Estonia, because only a few of the managers actually believed in the socialist doctrines.	09	32	06	40	14	3.20	1.24
The management cultural transition in Estonia will continue for several years, as, in the present conditions, many features not typical of the national culture of Estonia will be reflected in the Estonian management culture.	24	57	13	05	00	2.00	0.77

Scale:
1 = I agree completely
2 = I agree to some extent
3 = Difficult to say
4 = I disagree to some extent
5 = I disagree completely

Despite the positive transformation, it must be remembered that a transition is not a phenomenon which continues automatically once begun. The transition can proceed rapidly but also return toward the old direction. This does not necessarily mean that the transition as a whole should be regarded as having failed. It is precisely this unexpected nature of transition which makes its study so challenging. Furthermore, the transition may produce results of a cosmetic nature.

With regard to the burden of history in cultural transition, it is clear that the effects of the past have long roots into the future. Secondly, a cultural vacuum as such cannot exist, even though some researchers have claimed so. Rather than a vacuum, the situation could be better described as cultural chaos, in which a community is searching for its own cultural identity. In practice this means that the cultural past is always present today and thus also in the future. Hence the transition of both organisation and management culture can never begin from 'a cleared table'. In other words, the past is a part of the process in which a new organisation and management culture is formulated.

The cultural resistance to the recent Estonian management cultural transition has been surprisingly small, when it is remembered that the transition taking place has been both extremely wide and deep. This is mostly due to the fact that the transition process has evolved fairly naturally. The majority of Estonians have been ready for shock treatment when its reward has been independence and they have felt confident about its outcome adding to their well-being.

CONCLUSIONS

To conclude the observations made in this chapter, it could be stated that the strong transition of Estonian management culture was mostly caused by the emergence of new organisations. This 'new' organisation and management culture, however, was largely constructed of old components. In other words, this 'new' management culture is not totally without the evidence of a Soviet impact.

If the experiences of Estonian entrepreneurial and management cultural transition were to be applied to other former Soviet republics, such an exercise should be carried out with great care. It should be remembered that the market and economic remedy adopted for Estonia cannot be directly transposed into other transition economies. The generalisation of the organisation and management cultural transition should in fact begin from a more abstract level. Figure 3.1 shows the sub-areas in the organisation and management cultural transition and the most important message to be read from it is that the managers in transition economies hold a key position as its ultimate implementors. Secondly, the managers alone cannot accomplish a transition if they are not supported by other interest groups with an involvement in the transition.

A positive outcome of an economic transition begins with the ordinary people and ends with the companies actually implementing it. Therefore the outcome is not a game in which only the economic reformers and managers implementing those reforms can participate. The purpose of Figure 3.1 is to offer one proposition which aims at combining, at least in some manner, the political, macro-economic, micro-economic and national–cultural perspectives. Each of the sub-areas in this figure should be considered in the terms of the conditions prevailing in each transition economy. Each individual transition economy should be prescribed a specially constructed market economy remedy. The weakest alternative would be some kind of general prescription created by Western economists, a medicine which would fail to cure the problems of any transition economy. This is a trap that the developed West has too often fallen into in the past in various development programmes undertaken in many developing countries.

As regards Figure 3.1, some further comments are necessary. First of all, the triggering force of transition is people who feel a pressure to change the system when, for instance, they are striving to improve their

Figure 3.1   The role of organisational and management cultural transition in the overall transformation process

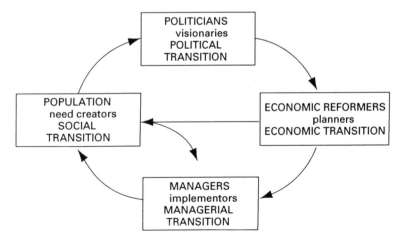

own welfare. An automatic result of this is that national culture(s) is reflected in the second part of the transition, namely, the part involving the political decision-makers. They in turn should try to represent the needs of their voters, create visions and ideas for the implementation of the needs of the society. The way in which the new democracies operate essentially influences the outcome of the economic transition. This is simply due to the transition depending on the occurrence of many thorough, simultaneous and sufficiently long-range actions. However, many transition economies are characterized by political disintegration and impatience, which have often prevented the planning and implementation of economic reforms. The role of the economic reformers is vital in the latter function. They need sufficient knowledge about the operations of the market economy, and they must have an ability to co-operate, as their work will mainly be accomplished in groups. The disagreements upon economic reforms often tend to result in blind alleys, from which the only way out is a sufficient amount of political consensus. Unfortunately, the transition conditions usually involve a power struggle, which in most cases prevents the parties reaching agreement. In consequence, political power struggles often result in considerable economic loss.

Given these conditions, the company managers in many transition economies face an entrepreneurial Wild East, where a former 'speculator' has a far better chance of survival than a law-abiding entrepreneur. Under the conditions of the Wild East the organisation and management culture is often forced to adopt illegal and unethical means. These negative characteristics are hardly ever a part of the traditional national management culture, but they may have long-term effects on the fragile national business culture.

If the enterprises fail to meet the goals for economic welfare set by the population, the transition becomes a vicious circle in which criticism directed against the decision-makers continuously increases. Finally impatience grows so strong that any visions, plans or implementation of economic reforms become impossible. In this kind of situation populist movements, whether ultra-nationalist or conservative, often gain strength. This vicious circle can be avoided by adopting methods that better link enterprises to the economic decision-makers. For example, if the economy of the country is in an unsatisfactory state, the politicians could try to come to an agreement on the necessary reforms in economic policies. Equally, the effective monitoring of the economic reforms is vital because without an economic policy that is consistent and sympathetic towards entrepreneurship the population will not generate more new entrepreneurs. This is the important interaction which is suggested in the middle of

Figure 3.1. Finally, if the transition means forgetting the impact of socialist ideology and if Andrei Sakharov (as quoted in the preface) was right about the effect of socialism in Soviet Estonia, economic transition of Estonia will proceed more rapidly than in several other former Soviet republics. In a similar manner, if the Estonians were right in claiming that the reason they were economically better off in the Soviet Union was a result of their own hard work, there is no doubt that the entrepreneurial transition in Estonia will be assured.

Note

1. Companies with at least 20 employees were classified as large companies.

REFERENCES

Aaltio-Marjosola, I. (1991) *Change in a Business Enterprise: Studying a Major Organisational Change and Its Impact on Culture*, Acta Academiae Oeconomicae Helsingiensis (Helsinki: Helsinki School of Economics).

Dyer, G.W., Jr (1985) 'The Cycle of Cultural Evolution in Organisations', in R.H. Kilmann and M.J. Saxton (eds), *Gaining Control of the Corporate Culture* (San Francisco: Jossey-Bass) 200–229.

Eesti Statistika (1935) *Toodang ja Tööjõud Suurtööstuses 1934* a. (Tallinn: Riigi Statistika Büroo).

Eesti 1920–1930 (1931) (Tallinn: Riigi Statistika Keskbüroo).

Feldman, S.P. (1986) 'Management in Context: An Essay on the Relevance of Culture to the Understanding of Organisational Change', *Journal of Management Studies*, 23(6), 587–607.

Gagliardi, P. (1986) 'The Creation and Change of Organisational Cultures: A Conceptual Framework', *Organisation Studies*, 7(2), 117–34.

Gersick, C.J.G. (1991) 'Revolutionary Change Theories: A Multilevel Exploration of the Punctuated Equilibrium Paradigm', *Academy of Management Review*, 16(1), 10–36.

Grancelli, B. (1988) *Soviet Management and Labour Relations* (London: Allen & Unwin).

Hendry, J. and Hope, V. (1994) 'Cultural Change and Competitive Performance', *European Management Journal*, 12(4), 401–6.

Hinkkanen-Lievonen, M.-L. (1984) *British Trade and Enterprise in the Baltic States 1919–1925* (Helsinki: Studia Historica).

Juuti, P. (1992) 'Yrityskulttuurin murros', *Aavaranta-sarja*, 31 (Tampere: Tammer-Paino Oy).

Kavass, I.I. and Sprudzs, A. (eds) (1972) *Baltic States: A Study of their Origin and National Development; Their Seizure and Incorporation into the USSR* (New York: William S. Hein).

Kozminsky A.K. (1993) *Catching Up? Organisational and Management Change in the ex-Socialist Block* (Albany: State University of New York Press).

Laurent, A. (1989) 'A Cultural View of Organisational Change', in P. Evans, Y. Doz and A. Laurent, (eds), *Human Resource Management in International Firms: Change, Globalisation, Innovation* (London: Macmillan), 83–94.

Liuhto, K. (1991) *The Interaction of Managerial Cultures in Soviet–Finnish Joint Ventures – including Estonian–Finnish Joint Ventures* (Turku: School of Economics and Business Administration, Institute for East-West Trade).

Liuhto, K. (1992) *Developing Estonian Entrepreneurship in Economic Transition* (Turku: School of Economics and Business Administration, Institute for East-West Trade).

Liuhto, K. (1993) *Creating New Managerial Concepts to Replace Management Sovieticus: Managerial Transition in Eastern Europe and in the Former Soviet Union,* (Turku: School of Economics and Business Administration, Institute for East-West Trade).

Liuhto, K. (1994) *A Comparison of Foreign Nepmen and Contemporary Joint Venturers in Russia: A Historical View in Predicting Future Development* (Turku: School of Economics and Business Administration, Institute for East-West Trade).

Liuhto, K. (1995a) 'Foreign Investment in Estonia: A Statistical Approach', *Europe–Asia Studies* (formerly *Soviet Studies*), 47(3), 507–26.

Liuhto, K. (1995b) 'Entrepreneurial and Managerial Evolution in Estonia: A Historical Approach to the Contemporary Phenomenon', *Proceedings of the Sixth ENDEC World Conference on Entrepreneurship, Shanghai,* 261–70.

Liuhto, K. (1996) 'Entrepreneurial Transition in the Post-Soviet Republics: The Estonian Path', *Europe–Asia Studies* (formerly *Soviet Studies*), 48(1), 121–140.

Lundberg, C. (1985) 'On the Feasibility of Cultural Interventions in Organisations', in P.J. Frost *et al.* (eds), *Organisational Culture* (London: Sage), 169–85.

Millar, J.R. (1988) 'The Little Deal: Brezhnev's Contribution to Acquisitive Socialism', in T. Thompson and R. Sheldon (eds), *Soviet Society and Culture* (London: Westview Press) 3–19.

Nove, A. (1989) *An Economic History of the USSR* (Harmondsworth: Penguin Books).

Pihlamägi, M. (1992) Tööstuspoliitika ja Tööstuse Arengu Üldjooni Eesti Vabariigis 1920, EMI Teataja, Tallinn:

Raud, V. (1987) *Developments in Estonia 1939–1941* (rev. edn) (Tallinn: Pestioodika).

Raun, T.U. (1987) *Estonian and Estonians* (California: Stanford University, Hoover Press).

Sakharov, A, (1991) *Muistelmat* (Juva: WSOY).

Schein, E.H. (1985) *Organisational Culture and Leadership: A Dynamic View* (San Francisco: Jossey-Bass).

Thompson, J.L. (1990) *Strategic Management: Awareness and Change* (London: Chapman & Hall).

Tiusanen, T. (1991) *The Baltic States: A Survey for Further Industrial Co-operation* (Copenhagen: Nordic Council of Ministers).

Torpan, N.I. (1984) Monopolistitsesky kapital v promislennosti Estony–90-e gody XIX veka–1917 god (Tallinn: Eesti Raamat).

Tööstus (1939) *Majandusloenduse andmed* (Tallinn: Riigi Statistika Keskbüroo).

Van Arkadie, B. and Karlson, M. (1992) *Economic Survey of the Baltic States: The Reform Process in Estonia, Latvia and Lithuania* (London: Pinter).

Wilkins, A.L. and Patterson, K.J. (1985) 'You Can't Get There From Here: What Will Make Culture-Change Projects Fail', in R.H. Kilmann, M.J. Saxton, R. Serpa *et al.* (eds), *Gaining Control of the Corporate Culture* (California: Jossey-Bass).

4 Collectivism and Individualism in Estonia: An Exploratory Study of Societal Change and Organisational Orientation

Maaja Vadi and Anthony F. Buono

INTRODUCTION

Estonia is currently being confronted by a rapidly changing set of challenges and concerns. Similar to the transformation taking place throughout Eastern Europe, Estonia's economic, political and cultural environment has changed very rapidly during the last six years. The liquidation of the Soviet Union, combined with the transition from a centrally-planned and centrally-managed economy to a market-driven one, with escalating inflation and novel forms of competition, have had significant repercussions on the basic fabric and nature of Estonian culture as well as on Estonian organisations, their management and their employees (see, for example, Uksvarav, 1991). Of concern in this chapter are some of the ramifications these changes pose for the management and organisation of Estonian business firms.

THE ESTONIAN CONTEXT

Historically, the Estonian national culture has been influenced by both the West and the East. Estonians have been living along the coast of the Baltic Sea and the Gulf of Finland for the past five thousand years and they are one of the oldest peoples in Europe. While the latitude for Estonia places the country in Northern Europe, longitudinally it is located in Eastern Europe. This twofold geopolitical dimension has had a significant influence on the history and culture of Estonia. The Estonian language, for example, belongs to the Finno-Ugric languages and its main religion is Lutheran. By the end of the 19th century, the vast majority (96 per cent) of Estonians were literate, and, despite the fact that the country is sparsely populated (approximately 34.8 persons/per sq. km), its language as well as its cultural traditions have survived under significant pressure from long-term Soviet domination.

The relatively small country (45.227 sq. km) had been occupied for 700 years by Germans, Russians and Swedes, and for the last fifty years by the USSR. Estonia has experienced only twenty years of independence, which it gained through the Tartu Peace Treaty of 1920, according to which Soviet Russia recognised the Republic of Estonia as an independent state. After the Molotov–Ribbentrop Pact (1939), which was the agreement between Stalin and Hitler, however, the country was occupied by the Soviet Union and incorporated into the USSR. Throughout the ensuing period, a significant number of Estonians continued to seek ways for action against, or at least passive resistance to, Soviet domination. The opportunity to re-establish an independent state arose in August 1991, and a wave of international recognition followed. Much of the current focus of Estonia's relations with former Soviet republics concerns the establishment of bilateral trade and financial relations. With respect to the Russian Federation in particular, negotiations have concentrated on resolving key issues relating to property, citizenship, and borders (see Odling-Smee *et al.*, 1992).

THE INFLUENCE OF SOCIETAL CULTURE

A notable body of research has indicated that societal culture has a large impact on the operating style and cultural orientation of organisations and their members, including such areas as employee motivation, leadership, supervision, and accepted ways of accomplishing daily tasks (for example, Harris and Moran, 1979; Schein, 1985; Smircich, 1983). In their seminal Hawthorne Study research, for example, Roethlisberger and Dickson (1956: 174) differentiated between American- and foreign-born persons who participated in the Relay Assembly Test Room experiment. The researchers suggested that there was a difference between the work-related values and traditions of the American- and foreign-born operators. More recently, such findings about the connections between national culture and work organisation have been echoed by Geert Hofstede's (1980, 1991) large-scale, comparative study of work-related values, and the myriad analyses comparing and contrasting US and Japan management and organisation (cf. Fucini and Fucini, 1990; Kang, 1990; Ouchi, 1981; Pascale and Athos, 1981).

At present, however, the views about the relative influence of national culture are diverse. Trice and Beyer (1993), for example, conclude that observers still disagree on how closely national host cultures bind and pattern the internal operations of work organisations. As they suggest (1993: 332), 'One view says that their external surrounding cultures largely determine organisations' formal structures and internal cultures. The opposing view argues that many patterns of organisational character-istics are universal and stem from inherent requirements of organising or doing certain kinds of work'. Thus, while some researchers suggest that the processes underlying industrialisation exert considerable influence on work-related values and goals (implying convergence), others point to per-sistent divergence, underscoring that cultural differences across societies persist even after controlling for industrial organisational differences (see, for example, Ricks *et al.*, 1990). As Morgan (1986: 117) argues, 'culture, whether Japanese, Arabian, British, Canadian, Chinese, French, or American, shapes the character of organisation'.

Culture, of course, is a complicated field of study. Most definitions of culture used currently in the social sciences are modifications of E.B. Tylor's (1871: 1) delineation of the concept as 'that complex whole which includes knowledge, belief, art, morals, law, custom, and any other capabilities and habits acquired by man as a member of society' (see Buono *et al.*, 1985). It appears, however, that researchers tend to only agree on two basic issues: (1) that culture affects peoples' minds, and (2) that there are many different aspects of these phenomena. An important dimension that researchers have focused on that may help to explain such divergent views concerns the strength of social forces that bring individu-als together in social groups. In Hofstede's seminal (1980) work, this influence was referred to as individualism–collectivism.

INDIVIDUALISM AND COLLECTIVISM

Hofstede (1980) argues that the most important differences between soci-etal cultures can be captured by finding out the extent to which members of disparate cultures differ with respect to four factors:

1. power distance (that is, the extent to which members of a society accept the fact that power in institutions and organisations is dis-tributed unequally);

2. uncertainty avoidance (that is, extent to which people feel threatened by uncertain and ambiguous situations);
3. the extent to which the dominant values in society reflect masculinity (gender roles are clearly distinct and reflect such characteristics as assertiveness, acquisition of money and things, not caring for others) or femininity (gender roles overlap and reflect collaborative and nurturing characteristics); and
4. the degree to which a society reflects individualism (a loosely knit social framework in which people are supposed to only take care of themselves and their immediate families) or collectivism (characterised by a tight social framework in which people distinguish between in-groups and out-groups).

His subsequent work (Hofstede, 1991; Hofstede and Bond, 1988) added a fifth dimension, initially referred to as 'Confucian dynamism', which reflects a long-term versus short-term orientation in life and work (for example, propensity toward thrift and saving versus immediate consumption). As a voluminous body of research based on this framework (for example, Boyacigiller and Adler, 1991; Buono *et al.*, 1983; Gudykunst and Ting-Toomey, 1988; Hofstede, 1983; Hofstede *et al.*, 1990; Kreacic and Marsh, 1986; Shackleton and Ali, 1990; Sondergaard, 1994) indicates, while this approach may not reflect the ultimate truth about cultural differences, it has proven to be a highly useful model for cross-cultural research and understanding.

The study reported in this chapter is based on the individualism–collectivism dimension. Several researchers have found that individualism and collectivism are related to different personality traits, life values, and socialisation processes (cf. Eysenck and Long, 1986; Ochse and Plug, 1986; Trofimov and Triandis, 1991; Triandis and Bontempo, 1986; Triandis *et al.*, 1990; Wheeler *et al.*, 1989). Collectivist cultures are different from individualistic-oriented ones, where individuals are more emotionally independent from groups, organisations and other social groupings and activities. Typical individualist cultures, for example, have been found in the United States, Britain and British-influenced countries, while collectivistic cultures have been found in various African, Asiatic and Latin-American ones. This broad cultural dimension has also been used to determine how people behave in uncomfortable or stressful situations and the ways in which they act when encountering somebody from their own group compared to a stranger group (Holtgraves and Yang, 1990; Miller *et al.*, 1990; Leung, 1987; Leung and Lind, 1986).

When seeking to determine if individualism or collectivism prevails in Estonia, several assumptions arise due to very different influences. For instance, in general, Estonians prefer to get by on their own, keeping personal distance even from other Estonians, dreading overflowing sentimentality and tending to mock any kind of state authority, suggesting a strong influence of individualism. Research has also suggested that Estonian managers operate more like their Western colleagues than they do their Russian counterparts (Uksvarav, 1991). At the same time, however, the influence of the old Soviet rule, with its emphasis on centrally-planned, centrally-managed economies and the powerful role of the state suggests a lingering collectivistic influence. In fact, recent studies of the changes taking place in Eastern Europe suggest that individualistic attitudes are often superimposed on collectivist belief systems (Reykowski, 1994). Thus, knowledge of the degree to which people depend on various groups and reflect individualistic or collectivistic tendencies can enable us to better understand and influence organisational life.

THE STUDY AND METHODOLOGY

Measures of individualism and collectivism

Although individualism and collectivism can manifest themselves in a number of different ways, there are three basic methods for measuring this cultural phenomenon. The preferred approach for assessing individualism and collectivism consists of measuring (1) the social content of the self, (2) the structure of values, and (3) attitudes toward different kinds of social behaviour (cf. Allik and Realo, 1994; Hofstede and Spangenberg, 1987; Reykowski, 1994). The present study draws on these three sets of measures to investigate the relative influence of collectivism and individualism in Estonia.[1]

Social content of the self

In the Twenty-Statement Test (TST) created by Kuhn and McPartland (1954), subjects were asked to complete twenty sentences which began with the words 'I am ...'. Responses were content analysed based on whether the responses referred to some kind of group. Following Triandis *et al.*'s (1990) conceptual and empirical development of this approach, the percentage of subjects' answers that had connection with groups is referred to as the per cent S score. The basic idea underlying the per cent S score is that people from collectivist cultures are more likely to emphasise social groups when they are asked to identify themselves than people from individualistic cultures. In the present study, subjects were asked to complete the Kuhn and McPartland 20-item TST.

Life values

Life values are general principles that people use as conceptual guidelines for their activities and decisions. In other words, these are preferences that people have for certain states and outcomes (for example, health, intelligence, general well-being, family security) that influence how we behave. Schwartz and Bilsky (1987, 1990), for example, argue that such preferences or values may serve individual interests (for example, pleasure, independence) or collective interests (for example, equality, responsibility) or both (for example, wisdom). Responses to these items thus provide additional insight into people's individualistic and collectivistic orientations. In the present study, the 56-item Schwartz-Bilsky inventory was drawn on in which subjects are asked to indicate on a 7-point, Likert-type scale the extent to which a particular value is important in their lives.

Attitudes toward social behaviour

The way one feels is a determinant and criterion of choices in human behaviour, and attitudes are the main source of variability across individuals. The extent of one's emotional involvement with particular groups derives from these issues. Several researchers have used the individualism–collectivism scale (INDCOL) developed by Hui (1984) to assess such involvement. Although the INDCOL scale consists of five subscales, and subsequent work by Triandis *et al.* (1990) improved on its capability, the reliability coefficients of the subscales are still relatively low.

   This method for determining relative individualism–collectivism orientations, however, did not take into consideration the reality that interpersonal relations can be classified into different categories. Thus, the present study differentiates three types of collectivist orientations – the family (C1), peers (C2) and society (C3) – as well as a cumulative scale (ESTCOL) to examine the collectivist orientation of the sample (see Allik and Realo, 1996). Using a Likert-type scale, subjects were asked to respond to the 24 items in the estimated collectivism (ESTCOL) inventory (see Appendix 4A) according to the importance of the different dimensions in their lives.

The sample

Societies includes different sub-populations and it is quite obvious that profession, family structure, social organisation and different living conditions among a host of other factors present disparate demands in terms of expected relations with others and the ways in which people conceptualise and fulfil their social roles. Such heterogeneity raises significant challenge to studies of culture and culture change, emphasising the existence of subcultures and cultural lag across different groups (for example, Martin and Siehl, 1983; Ogburn, 1922; Yinger, 1982). In fact, part of the post-modern criticism of management and organisational research focuses on the limited and highly homogeneous nature of most sample populations. As postmodernists argue, multiple truths exist in pluralistic settings and it is important to capture as much of this diversity as possible (cf. Brown, 1991; Cooper and Burrell, 1988; Parker, 1992).

Given this reality, it is useful to compare and contrast groups that are mainstream and marginal to the larger society. From a sociological perspective, the concept of marginality refers to individuals and groups who are unique to a given social situation, in essence reflecting a type of cultural hybrid, 'living in two worlds' (Park, 1928). While initial use of the concept focused on individuals who had crossed physical distances into new frontiers, the frontiers of contemporary society are more social in nature. In fact, society today can be characterised by a sense of 'pervasive marginality', where we all are, to some degree, marginal to some aspect of social life (Leventman, 1981). Thus, by studying a society's marginal groups, researchers are better able to map the boundaries of social phenomena, going beyond the potentially limited understanding posed by society's mainstream.

As a way of capturing such sub-population diversity, the study focused on eight distinctive groups, representing both mainstream and marginal groups, which represent a wide cross-section of Estonian society:

1. *Long-time members of a university sorority.* Twenty-two women, with a mean age of 78, were included in the sample. These women joined the sorority during their studies at the University of Tartu before Estonia was occupied by the Soviet Union in 1940. According to the rules of the Estonian students' associations, alumnae/alumni must remain connected to their sororities/fraternities after graduating from the university, in essence forming 'invisible colleges' in which the traditions and norms of the association are tightly held. These individuals represent adherent supporters of the restoration of the Republic of Estonia in the form that existed before the Soviet occupation.

2. *Inhabitants of Kihnu island.* Kihnu is a very small island (16.4 sq. km) in the Riga's Gulf area of the Baltic Sea with about 600 inhab-

itants. This sub-sample consisted of 17 people (16 women and 1 man, mean age was slightly over 31 years) who maintained a traditional fishing culture due to their isolation from the mainland. Traditions are very highly valued by inhabitants of Kihnu. Women, for example, wear the same national clothes as those worn one hundred years ago and accept the same basic norms as previous generations, and families with fishermen still provide fish to those neighbours or other village families where there are no fishermen. At times, such traditions are modified to meet the requirements of the present, but Kihnu's inhabitants attempt to follow their cultural heritage as much as possible.

3. *Representatives of the Estonian Army.* Ninety young servicemen of the Estonian Army were included in the sample. Military service lasts 12 months and is mandatory for all Estonian citizens over 18. The mean age of the servicemen was 19 years.

4. *Housewives with five or more children.* According to the Social Department of the Tartu City Council, among more than 100,000 inhabitants of Tartu, 93 housewives had five or more children who were less than 18 years old. Ten of these women were included in the sample; their mean age was 36.

5. *Athletes.* Sixty athletes were included in the sample, most of whom were semi-professionals, participating in group-oriented sports. The mean age of the 16 sportsmen and 44 sportswomen in the sample was slightly over 21 years.

6. *Students.* Eighty-nine students (56 women and 33 men of the University of Tartu) who studied economics and social sciences were included in the sample. Their mean age was approximately 20 years.

7. *Business managers and directors.* Forty managers of private firms and state institutions were selected; this sub-sample includes 18 men and 22 women with a mean age of 34.

8. *College and high school teachers.* Twenty-seven college and high school teachers participated in the survey; 5 men and 22 women with a mean age of 33.

FINDINGS

Since cultures and subcultures may vary in terms of the main target(s) to which collectivist orientations are linked (see Triandis *et al.*, 1990), the assessment of different groups provides an opportunity to generalise to a

broader population as well as to examine variations within that population. Obviously, within such diverse populations, different kinds of
collectivism exist – one could be very collectivist in regard to his or her
family, for example, but feel far more independent in terms of relationships with friends or the larger society.

Using the ESTCOL instrument on the sample of 355 respondents (163
males and 192 females, ages 15 to 84 with a mean age of 27.1), attitudes
toward social groups were examined based on principal component analysis with varimax rotation. Questionnaire items focused on relations with
the family (C1), their peers (C2), and society in general (C3). The cumulative collectivism index (ESTCOL = C1+C2+C3) suggested that collectivist orientations were higher for men than women (t=2.94, p=.01) and
that collectivism was also positively associated with increasing age (r=.12,
p=.05).

The differences between the sub-populations with respect to the cumulative collectivism scale (ESTCOL) were dramatic. Table 4.1 presents the
mean values and standard deviations of the three subscales and the total
score for each of these groups. Overall collectivist orientations were
highest among those subgroups that were isolated or closely linked to
either tradition and/or the past (for example, sorority members, Kihnu
Island inhabitants, military personnel), while those sub-samples which
were closer to the transformation of Estonian society (students, managers
and directors, teachers) fell significantly below the ESTCOL mean for the
entire sample. In general, identification with one's family and Estonian
society were more significant aspects of collectivism than identification
with one's peers.

Dependence on groups was determined by using the per cent S score,
computed from the content-analysed Twenty Statement Test (TST). The
main value for the sample was 35 per cent S, which is considerably higher
than the reported 19 per cent S for US samples (Illinois students) but
lower than the People's Republic China sample (52 per cent S) (Triandis
et al., 1990). Similar to the findings with the cumulative collectivism
index, the per cent S score increased with age. For the 27 respondents in
the sample who were younger than 19 years old, for example, their per
cent S score was approximately 19 per cent S, which is similar to their US
counterparts.

In addition, the responses to the TST were analysed as a simple text,
focusing on the nature and number of words used. Two-thirds of the 'I
am …' descriptors were unique to different respondents. Typically, subjects used approximately 34 words to respond to the 20 questions about
themselves and 24.3 of those words were unique. Five of the most fre-

Table 4.1 Collectivist orientations in Estonia

Sample (n)	Family (C1)		Peers (C2)		Society (C3)		Cumulative (ESTCOL)	
	Mean	SD	Mean	SD	Mean	SD	Mean	SD
Sorority members (22)	22.20	7.41	8.90	5.04	**27.00**	3.85	**58.10**	9.98
Kihnu Island inhabitants (17)	23.20	4.75	**12.90**	6.37	19.60	4.69	55.70	11.29
Servicemen (90)	24.30	5.11	12.70	5.85	19.30	5.65	56.30	11.51
Housewives (10)	**26.50**	4.81	9.20	3.55	19.10	5.74	54.80	8.82
Athletes (60)	22.10	5.25	10.10	5.27	15.80	6.25	48.00	12.46
Students (89)	18.30*	6.48	9.20	4.26	14.20	5.26	41.70	11.63
Managers and directors (40)	18.80	6.55	7.00*	4.57	15.30	5.45	41.10	13.67
Teachers (27)	18.40	7.59	7.20	4.15	11.70*	6.24	37.30*	14.67
Total population (355)	21.50	6.47	9.90	5.35	17.00	6.53	48.40	13.78

Note:
Higher scores reflect higher collectivism. Numbers printed in bold indicate highest levels of collectivism; asterisked numbers indicate the lowest levels of collectivism for the different sub-samples.

quent descriptors used were 'human being', 'mother', 'woman', 'good', and 'Estonian'. Finally, testing life values further enables us to understand how much peoples' guiding principles are connected to collectivistic or individualistic ideals. The three the most highly estimated values were health (m=5.58, sd=1.25), family security (m=5.12, sd=1.43), and intelligence (m=5.11, sd=1.32), suggesting individualistic tendencies. The lowest values in the rank-order were social power (m=1.35, sd=1.93), accepting my position in life (m=0.70, sd=1.65), and devotion (m=0.33, sd=1.50).

DISCUSSION: IMPLICATIONS OF COLLECTIVISTIC AND INDIVIDUALISTIC ORIENTATIONS

Individual psychological processes are influenced by various socio-cultural contexts within which the individual is embedded. At the same time, people bring their own attitudes, beliefs, and values into the organisations where they are engaged. Laurent (1993: 362), for example, argues that 'managers from different national cultures hold different assumptions about the nature of management, authority, structure and organisational relationships'. Within such broader cultural contexts, however, McGregor's (1960) seminal work continues to reinforce the notion that one's preferred managerial style is influenced by basic assumptions that the individual, not the society *per se*, holds about human nature. Thus, even within the same society and the same organisation, different managers can have Theory X (control-oriented) or Theory Y (participative, commitment-oriented) tendencies. This reality is further compounded by the type of rapid cultural change that is currently taking place within Estonia and Estonian organisations.

The introduction of a market economy, with high levels of competition and inflation, escalating demands on production and distribution systems, and changing customer attitudes – in essence a transformation of the basic nature of the business environment – have placed managers throughout Eastern Europe in a precarious position (see Culpan and Kumar, 1995; Shama, 1993). These forces have also exerted a strong influence on the nature of Estonian society, in addition to raising significant questions about how to structure and manage Estonian firms in the newly emerging economy.

The present study suggests that those Estonians who are likely to play a critical role in the transformation of the business sector – students, managers and directors, and teachers – are more individualistic than their more traditional counterparts: the elderly members of a university sorority, the inhabitants of Kihnu Island, military personnel, and women with large families. Younger Estonians also reflected similar levels of individualism compared to Triandis *et al.*'s (1990) assessment of US college students, and collectivism was related to increased age in the present study. Collectivism was also the lowest on the peer level (C2), and this subscale includes the relations with co-workers. It seems that in work organisations, Estonians tend to be even more individualistic in their orientations. Both managers and teachers, for example, had a lower C2 score than students and servicemen. Thus, at the organisational level, while collectivistic norms and behaviour patterns might have been effective in the past, they are unlikely to develop appropriate motivational and other work-related systems for the new Estonian economy.

People from cultures like China are more likely to stress collectivist life values (for example, social order, honouring parents and elders, accepting one's position in life) compared with more individualistic-oriented values (for example, equality, freedom, a varied life) (see Triandis *et al.*, 1990). Despite the years of Soviet influence on the country, at the top of Estonians' preferences was only one collectivistic life value – family security (C1). Moreover, in general, collectivistic life values were ranked lower than individualistic ones.

The emerging influence of individualism also helps to explain why the culture of present-day Estonian organisations was found to be more like American than Japanese firms. Vadi and Sirel (1994) found that the majority of the Estonian organisations they studied reflected an American-type of organisational culture, especially in terms of decision-making, responsibility and communication. In another study, in contrast, Estonian managers were asked to indicate their preferences on Fiedler's LPC scale (Vadi and Valeng, 1995). Fiedler proposed that a high LPC is connected to a manager's wish to maintain good relations with superiors and bosses (collectivism), and a low LPC score indicates a more task-oriented preference (individualism). Almost half (47 per cent) of the managers in the Vadi and Valeng (1995) study had a high LPC score compared to 42 per cent who had low LPC scores. Thus a significant portion of managers reflected a relationship orientation and wanted to maintain harmony with their co-workers, both features of collectivism. The Vadi and Valeng (1995) findings raise some caution about this chapter's conclusion that individualism is becoming the dominant orientation in Estonian work organisations.

While more study of Estonian organisations and management practices is thus necessary, as noted above it does appear that those individuals who are likely to play a key role in the transformation of the country's economy and business system are more individualistic than those respondents from more traditional backgrounds. These data suggest that this critical group will respond favourably to greater participation in organisational decision-making and greater latitude in supervisory relations than would an older, more conventional population. It is clear, however, that management and organisation training and development efforts focused on these individuals is necessary to facilitate the continued transformation of the Estonian economy. Kripps (1992), for example, found that older Estonian managers cling to a Soviet-influenced collectivist orientation and an autocratic leadership style that are increasingly subjugating and alienating their subordinates. Yet, while younger Estonian managers appear to be moving away from such collectivist beliefs, their lack of experience, skill and training influence them to act in an even more authoritarian manner than the senior leaders. Combined with other analyses of the need to transform managerial behaviour in companies throughout Eastern Europe (for example, Rondinelli, 1991), these findings underscore the importance of leadership, decision-making, interpersonal- and communication-skills training for these individuals.

The power to harness such emerging individualistic orientations is also an important organisational dimension of broader privatisation strategies (Culpan and Kumar, 1995; Moore, 1992; Savitt, 1995). As Estonia continues to privatise its business operations, for example, small- and medium-sized enterprises (defined as companies with up to 100 employees) are capturing the largest share of wholesale and retail trade (Ministry of Economic Affairs of the Republic of Estonia, 1995). While the Estonian government continues to concentrate on the broader public policy issues associated with privatisation (for example, restructuring the legal system, tax policy, determining property ownership and rental agreements), these emerging private firms must develop and capitalise on the skills and abilities of their employees if they are to continue to be successful. The dilemma these organisations face, however, is that, despite the emerging individualism in post-communist countries, employees are not accustomed nor trained to take the initiative on their own.

As Estonia continues its evolution toward a market-based economy, the importance of individualistic as compared to collectivistic orientations is likely to increase. Given this trend, organisations and their management must take advantage of this shift, aligning their motivation, compensation and training schemes accordingly. Organisational cultures and systems must be created that reflect and facilitate such development by focusing on explicit goals, ensuring timely and specific feedback, emphasising individual responsibility, and rewarding employees on the basis of results and stock ownership programmes. Such efforts will not only strengthen and develop effective and committed managers and employees but are likely to enhance the performance of Estonian organisations as well. While such transformation will be a time-consuming and difficult process, it appears that the attitudinal shifts necessary for such large-scale changes and transitions are beginning to take hold.

Note:

1.   The data used in this chapter were originally gathered by Anu Realo and Jüri Allik (Department of Psychology) and Maaja Vadi (School of Economics and Business Administration) at the University of Tartu, Tartu, Estonia.

REFERENCES

Allik, J. and Realo, A. (1996) 'The Hierarchical Nature of Individualism–Collectivism: Comments on Matsumuto *et al.*, 1996', *Culture and Psychology*, 2, 111–19.

Boyacigiller, N. and Adler, N. (1991) 'The Parochial Dinosaur: Organisational Science in Global Context', *Academy of Management Review*, 16 (2), 262–90.

Brown, D. (1991) 'An Institutionalist Look at Postmodernism', *Journal of Economic Issues*, 25 (4), 1092–4.

Buono, A.F., Nicolaou-Smokovitis, L. and Bowditch, J.L. (1983) 'A Comparative Quality of Work-Life Survey of Banking Institutions in Technological Change: A Cross-Cultural Study', *Greek Review of Social Research*, 51, 59–99.

Buono, A.F., Bowditch, J.L. and Lewis, J.W. (1985) 'When Cultures Collide: The Anatomy of a Merger', *Human Relations*, 38 (5), 4, 77–500.

Cooper, R. and Burrell, G. (1988) 'Modernism, Postmodernism and Organisational Analysis: An Introduction', *Organisation Studies*, 9 (1), 91–112.

Culpan, R. and Kumar, B.N. (eds) (1995) *Transformation Management in Postcommunist Countries: Organisational Requirements for a Market Economy* (Westport, CT: Quorum Books).

Eysenck, S. and Long, F. (1986) 'A Cross-Cultural Comparison of Personality in Adults and Children in Singapore and England', *Journal of Personality and Social Psychology*, 50, 124–35.

Fucini, J.J. and Fucini, S. (1990) *Working for the Japanese: Inside Mazda's American Auto Plant* (New York, Free Press).

Gudykunst, W.B. and Ting-Toomey, S. (1988) *Culture and Interpersonal Communication* (Newbury Park, CA: Sage).

Harris, P.R. and Moran, R.T. (1979) *Managing Cultural Differences* (Houston: Gulf).

Hofstede, G. (1980) *Culture's Consequences: International Differences in Work-Related Values* (Beverly Hills, CA: Sage).

Hofstede, G. (1983) 'National Cultures in Four Dimensions', *International Studies of Management and Organisation*, 13, 46–74.

Hofstede, G. (1991) *Cultures and Organisations: Software of the Mind* (New York: McGraw-Hill).

Hofstede, G. and Spangenberg, J. (1987) 'Measuring Individualism and Collectivism at Occupational and Organisational Levels', in C. Kapitcibasi (ed.), *Growth and Progress in Cross-Cultural Psychology* (Netherlands: Lisse) 113–22.

Hofstede, H.C. and Bond, M.H. (1988) 'The Confucius Connection: From Cultural Roots to Economic Growth', *Organisational Dynamics*, 14 (4), 4–21.

Hofstede, G., Neuijen, B., Ohayv, D.D. and Sanders, G. (1990) 'Measuring Organisational Cultures: A Qualitative and Quantitative Study Across Twenty Cases', *Administration Science Quarterly*, 35 (2), 286–316.

Holtgraves, T. and Yang, J. (1990) 'Politeness as Universal: Cross-Cultural Perceptions of Request Strategies and Influences Based on Their Use', *Journal of Personality and Social Psychology*, 59, 719–29.

Hui, C.H. (1984) *Individualism–Collectivism: Theory, Measurement and its Relationship to Reward Allocation*, unpublished doctoral dissertation, Department of Psychology, University of Illinois at Champaign-Urbana.

Kang, T.W. (1990) *Gaishi: The Foreign Company in Japan* (New York: Basic Books).

Kreacic, V. and Marsh, P. (1986) 'Organisation Development and National Culture in Four Countries', *Public Enterprise*, 6, 121–34.

Kripps, H. (1992) 'Leadership and Social Competence in the Declining Years of Communism', *Small Group Research*, 23 (1), 130–45.

Kuhn, M.H. and McPartland, T. (1954) 'An Empirical Investigation of Self-Attitudes', *American Sociological Review*, 19, 68–76.

Kumar, B.N. (1995) 'Evidence of Corporate Transformation in Postcommunist Countries: Towards a Theory of Transformation Management', in R. Culpan and B.N. Kumar (eds)., (1995) *Transformation Management in Postcommunist Countries: Organisational Requirements for a Market Economy* (Westport, CT: Quorum Books), 235–42.

Laurent, A. (1993) 'A Cross-Cultural Perspective on Organisational Change', in T.D. Jick (ed.), *Managing Change* (Homewood: Irwin), 361–4.

Leung, K. (1987) 'Some Determinants of Reactions to Procedural Models of Conflict Resolution: A Cross-National Study', *Journal of Personality and Social Psychology*, 53, 898–908.

Leung, K. and Lind, A.E. (1986) 'Procedural Justice and Culture: Effects of Culture, Gender, and Investigator Status on Procedural Preferences', *Journal of Personality and Social Psychology*, 50, 1134–40.

Leventman, S. (1981) 'Marginality and the Vietnam Vet', Luncheon Roundtable Discussion, American Sociological Association, Toronto, Canada, August 1981.

Martin, J. and Siehl, C. (1983) 'Organisational Culture and Counterculture: An Uneasy Symbiosis', *Organisational Dynamics*, 12 (2), 52–64.

McGregor, D. (1960) *The Human Side of Enterprise* (New York: McGraw-Hill).

Mead, G.H. (1956) *On Social Psychology* (Chicago: University of Chicago Press).

Miller, J., Bersoff, D. and Harwood, R. (1990) 'Perceptions of Social Responsibilities in India and the United States: Moral Imperatives on Personal Decisions', *Journal of Personality and Social Psychology*, 58, 33–47.

Ministry of Economic Affairs of the Republic of Estonia (1995) *Estonian Economy 1994–1995* (Tallinn: Ministry of Economic Affairs and Vastus Ltd).

Moore, J. (1992) 'British Privatisation – Taking Capitalism to the People', *Harvard Business Review,* 70 (1), 115–24.

Morgan, G. (1986) *Images of Organisation* (Beverly Hills, CA: Sage).

Ochse, R. and Plug, C. (1986) 'Cross-Cultural Investigation of the Validity of Erikson's Theory of Personality Development', *Journal of Personality and Social Psychology*, 50, 1240–50.

Odling-Smee, J., *et al.* (1992) *Economic Review: Estonia* (Washington, DC: International Monetary Fund).

Ogburn, W.F. (1922) *Social Change with Respect to Culture and Original Nature* (New York: B.W. Heubsch).

Ouchi, W. (1981) *Theory Z: How American Business Can Meet the Japanese Challenge* (Reading, New York: Addison-Wesley).

Park, R. (1928) 'Human Migration and the Marginal Man', *American Journal of Sociology*, 33, 881–93.

Parker, M. (1992) 'Postmodern Organisations or Postmodern Organisation Theory?' *Organisation Studies*, 13 (1), 1–17.

Pascale, R.T. and Athos, A. (1981) *The Art of Japanese Management: Applications for American Executives* (New York: Simon & Schuster).

Reykowski, J. (1994) 'Collectivism and Individualism as Dimensions of Social Change', in U. Kim, H.C. Triandis, C. Kagticibasi, S. Choi and G. Yoon, (eds), *Individualism and Collectivism* (Newbury Park, New York: Sage).

Ricks, D.A., Toyne, B. and Martinez, Z. (1990) 'Recent Developments in International Management Research', *Journal of Management*, 16 (2), 223–6.

Roethlisberger, F.J. and Dickson, W.J. (1956) *Management and the Worker* (Cambridge, MA: Harvard University Press).

Rondinelli, D.A. (1991) 'Developing Private Enterprise in the Czech and Slovak Federal Republics', *Columbia Journal of World Business*, 26 (3), 26–36.

Savitt, R. (1995) 'Critical Issues of Privatisation: A Managerial Perspective', in R. Culpan and B. Kumar (eds), *Transformation Management in Postcommunist Countries: Organisational Requirements for a Market Economy* (Westport, CT: Quorum Books), 17–28.

Schein, E.H. (1985) *Organisational Culture and Leadership* (San Francisco, CA: Jossey-Bass).

Schwartz, S.H. and Bilsky, W. (1987) 'Toward Universal Psychological Structure of Human Values', *Journal of Personality and Social Psychology*, 53, 550–62.

Schwartz, S.H. and Bilsky, W. (1990) 'Toward a Theory of the Universal Content and Structure of Values: Extensions and Cross-Cultural Replications', *Journal of Personality and Social Psychology*, 58, 878–91.

Shackleton, V.J. and Ali, A.H. (1990) 'Work-Related Values of Managers: A Test of the Hofstede Model', *Journal of Cross-Cultural Psychology*, 21 (1), 109–18.

Shama, A. (1993) 'Management Under Fire: The Transformation of Managers in the Soviet Union and Eastern Europe', *Academy of Management Executive*, 7 (1), 22–35.

Sondergaard, M. (1994) 'Hofstede's Consequences: A Study of Reviews, Citations and Replications', *Organisation Studies*, 15 (3), 447–56.

Smircich, L. (1983) 'Concepts of Culture and Organisational Analysis', *Administrative Science Quarterly*, 28 (3), 339–58.

Triandis, H.C. and Bontempo, R. (1986) 'The Measurement of the Ethic Aspects of Individualism and Collectivism Across Cultures', *Australian Journal of Psychology*, 38, 257–67.

Triandis, H.C., McCusker, C. and Hui, H.C. (1990) 'Multimethod Probes of Individualism and Collectivism', *Journal of Personality and Social Psychology*, 59, 1006–20.

Trice, H.M. and Beyer, J.M. (1993) *The Cultures of Work Organisations* (Englewood Cliffs, NJ: Prentice Hall).

Trofimov, D. and Triandis, H.C. (1991) 'Some Tests of the Distinction Between the Private and the Collective Self', *Journal of Personality and Social Psychology*, 60, 649–55.

Tylor, E.B. (1871) *Primitive Culture: Researches into the Development of Mythology, Philosophy, Religion, Language, Art and Custom,* Vol. 1 (New York: Henry Holt).

Uksvarav, R. (1991) 'From Planned to Market Economy: The Estonian Case', *Business and the Contemporary World*, 3 (4), 63–71.

Vadi, M. and Sirel, K. (1994) *Eesti organisatsioonikultuur on ameerikalik* [The Estonian organisational culture looks American], érielu, nr.10, lk. 11–14.

Vadi, M. and Valeng, A. (1995) *Juht kui leader* [Manager as a leader], érielu, nr. 2, 81–4.

Wheeler, L., Reis, H.T. and Bond, M. (1989) 'Collectivism–Individualism in Everyday Social Life: The Middle Kingdom and the Melting Pot', *Journal of Personality and Social Psychology*, 57, 79–87.

Yinger, J.M. (1982) *Countercultures* (New York: Free Press).

APPENDIX 4A

ITEMS IN THE ESTCOL SCALE FAMILY (C1)

In life, family interests are most important.

Family celebrations are the most important events during one's life.

A family should have one joint budget.

Children should not be an embarrassment to their parents.

The highest thing that a person can do in life is to dedicate him/herself to one's family.

The most important decisions in a person's life should be made within the family circle.

Children should not create worry for their parents.

In life, the interests of one's family are not the most important. (R)

PEERS (C2)

Neighbours should lend things to each other.

A person can only feel good in the company of others.

There should be no secrets between friends.

One does not have to tell everything to one's friends. (R)

Neighbours should live as one big family.

One does not have to lend money to co-workers. (R)

Everything should be equally shared between friends.

One must take into account the opinions of friends when making decisions.

SOCIETY (C3)

If necessary, one should die in the name of his/her nation.

A person should sacrifice him/herself for the future of his/her nation.

People who dedicate themselves to their nation deserve special recognition.

A person who renounces his/her nation deserves scorn and contempt.

The interests of nation outweigh the individual interests of its members.

A person cannot be content is his/her nation is suffering.

Every nation should remember and honor its heroes.

If required by the interests of the state, individuals must surrender their own comforts.

(R) denotes reverse scaling
Source: J. Allik and A. Realo, 'The Hierarchical Nature of Individualism–
Collectivism: Comments on Matsumato *et al.*, 1996', *Culture and Psychology*, 2
(1996).

5 Leftism, Achievement Orientation, and Basic Dimensions of the Socio-economic and Political Attitudes in Baltic Countries versus Other Central and East European Countries

Jan Jerschina and Jaroslaw Górniak

INTRODUCTION

The processes of political and economic transformation in Central and Eastern Europe are determined by several types of factors. Basically these are as outlined below.

Political framework   This consists of the institutions which were inherited from the communist era or which developed in the course of transition.

Economic institutional framework and economic conditions   These were also partly inherited from the communist times. For example, in all these countries part of both industry and services is in state ownership. The economic institutional framework has changed alongside the privatisation of state property but, paradoxically enough, even in the countries where this process has been rapid (the Czech Republic, Poland, Hungary), central power and control over the economy was not weakened at all. It is a common opinion that it has rather been strengthened and that without this the reforms would have not been possible.

Social structure and stratification   None of the countries entered the path of transformation with a fully developed middle class. As has been predicted, it is the stratum of intellectuals which takes the shape of the

80

new middle class and political class, whatever its background. The ranks of the post-communist bureaucracy, nomenklatura, or groups of dissidents and 'semi-dissidents', are most often endowed with higher education. However, the countries of this part of Europe are different with respect to the resources from which the middle and political classes could grow. In some of them, for instance in Poland, the private economy was never completely liquidated and the group of dissidents was relatively large. Conversely, in others, like Ukraine, no private economy existed before 1990, and the group of dissidents was very small. A rather important aspect of the social structure of the countries are the numbers of people working in agriculture. Poland and Hungary are countries where the proportion of people working in agriculture is very large, while Russia and the Czech Republic employ many fewer people in this sector. The political effects of this are quite visible. For instance, the new ruling coalition in Poland consists of the agrarians and neo-social democrats. Another important aspect of the social structure is the resource base of people with higher and full secondary education. The Czech Republic is one of the richest in this respect, and Poland one of the poorest. All these and other aspects are important as factors which determine the course of economic and political reform and the basis for political stability.

Social, political and economic attitudes of people In all these countries it is possible to identify a short period of time during which everyone, except the nomenclature and some communist party members, were pro-reform. However, shortly after that the people's attitudes changed significantly. Observers and students of opinion polls show that the privatisation of the economy in most of those countries was supported by relatively large groups of people whose market positions were strong (highly qualified specialists) and opposed by those whose market position was weaker or weak (semi-skilled workers or farmers). This differentiation of attitudes is growing and their content and dynamics is an increasingly important factor in the processes of transformation.

It was these latter observations which led to the beginning of the project upon which this chapter is based. It is called here the PSE Model. Jan Jerschina, Professor of Sociology at Jagiellonian University, and the Director of the Market and Public Opinion Research Institute, 'CEM' in Cracow, co-operated from 1990 with the Research Institute of Radio Free Europe/Radio Liberty. In 1993 they designed the first version of the method and the tools to measure the political and economic attitudes of the citizens of Central and Eastern European countries. These were subsequently improved in the course of the research which has been repeated every year from 1993 to 1996. The PSE Model now functions as a method of monitoring these changes in twelve countries: Russia, Ukraine, Byelorussia, Estonia, Latvia, Lithuania, the Czech Republic, Slovakia, Hungary, Poland, Bulgaria and Rumania.

The project was, and still is, supported by Audience and Opinion Research in Washington, led by Dr Mark Rhodes and the former Director of this research unit at the Research Institute of RFE/RL, Dr Eugene Parta. Both have had a substantial input in conceptualising the method and adding to it. Dr Jaroslaw Górniak, one of the authors of this chapter, executed (with assistance) most of the statistical work for the project. The method developed is too complicated to be described in detail in this chapter, which uses only some of its elements and analytical concepts. Some of the key issues are set out briefly in the following paragraphs.

The first component of this method is a set of Likert-type scales to measure attitudes as follows: *Authoritarianism* (political), *Nationalism* (economic and political), *Business Aptitude and Achievement Orientation* (in the course of this chapter the abbreviated term *Achievement Orientation* is used), *Economic Optimism, Economic Statism, Egalitarianism, Left Orientation* (which is a scale composed of the former two scales), *Regionalism, Pro/Anti-Americanism,* and *Political Mobilisation.* The PSE Model consists of fifteen other scales which are in the process of development, among them scales of *Political Repressiveness* and *Pro/Anti-Europeanism.* Together, they create a system for evaluating the conditions for political stabilisation and the pro/anti-reform socio-political climate in these countries for foreign investment (through the evaluation of investment risk in these countries in respect of economic and political trends), and for security (by the evaluation of possible trends in international policy of these countries). Taken together, these items explain the name of the system: *Political–Security–Economy (PSE) Model*: namely, a Decision Support Model for Strategic Planning and Risk Evaluation in Politics, Economy and Security Based Upon Measurement and Comparative Analysis of Socio-Political Values in Central Europe and the Former Soviet Union.

The second set of concepts is connected with the idea of the aggregates of political actors. The basic assumption is that there are four basic aggregates of political actors in all societies; *Conductors of Change, Passive Experts, Active Citizens and Silent Citizens.*

The analysis of data collected by researchers from the Research Institute of RFE/RL allowed for building a typology of four aggregates of people according to their allocation on the scales of control of political processes using political, cultural and economic means. The indicators of the possession of the necessary means are: possession of economic power (property and income), political power (position in political institutions) education (which is conceived as a means of intellectual capacity able to control the political processes), participation in politics (in elections) and interest in politics (declared interest).

In summary form, this typology can be stated as follows:

Conductors of Change are people who possess the means of control over political processes to a higher extent than others and who participate in political processes.

Passive Experts are people who possess the means of control over political processes but they do not participate in them and they declare their disinterest in participation.

Active Citizens are poorly endowed with the means of control over political processes but they are interested in politics and participate in it.

Silent Citizens are poorly endowed with the means of control over political processes and they are not interested in it, nor do they participate in the processes.

The additional assumption of this model is that political stabilisation depends mainly on the relationships between two aggregates: namely the *Conductors of Change* and *Active Citizens*. Then it is assumed that the value profiles (unity or differences between the profiles) determine conditions for communication, negotiation, compromise, achieving consensus and co-operation between the aggregates of actors. The use of the concepts and the model are presented later in the chapter in the course of analysing some relevant data.

The focus of attention in this chapter is on the attitudes of citizens in the Baltic countries. In order to present this method, the results of empirical research and statistical analysis, some initial questions are posed. What kind of supportive or emerging background exists for the processes of reforms in social consciousness? Are there any important differences in this respect between nations living in the Baltic region, Central and Eastern Europe? What kind of evolution in both economy and polity can be expected, taking into account the attitudes and orientations dominating in these societies and among the politically active strata? A further question is also critical – what is the relationship between the orientations of people who belong to different aggregates of political actors or occupy different positions in social stratification?

The central topic of this chapter is to show the differences between countries and within countries from the point of view of two orientations which were measured within the broader framework of the PSE-project. These are *leftism* and *achievement orientation*. Both are regarded as important as an output of the socio-economic situation in these countries, and, from another perspective, as socio-psychological forces influencing economic reforms and personal political choices. The background for the 'within countries' analysis is the concept of *four aggregates of political actors* and is briefly described below.[1]

The data used here is mostly from research conducted in Spring 1994, in ten Central and East European countries. It should be noted that in Bulgaria and Romania the scale of Business Aptitude was not used. To show the dynamics of attitudes, some data from 1995 survey are also used, especially in the last part of the chapter. The research was financed and organised at that time by the Media and Opinion Research Department of the Radio Free Europe/Radio Liberty which now operates as the Audience and Opinion Research Department of the Open Media Research Institute in Washington, DC. The concept of the PSE-model and the elaborating of scales is the result of the co-operation which was mentioned above.[2]

METHODOLOGY

Before presenting selected results, some brief comment is necessary about the methodology. The research was conducted, using the same core questionnaire, in twelve Central and East European Countries, namely, Poland, Hungary, Czech Republic, Slovakia, Estonia, Latvia, Lithuania, Russia (European), Ukraine, Byelorussia, Bulgaria and Romania.

Sample sizes varied between 1430 (Hungary) and 2430 (Russia) in each country in 1994 and between 1012 (Slovakia) and 2271 (Russia) in 1995. The target population were people aged 18 and over. People were randomly sampled within countries. Before the calculation of the results as presented here, each country sample was weighted (redressed) to model the structure of the population, in respect of some important aspects, such as age, sex and education. For comparative purposes each country sample was designed to have the same impact on the overall statistics. This was done by weighting the samples so that each country is represented in the total sample by an equal number of 1000 subjects (the total weighted sample is 20 000 for both the 1994 and 1995 waves).[3] The research team wanted an equal representation of each country, because the purpose was to show the differences between countries and not the overall estimation of the parameters of the East European population. Thus the overall parameters are statistical reference points rather than regional estimates. Weighting proportionally to the number of inhabitants would standardise the scales in such a way that it would have given an enormous weight to the results obtained from European Russia and Ukraine, with some Polish influence, against other, smaller countries. The intention was to avoid such an outcome.

The conceptual framework of the PSE Model contains a proposal to measure a set of socio-political and economic orientations.[4] The initial work in building the scales was done using secondary data analysis. In September 1993, the researchers checked the items from earlier research, which could potentially measure the desired set of orientations and attitudes. Then the team collected or invented a large set of statements representing each orientation or attitude. For example, the scale of leftism was inspired by the work of Anthony Heath and his team (Heath *et al.*, 1991). However, this scale is much larger and is of special relevance to the situation of East-European countries. The scale of business aptitude/achievement orientation was built under the influence of the classical concepts of McClelland (McClelland, 1964) and Heckhausen (Heckhausen, 1965).

The classical Likert-type scaling was chosen. Principal components analysis was used to check if the scale items build one dimension. Then the results of PCA and reliability/item analysis were used for the final selection of the items. The results from 5-point scales (after putting DK/NA in the middle) were summed up to give the score for each person.[5] The composition of the scales was discussed with a group of 'competent judges' and than tested in a small research project in Cracow using students of the final classes of Cracow secondary school. Then the improved results were put into a questionnaire on public opinion in Poland, in Autumn 1993. The scales were revised again and put into public opinion questionnaires and media research in the twelve (eleven in 1995) countries. Before proceeding further, some comment is necessary on the scales chosen for the chapter, namely Business Aptitude/Achievement Orientation, Leftism and Economic Optimism.

The scale of business aptitude/achievement orientation

Definition This scale measures the orientation towards economic achievement, associated with entrepreneurism and risk.

Assumption The higher the number of people in a society scoring high on this scale, the bigger is the capacity/dynamic of the society to cope with problems of economic development.

Composition This covers the preference for undertaking somewhat risky but profitable tasks and working on an individual's own account. This includes an orientation toward planning future undertakings, a feeling of being competent and strong enough to achieve goals and cope well with difficult problems.

The scale is stable across countries and social segments. In all cases factor analysis extracted one factor. The weakest item (but not one which decreased the overall reliability) was the orientation towards working on one's own account, but it was decided to preserve it due to the semantic meaning of the scale. Since business aptitude measurement is based on achievement motivation, so this item adding some of economic 'self-made-man' flavour to the scale is required.

The scale of leftism

Definition This measures the acceptance of the principle of equal distribution of wealth, the state responsibility for welfare, and attitudes towards state control of different aspects of economic life.

Assumption This is the scale of attitudes towards the syndrome of the three classical economic ideas of left-wing movements: economic egalitarianism, protection of jobs for everybody and state interventionism in the economy. Thus, the larger the number of people who score high on this scale, the stronger the opposition in a society against a free market economy and the differentiation of economic positions. The name 'leftism' has here, of course, only one of the possible meanings of this word, but one having historical relevance in this context. The practice of 'leftist' governments, both in the East and in the West, was more or less interventionist and egalitarianist.

Composition 'Leftist', in the sense of this scale, is the person who tends to accept the idea of the relative equality of income and wealth; the redistribution of income from the better off to the less off; a belief that a responsibility of government is to protect jobs and prevent state-owned enterprises and farms from being closed; state control over the profits of private entrepreneurs, wages of workers and prices of basic goods; and state ownership of heavy industry. The 'leftist' persons tends to claim, that 'ordinary working people do not get a fair share of the nation's wealth' and to evaluate system fairness from the point of view of differences in income.

The researchers started with the concept of two scales measuring egalitarianism and economic statism. After analysing the patterns of answers to the questions pre-selected for the scales of egalitarianism and economic statism, it was discovered that they consist of two factors which are stable across countries and segments. The hierarchical factor analysis procedure was applied to examine the structure of this phenomenon. As a result a correlation co-efficient between primary factors was found at the level 0.67 and a clear picture emerged of the common dimension (secondary factor) for the whole set of variables. So, it was decided to compose the main scale of the leftist orientation and, separately, two sub-scales measuring the two components of leftism, namely, egalitarianism and economic statism. The latter is not analysed further in this chapter. An analysis of the discriminating power of all items confirmed the statistical correctness of this decision.

In this presentation a *scale of economic optimism* and the segmentation of the societies according to *the social position and political activism of persons* are also used.

The scale of economic optimism

In the process of the exploratory data analysis it had been found in earlier Polish surveys that four items, typically used in public opinion polls for measuring economic satisfaction, tended to build a good scale. This was checked using the data from ten countries and interesting results were achieved. The scale of economic optimism was also important in explaining other dimensions in all these countries.

Definition This scale measures the satisfaction with both one's own economic situation and the economic situation and perspectives of one's country.

Assumption The larger number of people scoring high on this scale, the less conflict prone is the economic and social situation in a country and the greater the acceptance for the economic order and pro-market economy reforms.

Composition The scale was comprised of four items, typical for all public opinion research. The items referred to satisfaction of one's own and one's country's economic situation, the sense of improvement of one's living standard over the period of the last year, plus expectations concerning next year in the same respect. The reliability of the scale across the total sample of 10 countries was a=0.71 in 1994. Table 5.1 shows the reliability co-efficients for the described scales which were achieved in the 1994 and 1995 research. It shows that the scales are not only reliable but also that this reliability is stable over time.

Table 5.1   Reliability co-efficients for scales analysed in 1994 and 1995

	Business aptitude		Leftism		Economic optimism	
	1994	1995	1994	1995	1994	1995
All countries	0.74	0.73	0.81	0.84	0.72	0.74
Poland	0.79	0.74	0.84	0.85	0.71	0.68
Hungary	0.75	–	0.83	–	0.65	–
Czech Republic	0.79	0.77	0.85	0.89	0.73	0.75
Slovakia	0.80	0.78	0.82	0.85	0.70	0.70
Estonia	0.74	0.75	0.81	0.84	0.70	0.69
Latvia	0.69	0.65	0.77	0.80	0.70	0.67
Lithuania	0.75	0.76	0.77	0.81	0.69	0.70
Russia	0.69	0.66	0.78	0.82	0.66	0.71
Ukraine	0.75	0.71	0.77	0.78	0.70	0.70
Byelorussia	0.65	0.64	0.79	0.79	0.66	0.72
Bulgaria	–	0.81	0.82	0.85	0.71	0.72
Romania	–	0.73	0.79	0.82	0.74	0.76

Other scales

Some of the other PSE system scales are mentioned in this chapter. These can be briefly defined without going deeper into the methodology and assumptions behind them.

Authoritarianism The scale measures the acceptance of the general principle of hierarchy and obedience in society based on traditional values, combined with the acceptance of an autocratic and restrictive political order.

Nationalism This scale measures the strength of ethnocentrism and xenophobia, combined with the sense of being endangered by foreign cultural and economic influences.

Political Mobilisation The scale measures how prone individuals are to undertake political activities. The Rasch scaling approach was used to score these items. The scores were computed using the 1995 data and used both for 1994 and 1995 data. The scores are higher for political activities connected with the institutional framework of democracy, that is, the willingness to join a political party, the willingness to support political campaigns, or to support political candidates or a party.

The classification of the collective social actors

This classification was based on two dimensions, namely social stratification (simplified to two classes) and political activity, measured by taking part in elections and by interest in political issues.

An examination of the segments in the populations of the ten countries in 1994 shows that on average there are 12 per cent of 'Conductors of Change', 12 per cent of 'Passive Experts', 26 per cent of 'Active Citizens' and 49 per cent of 'Silent Citizens'. The greatest variations from this pattern are found in the Czech Republic and (though somewhat less different) in Slovakia, where stronger political mobilisation is evident. The top strata has been constructed in such a way that it comprises almost a quarter of each of the societies. The biggest differences from the average are observed in Hungary (18 per cent) and Russia (27 per cent). The composition of the samples in term of the four types of political actors has

	High position in social structure	Low position in social structure
Politically active	Conductors of change	Active citizens
Politically passive	Passive experts	Silent citizens

The definitions of the criteria employed in the chart are as follows:
High position in social structure: Logical sum (OR) of:

(i)   Education: Higher
(ii)   Income: Top decal
(iii)   Financial situation: Can afford everything
(iv)   Occupation:
     (a) Owner of own business
     (b) Manager/director of an enterprise or organisation
     (c) Department/division director
     (d) Higher professional/specialist
     (e) Professional/specialist

Low position in social structure: All not included in High position group.

Politically active: Scored high on the scale of interest in politics and took part in the last general election (or in Byelorussia: will take part in the next election).

Politically passive: All not included in the Politically active group.
The scale of interest in politics consists of general statements measuring how important it is for the respondent to stay informed about politics and what his general interest in politics is.

some impact on observed results, but the separate analysis within these segments will show that the actors also differ between countries.

PRESENTATION OF RESULTS

The methods of presentation

The analysis and presentation which follows is of an exploratory nature. Thus graphical presentation is used rather than statistical figures. However, some regression analysis results (with dummy coded categories) are also included, when describing the importance of grouping factors determining the differences in attitudes. In the perceptual mapping of the countries or political actors in the space created by the dimensions studied in this chapter the mean standardised scores computed for particular countries or actors are used. In the presentation of the results of factor analysis the means of factor scores computed for the groups of cases are employed, as is the factor loading of variables for labelling of the axes whenever this is applicable.

Countries in the space of leftism and achievement orientation (business aptitute)

The most leftist-oriented countries, if we use the mean score on the scale of leftism as a measure, are (European) Russia, Byelorussia and Ukraine, all scoring almost equally. The second level of leftism is represented by the Baltic Countries, Slovakia, and Hungary. The lowest level of leftism is found on average in Poland and especially in the Czech Republic. This picture is stable over the two waves of the research.

The differences according to achievement orientation are less obvious. However, it emerges that Poles and Hungarians tend to be more achievement-oriented than other nations. The differences between other countries are minor.

The differences in the leftist and achievement orientations between the four type of aggregates of political actors in ten countries

The picture is much more differentiated if the four types of political actors across countries are separately analysed. It emerges that the 'Conductors of Change', the influential and politically active stratum of the societies, tend to occupy the right lower rectangle of the scatter plot, namely they form a non-leftist, achievement-oriented cluster. When the positioning of the countries elites on the perceptual map are analysed, it can be observed

Figure 5.1   Leftism versus achievement: positioning using mean standardised scores, 1994

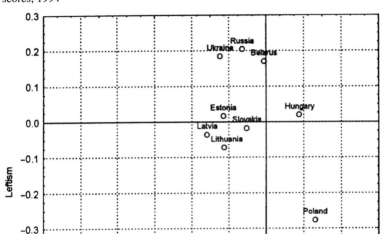

that the first end of the cloud of points representing conductors of change (as in the case of passive experts) is formed by the countries of Central Europe and the second end of the cloud is formed by Byelorussia, Russia and Ukraine. In the middle are Conductors of Change from Latvia, Lithuania (closer to the Eastern group) and Estonia (closer to the Western Group). The overall pattern of the plot is that the Silent Citizens are on average more passive and Active Citizens more leftist. It is also clear that both politically active segments in Byelorussia, Ukraine and Russia are more leftist oriented than the respective groups in the Central Europe.

Are the national minorities different? The problem of the post-soviet countries

The problem of national minorities often emerges in discussion about the East European countries, especially in the Baltics context. The problem is not so significant for countries like Poland (3 per cent of minorities

Figure 5.2   Leftism versus achievement: positioning of socio-political segments – 'actors' (means of standardised scales)

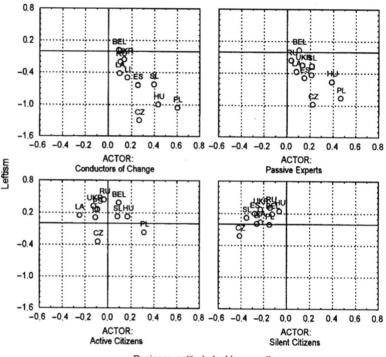

Business aptitude (achievement)

represented in the sample), Hungary (1 per cent), the Czech Republic (5 per cent), or even Slovakia (8 per cent). In contrast, this is more important in Estonia (37 per cent), Latvia (45 per cent), Ukraine (27 per cent), Byelorussia (22 per cent), Lithuania (18 per cent) and Russia (17 per cent).

Examining the perceptual map (Figure 5.3) it is evident, that the separate analysis of majorities does not change the basic pattern described above. Estonian, Lithuanian and Latvian minorities (mostly Russian) are more leftist oriented than the respective majorities, but the location of the majorities is not very different from the average country position. The differences on the scale of achievement orientation are smaller, though they seem to be stronger because of the aspect ratio of the scatter plot.[6] Of the Baltic countries, only Lithuania has a minority which seems to be significantly more achievement-oriented. There is another question which arises in this context, as to whether the ethnic minorities in Lithuania are differentiated. This cannot be addressed here, but it is an interesting question as to whether there are any differences between the Russian minority (most employed in cities, industry, and so on) and the Polish minority (large part of it connected with agriculture). This would, however, demand a separate study.

How economic optimism correlates with leftism and achievement orientation?

Leftist-orientation is correlated with the dissatisfaction with the economic situation of the country and an individual's own household, as measured by the scale of economic optimism. The least leftist Czechs are also the most optimistic and the leftists of Russia, Ukraine and Byelorussia are, in relative terms, those most dissatisfied with the situation. The Baltic countries emerge as a common cluster in the centre of the map.

It is, however, not the same with achievement orientation – the weaker discriminating scale. What is interesting is that the Czechs, who are very optimistic, score low on the scale of achievement orientation.

The impact of the country and belonging to the segment of the collective actors – exploratory regression analysis

The findings cannot only be explained in diagrams. In order to test the relative influence of belonging to particular segments of political actors, and to countries, regression analysis has been undertaken on both scales. The actors and countries were dummy coded. The reference categories (not included in the regression, that is, coded as double 0) were for political actors – Silent Citizens, and for countries – Byelorussia. The analysis was run on raw data.

When the betas and the significance of the regression coefficients are examined, it may be observed that Russia does not differ significantly from Byelorussia and Active Citizens from Silent Citizens in the influence on leftist orientation. The figures (Table 5.2) confirm the observations emerging from the scatterplots. Being a Conductor of Change decreases the standardised value of the scale of leftism by 0.23 points. The impact of being a Passive Expert is slightly weaker (0.17) but also negative. This means that belonging to higher social strata decreases the leftist orientation, as could be expected. Being a Czech or a Pole also decreases the leftist orientation, confirming the results of the graphical presentation. However, the explanatory power of countries as a group is weaker than the explanatory power of the belonging to the segment of political actors.

Figure 5.3 Positioning of ethnic majorities and minorities (1994)

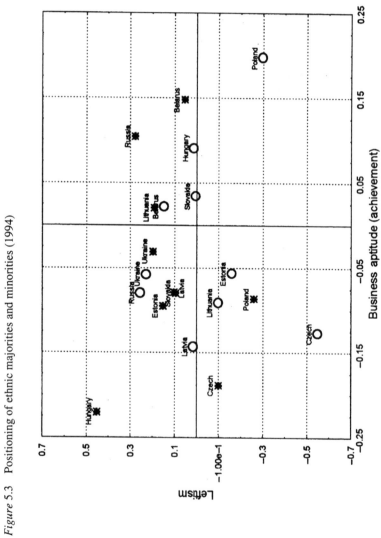

Figure 5.4 Leftism versus economic optimism (mean scores of standardised scales – 1994)

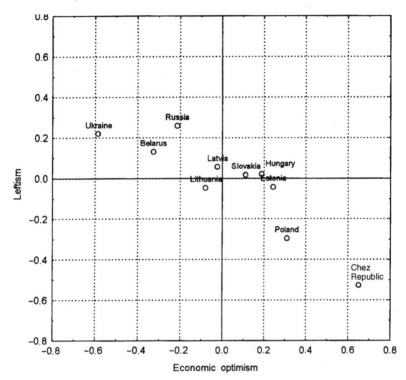

The model is much weaker at explaining the variance of achievement orientation (Table 5.3). It explains only 4 per cent of the total variance of the dependent variable, which is close to white noise. Especially weak is the influence of the country to which the individual belongs. This confirms the small differences observed on the plot.

One step more: positioning and clustering the countries and collective actors in the complex space of activism and national socialism

The analysis is now extended to show that the observed differences between countries and types of political actors are quite robust. Table 5.4 presents the results of the analysis of six scales used in the research.[7] The principal components analysis extracted two factors explaining respectively 36 per cent and 19 per cent of the common variance. The first factor represents a

Figure 5.5 Economic optimism versus business aptitude (1994)

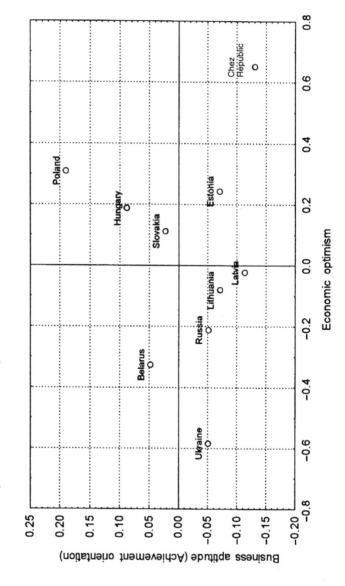

Table 5.2   Regression of the dummy coded types of the political actors'
segments and countries on the scale of leftism

Variable	B	SE B	Beta	T	Sig T
Conductors	–6.078971	.181010	–.234278	–33.584	.0000
Passive Experts	–4.469304	.178971	–.174822	–24.972	.0000
Active Citizens	.202881	.136410	.010588	1.487	.1370
Poland	–4.334006	.251432	–.154174	–17.237	.0000
Hungary	–2.402603	.251803	–.085461	–9.542	.0000
Czech	–6.239650	.252831	–.221938	–24.679	.0000
Slovakia	–2.190395	.252155	–.077904	–8.687	.0000
Estonia	–1.777522	.250782	–.063220	–7.088	.0000
Latvia	–2.283029	.251023	–.081216	–9.095	.0000
Lithuania	–2.661899	.251438	–.094682	–10.587	.0000
Russia	–.127704	.251078	–.004532	–.509	.6110
Ukraine	–.554003	.251332	–.019704	–2.204	.0275
(Constant)	44.790570	.188212		237.979	.0000

Multiple R	.34514			
R square	.11912			
Adjusted R square	.11859	Signif. F	.0000	
Standard error	7.92025			

syndrome, which can be labelled as National Socialism (Authoritarianism + Nationalism + Leftism). The second dimension can be called Activism (Achievement + Political Activism / + Economic Optimism).

The perceptual map (Figure 5.6) shows the same tendency to build clusters of countries as can be observed in the simpler case above. Ukraine, Russia and Byelorussia have similar profiles. The Czech Republic has the profile closest to liberal-democratic standards. Other countries are located between, with Poland, Slovakia and Estonia in the 'liberal-democratic quarter'. Hungary is in an untypical place on the map due to the high score on the scale of nationalism which, exceptionally, is not reliable in this country. Lithuania and Latvia are between, namely less 'national-socialist' but also less 'active'.

Turning to the plot presenting the profiles (means of regression factor scores) of the political actors across countries. There are some interesting observations to emerge from this analysis:

- Conductors of Change, who are the most influential stratum in these societies, tend to build the same cluster which was earlier observed in the plot showing average scores for countries.

Table 5.3   Regression of the dummy coded types of the collective actors'
segments and countries on the scale of business
aptitude/achievement orientation

	B	SE B	Beta	T	Sig T
Conductors	2.237903	.103610	.157154	21.599	.0000
Passive Experts	1.820167	.102477	.129687	17.762	.0000
Active Citizens	1.013252	.078123	.096302	12.970	.0000
Poland	.777926	.144007	.050395	5.402	.0000
Hungary	.663534	.144219	.042981	4.601	.0000
Czech	−.571962	.144808	−.037048	−3.950	.0001
Slovakia	−.131029	.144421	−.008486	−.907	.3643
Estonia	−.353278	.143634	−.022881	−2.460	.0139
Latvia	−.553541	.143773	−.035860	−3.850	.0001
Lithuania	−.373147	.144011	−.024170	−2.591	.0096
Russia	−.125382	.143631	−.008121	−.873	.3827
Ukraine	−.361198	.143949	−.023395	−2.509	.0121
(Constant)	16.740015	.107795		155.295	.0000

Multiple R	.20326			
R square	.04132			
Adjusted R square	.04074	Signif. F	.0000
Standard error	4.53631			

- Active Citizens represent similar order. They are at the same time more 'national-socialistic' oriented in all countries.
- Each type of aggregate of political actor tends to replicate the pattern observed for the countries and, at the same time, each type of actor is located in a somewhat different place on the perceptual map. Thus, Conductors of Change tend to be more active and less nationalistic, authoritarianist and leftist; Active Citizens are more nationalistic and socialist, Passive Experts are quite close to the Conductors of Change; Silent Citizens are first of all passive and somewhat more nationalistic and leftist.

The examination of differences between national minorities and majorities has shown it cannot be concluded that the position of Latvia or Lithuania is determined by their minorities. The Estonian minorities (mainly Russian) are first of all passive and they differ strongly from the national majority from this point of view.

Table 5.4   Summary of the factor analysis of the scales

Variable	Communality	Factor	Eigenvalue	Pct of Var	Cum Pct
Achievement	.57769	1	2.17286	36.2	36.2
Authoritarianism	.68211	2	1.15034	19.2	55.4
Nationalism	.56584				
Leftism	.76282				
Economic Optimism	.26576				
Political Activism	.46897				

Varimax rotated factor matrix of scales

Scale	Factor 1 National Socialism	Factor 2 Political-Economic Activism
Leftism	.86265	−.13656
Authoritarianism	.82589	−.00434
Nationalism	.75220	.00607
Achievement	−.03614	.75920
Political activism	.04168	.68355
Economic optimism	−.33757	.38962

SOME REMARKS ON THE DYNAMICS OF THE SITUATION IN CENTRAL AND EASTERN EUROPE: TRENDS 1994–1995

The second wave of the research, concluded in late spring 1995, has shown that the general dimensions of the socio-economic attitudes remained stable in all the countries. This is illustrated by the plot of factor loadings received in the principal component analysis based upon correlations between scales (Figure 5.8).

The maps enable both observation and analysis and, for the first time in the history of this project, the movements in the countries over time.

The population of the Czech Republic seems not only to be maintaining its pro-democracy and market orientation, but to be also moving further in this direction. The position of the country on Figures 5.9 and 5.10 makes the population a kind of a positive 'outsider'. It is commonly known that the economic and political developments in the Czech Republic confirm the conviction about optimistic perspectives taken on the economic and political reforms.

Figure 5.6   Positioning of ten Central and East European countries – in the factor space of the PSE Model

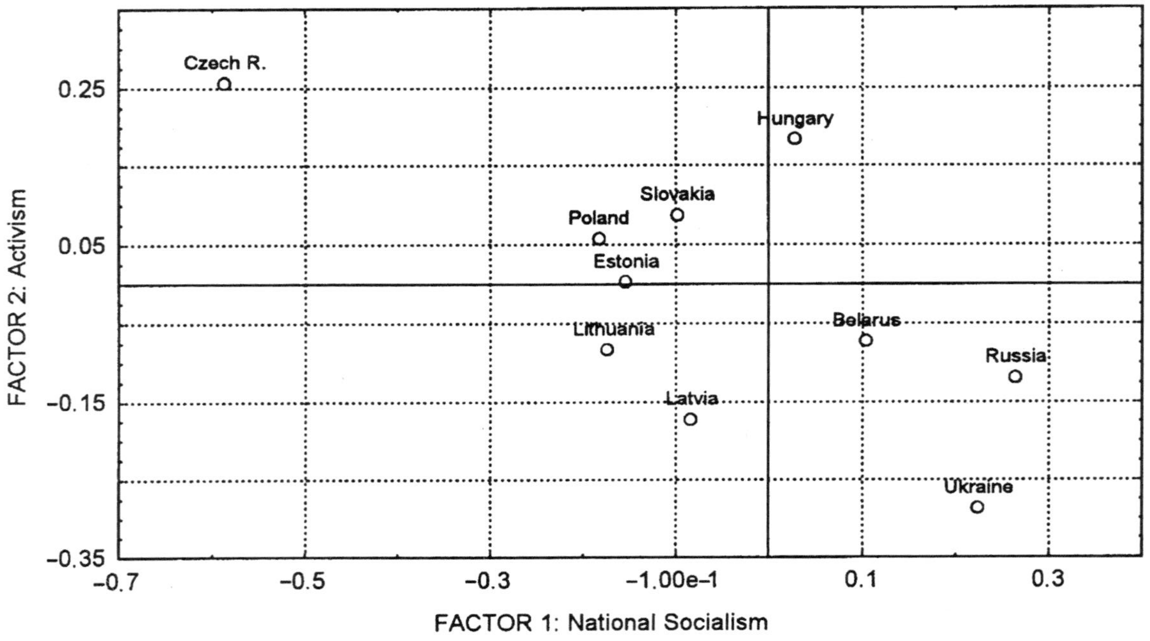

Figure 5.7   Political actors in ten countries (1994) – in the factor space of the PSE model

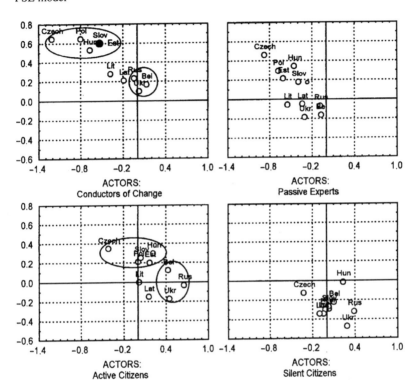

In contrast, Russia and Ukraine are strongly driving along the axis of 'national socialism'. Is this already a basis for prediction that the political events in these countries confirm their resigning from democratically based economic and political, reforms? Such a hypothesis begins to emerge from the results of this analysis. The events in Russia especially confirm that it is possible to infer political and economic predictions from the results of this research and on the basis of the model.

Byelorussia and Latvia are two countries where the situation is not subject to any easy interpretation. Both are driving along the axis of 'national socialism', but at the same time have slightly improved their position along of the axis of 'activism'. In the future it may be that the main tendency will be in one of the two directions, which conflict with each other.

Figure 5.8 Factor loadings (PCA) of attitude scales for pooled sample 1994–1995 of ten Central and Eastern European countries

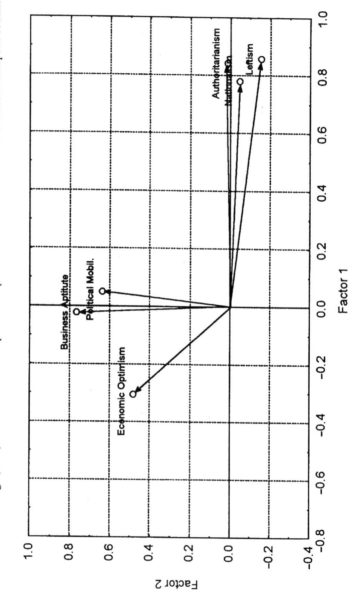

Figure 5.9 Mean factor scores (PCA) for countries – pooled sample 1994–1995

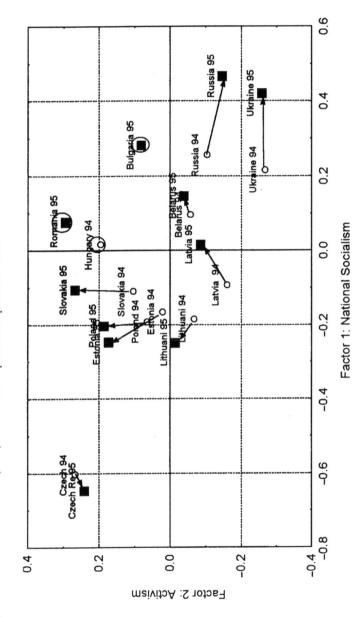

Figure 5.10   Position in PCA space of Conductors of Change (majorities *vs* minorities) in Baltic countries, Czech Republic and Russia

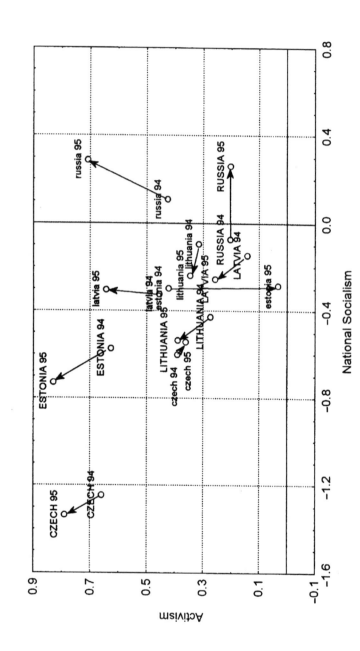

Two Baltic countries, Lithuania and Estonia, show, convincingly enough, that the pro-market and pro-democracy orientation prevails over national socialism. Estonia especially is moving energetically upwards. The same is true of Slovakia and Poland. The prevailing tendencies in Bulgaria, Rumania and Hungary, cannot be identified as there is no basis for comparison over time.

This part of the analysis confirms the hypothesis that there is polarisation process among the countries of Central and Eastern Europe. There is a group of countries which are increasingly tied to a market-oriented and democratic system, and which are developing in this direction, at the same time cultivating attitudes of acceptance for these reforms among their citizens. There is another group of countries in which market-oriented and democratic reforms may be rejected by elites and masses which do not want to pay their 'price'.

A thorough analysis of this problem requires a full set of data to be examined. In particular, more attention should be paid than was possible in this chapter to the differences of the value profiles of the Conductors of Change and Active Citizens and to their evolution over time. It is, for example, characteristic that the Conductors of Change and Active Citizens in Russia are rather strongly oriented towards 'national socialism' and that this allows them to find a basis for consensus on these grounds. Thus it could be predicted that this country may continue its contemporary movement along the axis of the 'national socialism'. The same situation may prevail in Ukraine. In other countries the differences between the value profiles of the two aggregates of political actors are deeper. This makes the political situation in these countries less stable as, for example, in Poland.

CONCLUSIONS

One of the crucial results of the study is the discovery of two basic dimensions of the socio-economic and political attitudes in all ten (now twelve) post-communist countries. The dimensions are stable in the statistical sense. Their meaning is sometimes not easily accepted by Western scholars who, on occasions, seem to dislike our associating leftist orientation with nationalism and authoritarianism or do not accept the name 'leftism' for the scale measuring a mixture of egalitarianism and economic statism. However, we know from history that egalitarianism and statism used to be very important points of the leftist movements' programmes. The correlation between leftism, authoritarianism and nationalism is an empirical fact in these countries and we know that such ideology might mobilise a broad range of people, especially from the lower social strata. Historical references are not necessary for this point to be taken.

The exploratory analysis of the survey results collected in the ten Central and East European Countries shows the tendency for three clusters of countries to emerge:

- A 'Liberal-democracy'-oriented group. This includes the Czech Republic, Poland, Slovakia, Hungary and Estonia, where the societies are less oriented toward leftism and generally less oriented toward the syndrome built of orientation towards nationalism (with the difficult exception of nationalistic Hungary?), authoritarianism and leftism, and more oriented toward activism and achievement in economy and polity.
- A 'National – socialist' oriented group which has an opposite orientation; namely an anti-liberal syndrome plus economic and political passivism as a mass response to the contemporary situation. The group comprises of Russia, Byelorussia and Ukraine.
- The 'in-between' countries: Lithuania and Latvia, driven by Conductors of Change towards the first group and by Active Citizens toward the second. Their future will depend on the advances in the transformation processes, the general economic and political situation and activities of the political elites. But the same is also true about other countries.

It is evident that in all countries surveyed the politically active elites are more 'progressive' from the point of view of Western values, than other segments of these societies. They drive the countries towards reform. But these elites differ also across the countries in orientation towards leftism or achievement and, more broadly, towards anti-liberal and anti-democratic values and activist orientation. They form the same clustering pattern as can be observed when studying whole societies. In some of the countries there are big tensions in attitudes between 'Conductors of Change' and 'Active Citizens'. The first group is very 'Western', the second is more leftist, nationalistic and authoritarian. In the most of the countries post-communist parties have gained the support of large fractions of the voters. In the Czech Republic both segments are not very different and they give a stable base for the liberal-democratic government of Klaus and Havel.

The Baltic countries are located in the intermediate position, not only in the geographic sense, but also in terms of attitudes and value orientations. It would appear that there will be a growing polarisation between developments in Central Europe and in Russia, Byelorussia and probably Ukraine. The position of the Baltic Countries is in the first group, but it is a considerable task for their elites to maintain this position.

It could be argued that the opinions formulated in this survey are independent from the real conditions of life in particular countries. But we have to remember, that the dominating attitudes and orientations affect the social behaviour and, in consequence, political and economic processes. Changing the economy and its institutions may change attitudes and orientation, but we cannot say that the reverse is not true. This makes the PSE method an efficient tool for diagnosing the situation in Central and Eastern Europe and for predicting, in general terms, the directions of their evolution in the course of transition.

Notes

1. The more complete description of the PSE project and the concept of four collective political actors may be obtained from M&PORI 'CEM' in Cracow (Director: Jan Jerschina).
2. Project directors of PSE Model project: Dr Eugene Parta, Dr Mark Rhodes and Professor Dr Jan Jerschina. Data analysis: Jan Jerschina, Jaroslaw Górniak and Elibietá Lesińska.
3. This was done for exploratory purposes. Care should be exercised when looking at the statistical significance of the tests, because the sample has been somewhat inflated. But in such a big overall sample the differences in significances are rather small and, from the other perspective, many tiny differences tend to appear significant.
4. The framework is presented in the paper of Jan Jerschina mentioned in note 1.
5. So, we built not the 'factor scales' but 'factor-based scales'. For discussion, see Kim J-O. and Mueller, C.W. (1994) 'Factor Analysis: Statistical Methods and Practical Issues' in M.S. Lewis-Beck (ed.), *Factor Analysis and Related Techniques* (London: Sage & Toppan) 138–40.
6. It was decided to use this aspect ratio to avoid overlapping points and labels, but readers should pay attention to the scaling of the axes.
7. The scales of authoritarianism and nationalism are described in the separate paper obtainable from M&PORI. The scale of political activism was computed from the classical set of questions about political mobilisation, using the Rasch scaling approach (in ALMO statistical package).

REFERENCES

Heath, A., Curtice, J., Evans, G., Jowell, R., Field, J. and Witherspoon, S. (1991) *Understanding Political Change: The British Voter 1964–1987* (Oxford: Pergamon Press).

Heckhausen, H. (1965) *Leistungsmotivation und Unternehmerinitiative,* Gavain 13, pp. 380–400.

McClelland, D.C. (1964) *The Achieving Society* (Princeton, NJ.: Van Nostrand).

6 Micro-Economic Differences between or within Baltic Nationalities?[1]

Richard Rose

INTRODUCTION

The distinction between macro- and micro-economics is familiar: macro-economics normally refers to properties of countries reported in aggregated national income accounts and central bank statistics, whereas micro-economics refers to individuals and household-level data. Although economists tend to specialise at one or another level of analysis, the economy as the whole can only be understood by bringing the two halves together. Not to do so risks committing gross errors. But just as total national income cannot be inferred from a statistic about the number in poverty, so household living standards cannot be inferred from data about the money supply. It is a basic ecological fallacy (cf. Robinson, 1950) to infer characteristics of individuals from characteristics of aggregates. Within a country we should not generalise about the distribution of poverty between regions or households from the mean figure for gross domestic product per capita. In a complementary fashion, it is an 'individualist' fallacy to infer properties of regions, impersonal organisations such as corporations, or such macro-economics measures as the balance of payments, from data about individuals (Scheuch, 1966).

In economies in transformation we must consider *What is the economy of account*? The literature of command economies was full of descriptions of multiple economies, variously labelled as a 'second' economy or a plurality of second or 'black' or 'rainbow' economies (see for example, Grossman, 1977; Dallago, 1990). The collapse of the command economy has created new conditions, but the skills cultivated in the multiple economies of the past remain important to help households cope with the impact of economic transformation (see Rose, 1993; Sik, 1995).

In the case of ethnically mixed countries, such as Estonia, Latvia and Lithuania, we must also ask: *What is the nation of account*? The national (*sic*) account of each Baltic state is effectively a multi-national account, reflecting the combined activities of Baltic, Russian and other former Soviet nationalities. Since nationality differences are patently important in politics, to what extent are they important in economic activities too? To answer this question we need micro-economic data disaggregated to the individual or household level, so that we can examine differences within as well as between nationalities in each Baltic state. We also need data about unofficial as well as official economies. As Herbert Simon (1969) has emphasised, choosing the appropriate level of aggregation or disaggregation is part of the 'art' of design.

THINKING ABOUT UNITS OF ANALYSIS

Official macro-economic data about the Baltics describes the collapse of the non-market command economy, consequent to the breaking of the power of the 'commanders' of the command economy (cf. Kornai, 1993). If official macro-economic statistics are taken at face value, the first stage of macro-economic transformation appears extremely negative for everyone in the Baltic states. The cumulative effect of annual changes in the size of the gross domestic product in aggregate and in the consumer price index since 1988 has been extraordinary, and it has also been negative. The aggregate national product of Lithuania has fallen by 55 per cent, of Latvia by 39 per cent, and of Estonia by 30 per cent. The cumulative effect of inflation is even greater, for the consumer price index has risen by more than 7700 per cent in Latvia, almost 12 500 per cent in Estonia, and inflation has risen by more than 31 000 per cent in Lithuania.

But are official macro-economic statistics a good guide to micro-economic conditions in a post-command economy? Logically, the answer must be 'No'. Only micro-economic data can report directly on micro-economic conditions. However, macro-economic data can be reliable if an economy is 'one-dimensional', that is, the great bulk of economic activity is monetised and also officially recorded. However, economies in transformation are *three-dimensional economies*; in addition to the division between macro- and micro-economies, we can also observe a division between officially recorded and unofficial economies and between monetised and non-monetised activities, producing a total of eight different types of 'economies', including at least four at the micro-economic level (Figure 6.1).[2]

Officially recorded and monetised. When the state employs the great bulk of the labour force, then *wages* of state enterprises and non-market

Figure 6.1   Three dimensions of economic activity

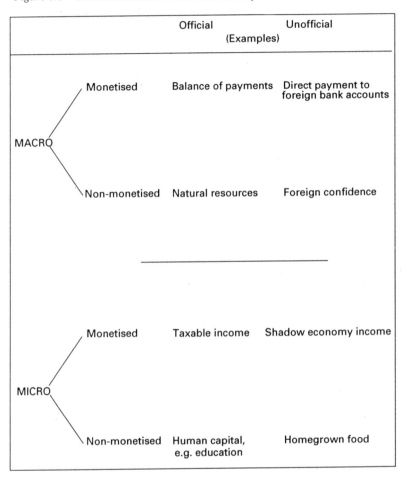

state agencies should routinely and readily be recorded in official statistics. However, transformation is about 'destatisation'; an incidental effect of this is the distancing of enterprises and their employees from official agencies, including those producing economic statistics. Inertia will lead many ex-state enterprises to continue filing statistics. But newly launched employers are unlikely to give a high priority to reporting statistics to ministries. Income-maintenance grants such as pensions are invariably recorded when paid by government ministries or their agents. Nearly every household in the Baltics is involved in the official economy, either as an employee or a pensioner, and many households receive two or more official incomes or combine the income of employees and pensioners (see Rose, 1995).

Official but non-monetised. The state's economic interests extend beyond its tax base; increasingly it includes assets that are not currently traded in the market. Natural resources, such as oil, are a macro-economic example; so too is clean air and water. At the micro-economic level, the parallel is human capital, education and training that give individuals marketable skills that can be used in the official economy (Seragheldin and Steer, 1994).

Monetised but not officially recorded. Command economies were officially non-market economies, but there were 'unofficial' markets in which farmers could sell their produce, tradespeople could sell their services, and bureaucrats could sell favours. The collapse of the command economy has greatly expanded the scope of economic activities outside state control, including opportunities to make money in 'second' economies, typically as a supplement to household income. The New Baltic Barometer II found upwards of a quarter of households are involved in 'uncivil' economies.

Social economies, unofficial and non-monetised. There was nothing illegal in a command economy in growing food on a garden plot, or in exchanging help with friends and relatives; compare the old Russian saying, 'Better to have a hundred friends than a hundred roubles' (cf. Rose, 1995b). Frequent shortages were incentives for individuals to rely upon producing some goods and services without any money changing hands. Such activities continue today; New Baltic Barometer II shows that nearly all Baltic households are involved in the production and consumption of goods and services in social economies in which no money changes hands.

ECONOMIC DIFFERENCES WITHIN AND BETWEEN
NATIONALITIES

Comparing economic conditions is the stock-in-trade of international organisations such as OECD and the World Bank; the basic unit of analysis is the country. But such data cannot tell us anything specific about economic conditions within a country, for that requires information about distributions around the mean. Micro-economic data can be used in making many types of within-country comparisons. For example, in the

United States, comparisons between racial groups, especially blacks and whites, are now standard practice in official statistics.

Comparing nationalities within a state

In the Baltic states, nationality is a fundamental fact of life. In Estonia and Latvia the population is divided into two groups nearly equal in size, a Baltic nationality and Russians or nationals of other republics of the former Soviet Union. The majority population in Lithuania is relatively large, but Russians and Poles constitute distinctive minorities. Whereas in earlier centuries the mixture of nationalities in the Eastern Baltic was the result of a lengthy process of migration, today's bi-nationalism was caused by the forced integration of the three Baltic states into the Soviet Union as a consequence of the Second World War.

If nationality influences economic life, its effects should alter with radical changes in the structure of the state. As the politically dominant nationality, Russians should have benefited from four decades of rule by Moscow. The achievement of independence by the Baltic states has reversed the significance of nationality. In Estonia and Latvia a majority of Russians are not citizens. Insofar as political differences cause economic differences, then Estonians and Latvians should be better off than people of Russian nationality. From this it follows that in Lithuania, where Russian nationals have readily acquired citizenship, there should be no economic differences between Lithuanians and Russian nationals.

Yet economic achievement need not depend upon citizenship or the right to vote; successful entrepreneurs can be foreigners and people can prosper while denied the right to vote. The Industrial Revolution occurred in England when the majority of industrialists as well as workers were denied the right to vote. In the old Eastern Europe, Jews played a significant part in economic sectors, even though they usually laboured under civil disabilities. In a modern welfare state, the relationship of the individual with the state creates 'rights' well beyond the right to vote, such as the right to work or receive a pension in return for contributions paid. Legal residence is usually sufficient for an individual to participate in the economy, and to receive benefits from the welfare state, and this is the case in the Baltic as in Western Europe.

From a legal and political perspective, nationality matters, especially in Estonia and Latvia. Yet within a country the economy is meant to be blind to distinctions of nationality, religion or skin colour; it is the cash value of income and wealth that matters. This chapter tests whether or not nationality affects the economic conditions of individuals in Baltic states. Lengthy arguments can be summed up in two conflicting propositions:

*   *Nationality matters.* In each Baltic state, economic differences between nationalities are large, and within-nationality conditions much the same.
*   *Within-nation differences.* In each Baltic state, economic differences between individuals of the same nationality are primary, and economic profiles of different nationalities similar.

Data for analysis

Relying upon official data about economies in transformation has a substantial built-in bias. It overstates the degree of contraction because the readily measured sector, the state sector, is contracting most. Insofar as the introduction of market prices increases the validity of GDP figures as against the 'prices' used to calculate Net Material Product, the extent of contraction will be increased (cf. Marer *et al.*, 1992; Holzmann *et al.*, 1995). 'Second generation' evidence of economic growth may also be exaggerated, as some increases in official GDP will simply reflect the entry into official accounts of activities that were previously unrecorded.

It is unnecessary to use macro-economic data to analyse micro-economic activity in economies in transformation. The normal social science methodology of a sample survey can provide very detailed empirical data about activities of individuals and households. Insofar as questionnaires in economies in transformation simply repeat questions asked in 'one-dimensional' market economies, the results risk repeating biases of macro-economic statistics.

The questionnaire used in the New Baltic Barometer follows the design established by Rose in a series of 1991 surveys about mass response to economy transformation in Bulgaria, Czechoslovakia, Poland and Russia, and continued since across more than a dozen post-communist countries (see Rose, 1993; Rose and Haerpfer, 1994). The surveys focus upon micro-economic behaviour in its multi-dimensional entirety, unofficial and official, monetised and non-monetised. In the Baltic states, there are a significant number of additional questions about nationality, language and citizenship.

This chapter reports results from the New Baltic Barometer II conducted from 3 to 17 April 1995 with separately drawn representative samples of six different nationalities (for full details, see Rose, Vilmorus,

Lasopec and Emor, 1995). Emor interviewed 651 Estonians and 650 Russian nationals in Estonia; Lasopec interviewed 656 Latvians and 517 Russians in Latvia; and in Lithuania Vilmorus interviewed 631 Lithuanians and 239 Russian nationals. The smaller number of Russian interviews in Lithuania reflected the smaller proportion of Russians in the population there; they had to be over-sampled to secure statistically reliable results. The total number of interviews – 3344 – is thus substantial.

Drawing separate samples increases the reliability of the results, for Russians are geographically concentrated, especially in Estonia and Lithuania. As in all samples – including those used to create price indices and national income accounts – there is a margin of sampling error; hence, differences of a few percentage points may not be statistically significant.

Literary discussions of nations imply a homogeneity based upon mother tongue, religion or another unifying characteristic. But economic exchanges within a nation presuppose differences between people speaking the same language and religion, for example, between factory workers and farmers. When we compare two nationality groups, each of which is internally differentiated, we must measure similarity or dissimilarity in the distribution of resources within each group.

Because similarities and differences are matters of degree, we need an easily understood measure applicable to economic conditions. The Difference Index provides this; it is a simple arithmetic description of the extent to which two groups differ, here, Baltic and Russian nationals living in a given Baltic state. It is calculated by taking the percentage point difference between the groups for each alternative value of a variable, summing the differences without regard to a plus or minus sign, and dividing the sum by two. It thus takes into account the distribution across all values of a polychotomous variable, whether nominal, ordinal or continuous. The Difference Index (DI) can thus range from 0 (*total similarity*) to 100 (*total difference*). For example, the calculation of the Difference Index for unemployment among Latvians and Russian nationals shows zero difference in the rate of current unemployment among the two nationalities, but in the course of a year Russians are more likely at some time to be unemployed. Yet the majority of the labour force and the median adult in both nationalities are employed all year. The Difference Index is low: 12 percentage points. However, when attention is directed at whether a person is born in the Baltic state of residence, the Difference Index between Estonians and Russians in Estonia is 55 per cent; in Latvia, 52 per cent; and in Lithuania, 58 per cent. For while nearly all Baltic nationalities were born in the Baltic states, about half non-Baltic nationalities were born there.

ECONOMIC ACTIVITIES

Because every Baltic household is involved in the officially recorded economy, economic transformation places everyone at risk of losing a job or being placed on short time and not paid for a full working week. Because the great majority of families depend upon two or more wage-earners, individuals are indirectly at risk if another member of their family becomes unemployed. However, the turbulence of economic transformation creates difficulties for people in work as well as for the unemployed. When people are asked whether they earn enough from the job they have to meet their basic needs, the great majority in the Baltics reply in the negative (Table 6.1); a similar response is given in the great majority of post-communist countries. In Latvia, five-sixths in the labour force say they do not earn enough to buy what they really need and in Estonia and Lithuania more than three-quarters cannot earn enough from their regular employment to buy necessities. A striking feature of Table 6.1 is that incomes are inadequate in all groups; Baltic and Russian nationals are equally likely to have trouble making ends meet with what they earn in the 'first' dimension of the economy.

However, economies in transformation are multi-dimensional, and every household is involved in a *multiplicity of economies*, official and

Table 6.1   Inadequacy of earnings from regular employment

Question: Do you and your family earn enough from regular work in the official economy to buy what your household really needs?

	Est %	EstRus %	Lat %	LatRus %	Lit %	LitRus %
Definitely enough	–	1	1	–	–'	1
Just enough	25	22	17	16	25	21
Not quite enough	52	48	38	41	43	43
Definitely not enough	23	29	43	42	31	34
	DI*	= 7	DI	= 3	DI	= 4

Notes:
* DI describes the Difference Index as defined in the text (p. 115) and employed in Tables 6.1 to 6.5.
Table excludes all respondents outside the labour force, principally the retired.
Source: Rose *et al.* (1995); New Baltic Bonometer II data in Tables 6.1–6.5 and reproduced with the permission of Professor Richard Rose.

unofficial, monetised and non-monetised. The New Baltic Barometer collects data about involvement in nine different economies. Only two are officially recorded and monetised: earnings in the first job or a pension or regular income-maintenance grant from the state, and another is usually officially recorded, benefits at the place of work. Three are monetised but not officially recorded: second jobs, being paid money on the side as tips or bribes, and dealings in foreign currencies; and four are unofficial and not monetised: growing food and repairing or building one's own house, exchanging help with friends, and getting favours, unpaid, from friends of friends. Detailed studies in the first New Baltic Barometer (Rose and Maley, 1994: 18) found that the average number of economies per household ranged from 3.8 among Russians in Estonia and 3.9 among Estonians to 4.2 among both nationalities in Lithuania.

The resources of a multiplicity of economies can be combined into very different kinds of *portfolios* (Rose, 1993). People are not seeking to protect themselves by looking to the state or their employer to provide welfare or by earning lots more money in an official economy that is, at best, in a Schumpeterian phase of 'creative destruction'. Instead, people are making meta-choices *between* different economies. For example, a person who loses a job in a state enterprise may substitute income from uncivil cash-only activities. If inflation makes food in shops too expensive, an employed person can fall back on non-monetised household production. Unofficial or household activities can compensate, to a greater or lesser degree, for the decline of official resources.

When people are asked to say which two economies are first and second in importance for their family, the largest group relies upon a *defensive* portfolio, combining resources from the official economy and from non-monetised resources, typically growing food (Table 6.2). A second group is *enterprising*; since a money income from the official economy is not enough, earnings are also obtained in second economies. The limited size of the enterprising group is less a reflection of the unwillingness of people to be paid cash-in-hand than it is of the limits of effective demand, for not many people in the Baltics are able to pay others to work for them in shadow economies. In an economy in transformation, those who depend solely upon their official earnings or pension are *vulnerable* to the effect of shocks from economic turbulence. The vulnerable group is substantial too. A fourth group are *marginal*; they do not depend upon cash earnings or a pension.

Nationalities in Estonia and Latvia differ to a degree in *how* they assemble portfolios that will protect them amidst the turbulence of transformation. In all three Baltic states, Russian nationals are more likely to be vulnerable than are Baltic nationalities, a likely result of being looked after

Table 6.2   Portfolios of most important economies

	Est %	EstRus %	Lat %	LatRus %	Lit %	LitRus %
Defensive (Official + non-monetised)	48	35	43	37	44	31
Enterprising (Official + shadow)	24	16	25	16	12	16
Vulnerable (Solely official)	20	38	22	40	35	44
Marginal	8	11	10	7	9	9
	DI	= 21	DI	= 18	DI	= 10

Note: All respondents included, whether or not in labour force.
Source: Rose *et al.* (1995).

at their work in the days when the Baltic states were part of the Soviet Union. Baltic nationals are more likely to be on the defensive, since Baltic people are more likely to live in the countryside where it is easier to grow food and build one's own house. Marginal groups are limited in number in all nationalities.

The object of combining resources is to 'get by', for survival is a pre-condition of individuals investing efforts in pursuit of wealth, and the likely alternative to getting by is to become destitute. People can get by at many different levels of economic wellbeing. 'Getting by' means matching resources to consumption; as long as this is the case a household can sustain itself indefinitely. The New Baltic Barometer therefore asks people whether or not they have had to spend savings or borrow money in the past year, for a household cannot sustain itself in the long term by consuming capital and running up debts, for sooner or later its capital and credit will be used up.

In the past year two-thirds to three-quarters of Baltic people have been able to get by on a basis that can be sustained indefinitely (Table 6.3). The proportion able to do so is as high as three-quarters of Latvians and 72 per cent of Russians in Latvia. The differences between nationality groups within each of the Baltic states is low. In view of the big differences in reported first economy GDP per capita, the difference in the percentage getting by is also very small between Estonia, Latvia and Lithuania.

Table 6.3   Getting by amidst the turbulence of transformation

Question: In the past year, has your family been able to (a) save some money, (b) just get by, (c) had to spent savings, (d) borrow money, or (e) spend savings *and* borrow money?

		Est %	EstRus %	Lat %	LatRus %	Lit %	LitRus %
(a)	Saved money	6	4	5	5	8	4
(b)	Just got by	65	70	70	67	59	64
	(Total)	(71)	(74)	(75)	(72)	(67)	(68)
(c)	Spent savings	18	11	11	10	14	16
(d)	Borrowed money	7	10	5	8	10	6
(e)	Spent savings, borrowed	3	5	9	10	9	10
		DI = 9		DI = 4		DI = 8	

Note: All respondents included, whether or not in labour force.
Source: Rose *et al.* (1995).

The impact of multiple economies is made evident by comparing the proportion of people earning enough from the official economy job with the proportion able to get by on the basis of a portfolio of activities. Whereas 75 per cent of Latvians manage to get by with a portfolio of activities, only 18 per cent of Latvians in the labour force and 10 per cent of all Latvians earned enough from their official economy job to get buy. A similar pattern is found in Estonia and Lithuania. In almost all post-Communist countries, *for the majority of people involvement in a multiplicity of economies makes the difference between sinking into destitution or getting by.*

The contrast between an economy in transformation and an established economy can be illustrated by comparing how people get by in countries such as Austria with what happens in the Baltic states. In Austria, the percentage reporting that they are able to get by is 82 per cent, not much higher than among Baltic peoples. The difference is that 70 per cent of Austrians say that they earn enough from their first job to get by, compared to less than a quarter of Baltic people (cf. Rose and Haerpfer, 1992: Appendix, Tables 1, 10).

Differences between portfolios appear to reflect opportunistic circumstances: amidst the turbulence of transformation people make do as best they can with the resources at hand. Differences between nationalities are small and usually within the range of sampling fluctuations. What is stamped on a citizen's passport or identity card is unimportant in the face of pressures to match resources with consumption needs.

DOING BADLY OR DOING WELL?

The study of income distribution is a recognised field within micro-economics; invariably, it is based upon the distribution of money income. There are big debates about measures of poverty in market economies (see for example, Polish Statistical Association, 1992; Atkinson, 1987), but there is agreement on one point: money is a sufficient measure of poverty. However, the above shows that in an economy in transformation it is misleading to treat a single dimension as if it were the total resources of a micro-economy. It is also misleading to impute money values to the production of goods that are consumed without money changing hands, or to the exchange of services between friends and relatives on an unrequited basis. Moreover, empirical analysis of Russian survey data has shown that money income is *not* a determinant of a household's capacity to get by (Rose and McAllister, 1996).The incommensurability of resources and the elusiveness of unofficial activities need not be a barrier to identifying individuals who are doing well or doing badly, as long as *direct* measures are employed rather than the proxy of money. The New Baltic Barometer uses just this strategy.

Whatever a household's income may be, if it must frequently do without the essentials of food, clothing, heat and electricity, it is in bad shape. This is true whether the cause of doing without is the shortages of a command economy or the cause of enjoying heat and electricity is the continuance of sub-market prices for housing and energy in an economy still being transformed.

Across the Baltics, households do not lack heat and electricity; price levels and methods of charging for domestic energy compensate for incomes that are low by world market standards. People are more likely to do without clothing and food, but no nationality group is often without these necessities. The median person in each group is sometimes or rarely without clothing and food (Table 6.4). In Latvia there is very little difference between nationality groups in doing without. In Lithuania the differences are small but consistent; Russian nationals are more likely to do without. In Estonia, the average person is less likely to be often without necessities; however, those frequently doing without necessities in Estonia are disproportionately in the Russian community, and there the Difference Index rises to 30 percentage points for doing without food.

Destitution is a matter of duration: the more often people have to do without necessities, and the more necessities households must do without, the more appropriate it is to describe people as destitute (see for example, Rose, 1995c). A scale measuring destitution can be created, with people never doing without scored 0, rarely doing without scored 1, sometimes 2, and often 3, and the scores summed for food, clothing and heat. The maximum destitution is a score of 9 and the greatest sufficiency a score of 0.

Across the Baltics, few people are destitute, that is, often doing without at least two basic goods and sometimes doing without a third (Table 6.4). The percentage avoiding destitution is as high as 96 per cent among Estonians and even when least high, it is 83 per cent among Russians in Latvia and Lithuania. In most nationality groups, the median block are in and out of difficulties. In such circumstances, people rely upon a variety of coping strategies. When there are difficulties in obtaining food, households can eat cheaper foods, eat less meat and more potatoes, or simply eat less overall. When there is no money for new clothes, secondhand clothes can be bought or a household can mend and make do, patching clothes or wearing available clothing that is out of fashion or shabby. A third or more of people in the Baltics are all right for basic necessities; only among Estonians is an absolute majority consistently all right. The Difference Index again reflects less similarity among nationalities in Estonia than in the other Baltic states.

Material possessions are a classic indicator of income and wealth. In countries where tax administration is weak and households resistant to paying taxes, the possession of material goods can be the basis of assessing taxes on income. Barometer surveys have found three consumer goods – a colour television set, a telephone and a car – are good indicators of having an income above the bare level of subsistence. Each costs a significant amount of money to purchase; a colour television set cannot be made in the household or produced by voluntary labour, as can an extension to a house. A telephone can involve a monthly bill, and a car significant monthly running costs. Furthermore, these are goods that the great majority of families in advanced industrial societies have, indicating that the propensity to have such consumer durables rises with household income.

In the Baltic states, a majority of nationalities have a colour television set, and there is little difference between countries or between nationalities (Table 6.5). A majority of all nationalities also have a telephone. Here again there is very little difference between countries or between Russian

Table 6.4   Tightening belts but not destitute

	Est %	EstRus %	Lat %	LatRus %	Lit %	LitRus %
Destitute (*score 7–9)	4	15	15	17	12	17
Tightening belts, mend and make do (*score 3–6)	31	48	50	55	46	51
All right for necessities (*score 0–2)	65	37	35	28	42	32
	DI = 28		DI = 7		DI = 10	

Notes: All respondents included, whether or not in labour force.
* Frequency of doing without food, clothing and heat, electricity,
   scored: 3 points = Often; 2 points = Sometimes; 1 point = Rarely; 0 points =
   Never.
Source: Rose *et al.* (1995).

nationals and a Baltic group within a country. Car ownership is more vari-able. In no country do half the households yet have a car, but large minor-ities have a car in every nationality group except the older and more urban Latvian Russians. The level of material possessions in a society where people are not always sure of food or clothing is a reminder that while transformation may disrupt daily routines, many households have a sub-stantial capital stock of goods that remain in their possession even if they sometimes have difficulties in obtaining basic necessities.

When we look at the distribution of consumer goods among households and nationalities, a familiar pattern once again emerges. In every national-ity group, most people are in the middle, having one or two major con-sumer goods rather than all or none. Furthermore, households who have all three consumer goods outnumber those with none in every nationality group. Moreover, in every Baltic state the proportion of households with all three consumer durables is higher than the proportion of destitute households.

'Getting on', that is, improving living standards by acquiring more con-sumer goods, is the other extreme from avoiding destitution and just getting by. The *New Baltic Barometer II* sought evidence of rising living standards by asking people whether they were planning to buy a major consumer good in the next twelve months. While a majority of all nation-alities do not yet have the money (or, in a few cases, the need) to buy con-

Table 6.5 Distribution of consumer goods

	Est %	EstRus %	Lat %	LatRus %	Lit %	LitRus %
A. *Household has:*						
Colour television	75	82	76	77	74	78
	(DI =	7)	(DI =	1)	(DI =	4)
Telephone	60	55	72	69	69	75
	(DI =	5)	(DI =	3)	(DI =	6)
Car	45	30	39	26	43	37
	(DI =	15)	(DI =	13)	(DI =	6)
B. *Household owns consumer goods*						
All three	31	19	29	17	31	27
Two	32	39	39	48	36	45
One	23	31	21	24	20	19
None	14	11	11	10	12	9
	DI =	15	DI =	12	DI =	8

Note: All respondents included, whether or not in labour force.
Source: Rose *et al*. (1995).

sumer durables, a sixth of Baltic people are planning to make some purchases; the percentage is highest in Estonia, 20 per cent; second in Latvia,
16 per cent, and lowest in Lithuania, 13 per cent.

If household resources were constant, then only the 'haves' would be
planning to buy consumer durables, replacing goods that were wearing out,
or improving the quality of what they owned, for example, buying a new or
second-hand Western car in place of a Lada. Those without would remain
without. But this is not the case. Most people planning to buy a car, 7 per
cent of all respondents, will be buying a car for the first time, a sure sign of a
rising living standard among the middle income groups in society. Among
the 7 per cent planning to buy a new colour television set, the proportion
replacing their old set with a better set is slightly larger than the proportion
buying a set for the first time. Among the 6 per cent expecting to get a telephone, three-quarters will be first-time possessors of a telephone.

The projected consequences of expanding consumer demand in Estonia,
Latvia and Lithuania show the pattern is the same – a small increase in the
possession of goods associated with a middle-income lifestyle in a market
economy. The number of households acquiring a colour television set for
the first time is expected to rise by 4 per cent in the next year in Estonia
and Lithuania and by 2 per cent in Latvia; acquiring a telephone, by

6 per cent in Estonia, 4 per cent in Latvia and 3 per cent in Lithuania; and a car, by 5 per cent in Latvia, 4 per cent in Estonia, and 3 per cent in Lithuania. The same pattern holds among nationality groups; the detailed figures are not presented to focus on the big picture. The plans of a household to buy consumer goods may not be realised, just as some households not currently planning to make a major purchase may end up doing so. The important point is the cumulative effect of small but regular increases in owning major consumer goods over a period of years. *The Trend in ownership of consumer durables is irreversibly up*, because these goods are durables unlikely to wear out in a few years time and, if a recession occurred, they could not be sold on the second-hand market, for a recession would lower demand.

In the medium term, say, five years, micro-economic analysis suggests that Baltic peoples are likely to make progress as an increasingly large proportion of the population attains a higher standard of living. This forecast is very different from that of World Bank economist Larry Summers (1992: 23ff). He confidently declared that Central and East European countries had incomes at the level of the United States in 1900, overlooking the fact that even well-to-do Americans did not own cars, colour television sets or telephones at that time – and television had not been invented. Moreover, he said that 'conservative estimates' indicate that it will take until after the year 2000 for many post-communist countries to regain their 1989 standard of living. The reason for his pessimism is easily explained; Summers was basing his pessimism on 'one-dimensional' macro-economic data![3]

WITHIN-NATION DIFFERENCES CREATE BETWEEN-NATION SIMILARITIES

Every micro-economic measure of economic conditions shows substantial differences within each Baltic nationality. Some people are able to get by amidst the turbulence of transformation, others are in great difficulties, and the median Baltic person is in and out of difficulty.

In theory, divisions within a nationality are consistent with differences between nationalities – if distributions are highly skewed in opposite directions in both groups. But this is not the case. On a scale from 100 to 0, the Difference Index consistently registers similarities, as more than half the values are single digit. In Lithuania, there is an average difference of only 7 points between Russian nationals and Lithuanians; in Latvia, 8 points between Russian nationals and Latvians; and in Estonia, 16 points between the two nationalities. Another way of making the same point is that economic conditions of Russian and Baltic nationals average 84 per cent similar in Estonia, 92 per cent in Latvia, and 93 per cent in Lithuania.

The evidence rejects two mutually conflicting political allegations, namely, that Russians have prospered greatly at the expense of Baltic nationalities or that the Baltic peoples are prospering at the expense of Russian nationals. In every nationality group, there are a small number prospering and a large number who are not – and a lot in between.

Another test of the impact of citizenship upon economic conditions is to compare the position of Russian nationals in the three Baltic states. If citizenship improves economic conditions, then Russian nationals in Lithuania, where a big majority are citizens, should be different from and much better off than Russian nationals in Latvia and Estonia, where only a minority are citizens.

In fact, citizenship does *not* make a significant difference in economic conditions between Russians in the Baltic states. The mean Difference Index for Russian nationals living under differing citizenship laws is usually a single-digit figure, and, given the nature of sampling fluctuations, is often statistically insignificant. The similarity between Estonian Russians and Lithuanian Russians is 92 per cent, for across a dozen measures the mean Difference Index is only 8 per cent. Between Latvia and Lithuania, the mean of the Difference Index is 7 per cent.

When individuals in Baltic states are interviewed they appear less different than when their economic conditions are inferred from statistics about gross domestic product per capita. The World Bank (1994: 18f) per capita figures show that Estonia is the richest (or least poor) country in aggregate; its 1993 gross domestic product in current US dollars was credited as $3 040. The GDP per capita of Latvia was 67 per cent of Estonia, and Lithuania 43 per cent. When the aggregate calculations are adjusted for purchasing power parity,[4] a similar pattern is found. Estonians appear to have more than twice the PPP per capita income as Lithuanians, and to be a third better off than Latvians (Figure 6.2).

By definition, 'missing' economies are left out of the accounts – though they are not left out of everyday life (see Table 6.5). Nonetheless, as long as there is a consistency of bias (or even what Alec Nove described as a 'constancy of cheating'), the figures ought to give a good idea of the relative position of the three countries.

But do macro-economic statistics give a full and fair portrayal of micro-economic conditions in the Baltic states? In the literal sense, they cannot, for the statistics are compiled at the state level and, unlike census and survey data, they do not take account of nationality. Secondly, the statistics do not describe distributions; a mean figure for GDP per capita cannot say how many people are better off or how many are destitute. Nor can it provide information about the distribution of income or the number of households negatively affected by the transformation of national economies.

Micro-economic surveys indicate that drawing inferences about economic conditions from GDP figures compounds logical and empirical fallacies. Figure 6.2 summarises the relative position of Estonians, Latvians and Lithuanians on a variety of micro-economic indicators. Across the seven indicators, Latvians and Lithuanians tend to be less well off than Estonians – but not by so much as macro-economic statistics suggest – and in many cases their conditions are the same or even slightly better. For example, ownership of consumer durables is at virtually the same level in all three Baltic states, and the capacity of individuals to get by is actually higher in Latvia than it is Estonia, notwithstanding the lower reported GDP per capita of Latvia.

The level at which people find an equilibrium differs from country to country. The fact that most Lithuanians, like most Austrians, can get by without spending savings or borrowing money, does not mean that people in Vilnius have the same standard of living as in Vienna. Nor does the fact that the majority of people in every member state of the European Union have economic resources sufficient to get by from year to year

Figure 6.2   Macro- and micro-comparisons of economic conditions (Latvia and Lithuania as % of Estonia)

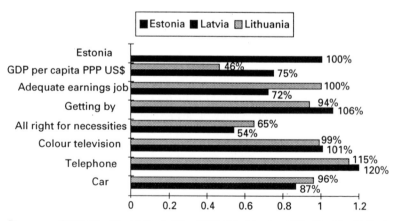

Sources: GDP: *The World Bank Atlas 1995* (Washington, DC: *The World Bank*, 1994), pp. 18–19. Microdata for Baltic nationals: Rose *et al.* (1995)

mean that most Portuguese or Greeks have the same standard of living as most Swedes or Germans. But such points too are outside the world of macro-economic data. The only logical way to show the extent to which Mediterranean and Nordic populations differ is with micro-economic data, and the same is true in examining differences between nationalities in Baltic states.

Notes

1. The data analysed in this paper were collected with the aid of grants from the European Commission under the Copernicus (COST) programme (CIPA-CT192-3012) and the East/West Initiative of the British Economic and Social Research Council Y309 253 047.
2. Meso-level subjects such as privatisation can be studied from a 'top down' macro-economic approach (e.g. strategies of privatisation) or from a 'bottom up' approach (e.g. worker participation in privatisation; studies of individual firms, as in Gurkov, 1995).
3. Had Summers used the World Bank's *social* data, a better picture would have been obtained. For example, infant mortality data show that the distance between the Baltic states and OECD and European member states is much less than official GDP statistics imply (see Rose, 1994).
4. Giving both current and PPP-adjusted GDP per capita is in keeping with standard international agency practice. However, the result is that what you conclude depends upon where you look. In current money terms, the Estonian GDP per capita is 16 per cent of Finland; in PPP terms, it is 45 per cent that of Finland.

REFERENCES

Atkinson, A.B. (1987) 'On the Measurement of Poverty', *Econometrica* 55, 749–64.

Dallago, B. (1990) *The Irregular Economy: The Underground Economy and the Black Labour Market* (Aldershot, Hants: Dartmouth).

European Bank for Reconstruction and Development (1995) *Transition Report Update* (London: EBRD).

Grossman, G. (1977) 'The Second Economy of the USSR', *Problems of Communism*, 26(5), 25–40.

Gurkov, I. (1995) *Popular Response to Russian Privatisation: Surveys in Enterprises*, Studies in Public Policy No. 245 (Glasgow: University of Strathclyde).

Holzmann, R., Gacs, J. and Winckler, G. (eds) (1995) *Output Decline in Eastern Europe* (Dordrecht, Netherlands: Kluwer).

Kornai, J. (1993) *The Socialist System* (Princeton, NJ: Princeton University Press).

Marer, P., Arvay, J., O'Connor, J., Schrenk, M. and Swanson, D. (1992) *Historically Planned Economies: A Guide to the Data* (Washington, DC: World Bank).

Polish Statistical Association (1992) *Poverty Measurement for Economies in Transition in Eastern European Countries* (Warsaw: Central Statistical Office).

Robinson, W.S. (1950) 'Ecological Correlations and the Behavior of Individuals', *American Sociological Review*, 15, 351–7.

Rose, R. (1992) 'East Europe's Need for a Civil Economy', in R. O'Brien (ed.), *Finance and the International Economy 6: The AMEX Bank Review Prize Essays* (Oxford: Oxford University Press), 5–16.

Rose, R. (1993) 'Contradictions between Micro- and Macro-Economic Goals in Post-Communist Societies', *Europe-Asian Studies*, 45(3), 419–44.

Rose, R. (1994) 'Comparing Welfare Across Time and Space', *Eurosocial Report* 49 (Vienna: European Centre for Social Welfare Policy and Research).

Rose, R. (1995a) *Pensioners, Gender and Poverty in the Baltic States*, Discussion Paper IDP-151 (Washington, DC: World Bank).

Rose, R. (1995b) 'Russia as an Hour-Glass Society: A Constitution without Citizens', *East European Constitutional Review*, 4 (3), 34–42.

Rose, R. (1995c) 'Adaptation, Resilience and Destitution: Alternatives in the Ukraine', *Problems of Post-Communism*, 42(6), 52–61.

Rose, R. and Haerpfer, C. (1992) *New Democracies between State and Nation: A Baseline Report of Public Opinion* Studies in Public Policy No. 204 (Glasgow: University of Strathclyde).

Rose, R. and Haerpfer, C. (1994) 'Mass Response to Transformation in Post-communist Societies', *Europe-Asia Studies* 46(1), 3–28.

Rose, R. and Maley, W. (1994) *Nationalities in the Baltic States*, Studies in Public Policy No. 222 (Glasgow: University of Strathclyde).

Rose, R., Vilmorus, Lasopec and Emor (1995) *New Baltic Barometer II*, Studies in Public Policy No. 251 (Glasgow: University of Strathclyde).

Rose, R. and McAllister, I. (1996) 'Is Money the Measure of Welfare in Russia?' *Review of Income and Wealth*, 42(1) pp. 75–90.

Scheuch, E.K. (1966) 'Cross-National Comparisons Using Aggregate Data', in R.L. Merritt and R. Stein (eds), *Comparing Nations* (New Haven, CT: Yale University Press), 131–68.

Seragheldin, I. and Steer, A. (1994) *Expanding the Capital Stock* (Washington, DC: World Bank), 30–32.

Sik, E. (1995) 'Measuring the Unregistered Economy in Post-communist Transformation', *Eurosocial Report* No. 52 (Vienna, European Center for Social Welfare Policy and Research).

Simon, H.A. (1969) *The Sciences of the Artificial* (Cambridge, Mass.: MIT).

Summers, L. (1992.) 'The Next Decade in Central and Eastern Europe', in C. Clague, and G. Rausser, (eds), *The Emergence of Market Economies in Eastern Europe*, (Cambridge, Mass., Blackwell), 25–34.

World Bank (1994) *The World Bank Atlas 1995* (Washington, DC: World Bank).

SECTION TWO

PROCESS AND POLICY

7 Privatisation and Employee Ownership: The Development in the Baltic Countries[1]

Niels Mygind

INTRODUCTION

Different forms of insider ownership are quite important in many countries in Eastern Europe, for example Poland, Russia, Slovenia and Ukraine. Also in the three Baltic Countries insider ownership in the form of both employee and management ownership plays a considerable role, especially in Lithuania. While management groups have taken over some enterprises, broader groups of employees have also been influential in taking over a substantial number of enterprises.

This chapter seeks to give an overview of how different forms of insider ownership have developed in the Baltic countries, paying specific attention to employee ownership with broad groups of employees as the dominating owners. First, the background situation in the three Baltic countries is presented, emphasising existing differences. There follows an analysis of important political developments relating to employee ownership, followed by a section describing the legislative development and the actual results on the incidence of employee ownership. Concluding the chapter, the main factors behind the different paths of development of employee ownership are identified within the three countries.

BACKGROUND CONDITIONS

The Baltic countries differ in many ways, yet they also share some characteristics. Explaining why employee ownership has developed in different ways within the three states must therefore include a description of these similarities and differences. Hence, the division in the four subsystems presented in Mygind (1994) is used as the structure in this summary. Also some of the conditions set by the surrounding world will be included. (See Table 7.1.)

The *institutional system* is the formal set of rules governing the political process and the co-ordination of the economy. The Soviet command system dominated this institutional system in all three countries. The system was based on state-owned enterprises mainly controlled by the All Union authorities in Moscow. Nevertheless, local authorities did control some enterprises. The economic experiments of the Gorbachev period affected all three countries, Estonia in particular. Employee ownership was also included in these experiments although only to a limited degree. These experiments took the form of Workers' Councils that were formally given certain rights to participate in the running of the enterprise. New co-operatives with participation of some of the employees as members were developed, especially in Estonia, (Table 7.1). Many experiments, including the 'small state Estonian enterprises' could be used by insiders to initiate a process of 'wild privatisation'. Managers, in particular, were involved in the process of getting state owned assets under their own control in a more or less legal acceptable way.

The *social system* is the different social groups and their interaction with each other. An important difference within the social system was that the Russian-speaking minority comprised a substantial part of the populations in Estonia and Latvia. This was especially the case for industrial workers where the titular population was a minority. In Lithuania, the Russian minority was less than 10 per cent of the population.

The *value system*, the culture, is also shaped by different religious beliefs. Estonia and Latvia are generally considered to be Protestant countries with a more 'modern', German-inspired culture. Lithuania with its Catholic tradition tends to be influenced more by Polish and traditional values. Individualism predominates in the northern countries, collectivism in Lithuania.

The *production system* is the resources of the society such as the natural resources, physical means of production and human knowledge. Within this system, it is important to note that Estonia and Latvia undertook the industrialisation process before the Soviet planning system took over. This was not the case in Lithuania. Therefore, the emphasis is more on large, heavy Soviet-type enterprises in Lithuania. All three countries were strongly integrated within the specialisation in the Soviet Union making them later strongly dependent on partners in the former USSR. Concerning the relationships with the surrounding world, the geographic

Table 7.1 Background conditions: before 1989

	Estonia			Latvia			Lithuania		
	1988	1989	1990	1988	1989	1990	1988	1989	1990
Institutional system[1] History, foreign dominance. During Perestroika centres for experiments	Co-ops Jobs Sales[2]			Co-ops Jobs Sales[2]			Co-ops Jobs Sales[2]		
Co-ops	256	969	2087	245	1190	4086	503	1569	4495
Jobs	4500	21500	42100	5200	28700	134800	5900	25500	81400
Sales[2]	8	102	385	10	190	1079	13	118	652
% of republic turnover	Leasing			Leasing			Leasing		
Leasing	–	0.9	3.3	–	1.0	5.6	–	0.5	1.6
Social system[3]	Emigration and deportations of Estonians and immigration of Russians increased the non-Estonian speaking minority to 39% in 1989, majority of workers are non-Estonian			Emigration and deportations of Estonians and immigration of Russians increased the non-Latvian speaking minority to 48% in 1989, majority of workers are non-Latvian			Emigration of Lithuanians, but no large immigration of Russians. Labour from agriculture to new industries. Non-Lithuanian speaking minority – 21% in 1989.		
Value system Language Religion Foreign influence	Finnish/Agrarian Protestant Mainly German			Baltic Protestant Mainly German			Baltic Catholic Mainly Polish/traditional		
Production system Industrialisation	Quite early			Quite early			Soviet industrialisation		
Surrounding world All three dependent on 'trade' with rest of USSR	Strong ties with Finland								

Notes:
1 Arkadie *et al.* (1992), 307.
2 Mill Rb.
3 Hanson (1990).

and linguistic proximity between Estonia and Finland made a better starting point for Estonia in its turn to the West (Dellenbrant, 1992).

POLITICAL DEVELOPMENTS AND EMPLOYEE OWNERSHIP

The political process is the main link between the initial conditions and the transition of the institutional system. These changes also decide which transitory path is chosen, including the choice of privatisation models.

Early economic and political changes in all three countries were interconnected with their fight for independence. Republican leadership adopted a more radical stance in Lithuania than in the other countries. One explanation behind this might be that Lithuania alone had a rather small Russian-speaking minority. In the aftermath of the August coup, the national question was just a decisive factor in Estonia and Latvia. As a result of this, a vacuum existed on the left of the political spectrum in the two Northern countries. Because the majority of industrial workers were Russian-speaking with very limited political power, workers were split and unions weak. Hence, the political debate during the early years of transition was not focused on the economic problems, but rather on the national question. In Estonia, quick and radical reforms aligned with this tendency as a part of change in orientation towards the Western world – a change which was made easier by the close geographical, cultural and linguistic links with Finland. In Latvia, a similar pressure for quick economic reforms did not exist. Here, the national question was to a larger extent a barrier which for a long period brought the political system into a deadlock.

The importance and influence of these different social groups are obviously linked to the above-mentioned development. Since this chapter deals with employee ownership, it is necessary to concentrate on the group of employees. The group of employees was split between the titular-speaking and the Russian-speaking group in Estonia and Latvia. They were able to use some of their power related to the Workers' Councils during the initial stages of the transition process. The councils were quite important, especially in Estonia. However, they were split into two organisations; a pro-Russian and a pro-Estonian. This split-up occurred soon after the transition process had taken off (Terk, 1996). During the transition especially, the Russian speaking part of the employees lost influence. The decreasing importance of employee-ownership in the beginning of the 1990s was most likely a result of the decline in 'Russian power'. Employee ownership was not promoted by the fragile unions.

Table 7.2 Political development, privatisation and employee ownership

Balticum	Estonia	Latvia	Lithuania
Fight for independence Economic policy: from experiments to preparation for a 'mixed economy'.	IME programme, May 1989: Mixed economy with 'peoples enterprises'. Employee ownership seen as instrument for liberalising enterprises from Soviet rule. Employee ownership gets lower priority as claims for independence and market economy gain ground.	Workers' Council some role at the enterprise level. Weak labour organisations.	Early preparation of reforms: employee shares Feb 1990, equalitarian values => voucher privatisation Feb 1991. Restitution important in agriculture for citizens living in Lithuania.
After independence before elections National forces split, Complex choices on citizenship, constitution, economic policy => new conflicts, unclear interests, volatility	Fight between *national line* for voucher-privatisation and restitution and *technocratic line* favouring direct sale of enterprises. Small privatisation: advantages for employees, diminished from May 1992. June 1992 intro of KROON, no citizenship and voting rights to Russians, liberal economic policy, privatisation slow.	Using part of old constitution, no citizenship and voting rights to Russians, privatisation fast in agriculture (few Russians), government and parliament in a deadlock on citizenship and economic policy. Decentralisation and privatisation of municipalities: small privatisation, branch ministries: large privatisation, some scope for insiders, more emphasis on restitution	Minorities full citizenship; unions somewhat involved. Protests from employees against early privatisation => 30% shares to employees at preferential price. Also other preferences for insiders mainly supported by strong industrial lobby.
After first elections More homogeneous and well-defined interests. Russian troops out August 1993 in Lithuania, August 1994 in Estonia and Latvia	Election September 1992. New constitution approved. Centre-right government programme: ultra-liberal, focus on the West, hardline nationalism, THA-privatisation introduced summer 1992. No advantage for employees. Sept 1994 Prime Minister steps down after scandal. Election March 1995. Opposition wins. Unchanged privatisation policy.	Election June 1993. Centre-right government, continued reform. Privatisation centralised, with privatisation agency. Summer 1994, voucher system slow start. July 1994, government crisis. Sept 1994, centre-left government. Dec 1994, first international tender. 1995, public offerings; election, Oct 1995. Deadlock, centre-left nationalist government.	Election Oct/Nov 1992. Presidential Feb 1993. Labour party majority. Support from workers and agro-workers dissatisfied with privatisation policy. Adjustments of privatisation. Employee share rises to 50%. Privatisation slows down in 1993, but accelerates 1994. Voucher programme finished 1995. Managers/old networks still in strong position, foreign capital not important.

Managers would often align themselves with the unions in order to push through different forms of insider take-overs. This occurred in the early years of transition when the employees could still influence decisions taken at the enterprise level. During the transition, the manager groups were able to establish a firmer power base, enabling them to build up capital resources. In this way, take-overs were realisable without involving the broad group of employees. In Estonia, this was combined with a quite early shift in the direction of the direct sale of enterprises, promoted by the Estonian Privatisation Agency. As a result the bureaucrats from the early stages were able to implement a 'technocratic' line. That is to say that take-overs either by a core investor (often based on foreign owners) or the existing management team were given priority. Changing governments did not lead to new policy directions. The election in 1992 resulted in an ultra liberal, nationalist government. The following election in 1995 was a step away from the extreme right-wing policies and led to a re-orientation of policy by the new consensus-seeking government which covered the middle of the political spectrum. However, the privatisation process was not halted, including quite an ambitious programme for the privatisation of public utilities.

Latvia implemented its privatisation process at a somewhat slower pace. Bureaucrats in the ministries and enterprise managers were able to forge an important alliance. At first, the insiders were supposedly at an advantage because it was hard to control the privatisation process. It is possible that in some cases the managers might also have included a broader group of employees. Local administrative bodies kept on adding certain advantages to insiders, in spite of the fact that actual legislation limited insider advantages in the small privatisation process in early 1992. The re-organisation of the privatisation process in 1994 gave the Latvian Privatisation Agency a key role and led to a significant change in this trend. The role of managers and their networks in the branch ministries declined after the 1994 legislative change. At the same time greater emphasis on foreign investment with international tenders, starting in the autumn of 1994, meant more competition among the potential new owners. Still, the privatisation process was slower than expected, and the banking crisis from the summer of 1995 created another barrier (Mygind, 1996b). The election in October 1995 was a delayed reaction to the economic crisis; but it did not result in a more clear political majority in parliament. The political deadlock continued first with months of negotiations to form the new government and later resulted in a broad government based on alliances which did not look promising for stability and decisive action.

Privatisation had a different face in Lithuania. Leading politicians believing in egalitarianism, implemented a different course of action from

1991 (Cicinskas, 1994). Distribution and some sort of employee owner-ship were also on the agenda of the labour unions at this time. A voucher system and employee advantages were underlined. The result of the 1992 election showed that this approach had public backing. Unlike the two Northern Baltic countries, this election was a strong reaction against the ruling politicians and the steep fall in production and material standard of living. The winning labour party extended the policy of advantages for employees in the privatisation process. The previous government had attempted to provide foreign investors with a large role in the country's economy, buy the steps aiming at implementing this policy approach were only sporadic. As a result, they did not really make an important impact on the privatisation process. The group of managers usually had to make alliances with broader groups of employees if they wanted to take-over an enterprise.

THE LEGISLATION AND IMPLEMENTATION OF PRIVATISATION

Table 7.3 sums up legislation and privatisation measures of relevance to employee ownership. The first transformation of state ownership in the form of 'semi private' 'small state-owned enterprises' and the 'new co-operatives' developed quickly. In fact, the process was started already in Estonia in 1987. Generally, it must be assumed that these enterprises were primarily taken over by managers.

Estonia

The political debate in Estonia was often centred around employee owner-ship. Legislation focused on this area and employee ownership was imple-mented to a certain extent in the early years of transition. Leased enterprises under the Soviet legislation of 1989 were part of this develop-ment (Frydman *et al.*, 1993). The law did not last very long, however. An alteration was made to correspond with the new specific Estonian legisla-tion and another 200 of such enterprises were started.

Before this, the legislation about 'People's enterprises' was passed. These enterprises were collectively owned by the employees and, in the initial political debate, many people expected this type to be the dominant form of ownership in the years to follow. However, only five to seven of these enterprises with full employee ownership were established (Terk, 1996), and political attitudes were not to favour this form over a prolonged period of time. The Estonian independence in August 1991 marked a

Table 7.3 Overview of privatisation and employee-ownership

Period	Estonia	Latvia	Lithuania
Before full independence	'Small state enterprises' and new co-operatives most management-owned; Soviet leasing systems, 12 large employee-owned, Estonian leasing (1990/91) 200 management-owned 'people's enterprises' (1991) 7 employee-owned.	New co-operatives; most management-Soviet leasing systems employee owned.	New co-operatives mainly management-Soviet leasing systems, 60 mainly employee-owned, temporary law on employee-shares, 1990–91, 2–3% of assets, LIPSP small and large privatisation starts 1991.
First stage after independence	Small privatisation insider preferences (Jan 1991–May 1992). 350 employee owned (May 1992–June 1993) less employee ownership. 7 large experiments most employee owned.	Small privatisation 1992–1993. 200 employee owned 6 large experiments 1991, mainly employee owned decentralised privatisation (1992–94) 200 insider owned.	LIPSP: shares for employees, 30% reserved from 1992, 50% from 1993, payment mainly by vouchers, from 1992, reserves can be used for employee shares, increasing employee ownership in large privatisation. By July 1994 all industrial JSC have employee ownership, 57%: 11–50% 21%: more.
Second stage	Large privatisation by (Nov 1992–Dec 1995). 2000–3000 insider owned, mainly by management, 200–300 foreign owned. Vouchers used for minority shares from end of 1994.	Large privatisation LPA 1994–95, few insider take-overs, foreigners increasing role, vouchers used for some public offerings.	Sale to foreigners of minor importance, from 1996 the remaining state owned enterprises to be sold by Privatisation Agency for cash.

turning point as politicians started to go against the concept of employee ownership. The development in small privatisation is an example of this. Whereas the initial legislation from January 1991 favoured the insiders, the great majority of preferences were removed from May 1992 onwards. An estimated 80 per cent of the first wave of 450 small enterprises were taken over by insiders prior to the policy reorientation (Kein and Tali, 1994).

A strong element of employee ownership was observable at the time when no significant policy change had yet occurred. Thus seven large experimental cases of privatisation were carried out. Employees were no longer given specific preferences once the summer of 1992 had come to an end. The large privatisation implemented by the Estonian Privatisation Enterprise, later the Estonian Privatisation Agency, did not give any benefits to employees. A tender process formed the basis of this kind of privatisation. The capital contributions of buyers and investment guarantees became significant aspects of the privatisation process. Thus existing capital owners were at an advantage. At this stage, the managerial group had accumulated some capital. They also gained access to credits in private banks which were developing quite fast at this stage. Furthermore, domestic capital was allowed to be paid in instalments. Hence, the managers' alliance with the broad group of employees was no longer necessary. In addition, foreign capital was permitted to enter the country and participate in the large privatisation. According to certain sources, foreign investors got around 40 per cent of the privatised assets (Baltic Independent 19 February 1994).

There is also other statistical evidence to back up the claim that foreign ownership increased greatly in this period. Thus, the PFPB-project carried out a survey in January 1995 in co-operation with the Statistical Office of Estonia involving 414 enterprises. They were a stratified random sample of private enterprises representing all branches and different size groups with five or more employees. The survey showed the following results (Mygind, 1996c). When the sample was normalised to represent the whole economy it is found that foreign ownership in the privatised part of manufacturing is as large as 52 per cent of the capital. For the whole privatised Estonian economy it is 37 per cent of the assets. Majority insider ownership covers around 36 per cent of the private enterprises. In about half of these enterprises managers dominate, while in the other half the broad group of employees own more than management. Forty per cent of the enterprises covering 29 per cent of the employees have no employee ownership. The survey estimated that about 25 per cent of all Estonian employees own part of their own enterprise in the private sector.

Employee ownership is especially widespread within the field of agriculture. Approximately 50 per cent of the enterprises are owned by a broad group of employees. Other branches such as construction, fishing, and mining can also show high percentages. In the manufacturing of textile and leather, instruments, petrol and chemicals, a broad group of employees have majority ownership in a relatively high proportion of the enterprises. The degree of employee ownership is relatively low in sectors such as wholesale trade, transport, finance and liberal services.

After the main parts of the Estonian privatisation process had ended, insiders rarely sold their shares. The situation has also remained the same up to at least January 1995. It might however be worthwhile to look at a number of changes that have taken place within other areas. There has been a noticeable decline in the cases where insider ownership did not exist and full insider ownership was present. Managers have more often tended to be the buyers and employees than those selling their shares, thus managers increased the proportion of shares in their possession. The number of majority management-owned enterprises increased from 76 to 88, while the number of majority employee-owned enterprises decreased from 102 to 82, see Jones and Mygind (1996).

Approximately 50 per cent of the employees were not owners in the enterprises with majority broad employee ownership. In agriculture, fishing and mining as well as other sectors the percentage is 25 per cent or lower. In 65 per cent of the small enterprises with employee ownership the distribution is quite equal among the employees who are owners. In large enterprises with more than 99 employees this percentage has fallen to 31 per cent. In this group about half of the cases indicate a very unequal distribution with differences typically more than 1:10. Broad employee ownership of capital does not necessarily mean that the employees have the same degree of control. There is a tendency that the system of non-voting shares of employees is especially frequent in cases with a high degree of broad employee ownership. 50 per cent of the large enterprises with majority employee ownership had this type of governance structure.

Latvia

Latvia underwent many of the same development processes as Estonia in the early years of transition. Many new co-operatives were established. Of importance was also leasing according to the Soviet legislation. The first legislation about small privatisation included some preferences for the employees just as was the case in Estonia, but these were also formally removed in 1992. However, the advantages for employees appear to have prevailed also in 1993 in the actual implementation in many municipalities (Vojevoda and Rumpis, 1993).

Employees buying 10 to 20 per cent of the shares in their enterprise were allotted some benefits (Frydman *et al.*, 1993). A strong case could, however, be made for the claim that the decentralised nature of the privatisation process constituted a key advantage in the sense that different ministries were given a central role in the process. Insiders were able to make use of already established contacts. One of the most frequently utilised forms for privatisation was leasing, and this method was mainly used by insiders. However, until 1994 privatisation was rather slow. Therefore, this type of privatisation only included around 200–300 enterprises, of which most were insider take-overs mainly controlled by management. Even so, this included more large enterprises than was the case in Estonia, and insiders had more time to benefit from this privatisation method in Latvia. What had happened in Estonia in the summer of 1992, only took place in Latvia in the summer of 1994. From mid-1994 the Latvian Privatisation Agency centralised the privatisation process to a great extent. Foreign capital as well as vouchers distributed mainly to Latvian citizens were given priority. The strategy of the Latvian Privatisation Agency was, as in Estonia, to first encounter a core investor in a tender process and subsequently to sell the minority shares for vouchers in public offerings. In the first months of 1995, three enterprises were sold in this way. Another 13 companies followed during the second round in mid-1995.

Figures describing the distribution of ownership among state, municipalities, domestic outsiders, foreigners and insiders have been collected by the Latvian Department of Statistics. These data show the total group of enterprises with 20 or more employees and a random sample of smaller enterprises. More precisely, results for 5585 enterprises exist for January 1995. Typically, one group of owners have more than 50 per cent of the ownership. In fact, only 3 per cent of the enterprises had mixed ownership in the sense that no group of owners had a majority. 16 per cent of these 5585 enterprises were mainly owned by the state and municipalities, 4 per cent by foreigners; 26 per cent by domestic outsiders and in 51 per cent of the enterprises insiders owned more than 50 per cent. A subsample of 685 enterprises shows that more than 80 per cent of the insider owned enterprises were 100 per cent owned by insiders. Majority insider ownership increases with smaller size measured as the number of employees. 67 per cent of the enterprises with one to four employees were majority insider-owned. The number is only 18 per cent for enterprises with more than 500 employees. State ownership dominates this group. Unfortunately, data distinguishing insiders as managers and other employees are not available.

Nevertheless, it would probably be a fair estimation to say that the bulk of especially the small insider enterprises are owned primarily by managers.

Lithuania

Lithuania was the absolute frontrunner of the three Baltic countries as far as the implementation of the privatisation process is concerned. This was particularly the case in the first years of the transition although privatisation in the form of new co-operatives and leasing as laid down by Soviet legislation was probably not as developed as in the two other Baltic states. However, the Lithuanian legislation for both small and large privatisation was already passed early in 1991. This was done according to the so-called LIPSP programme. The second part of 1991 marked the beginning of the implementation of this programme, which dominated most of the privatisation process in Lithuania. Therefore, the early egalitarian notions influenced most of the Lithuanian privatisation programme.

A temporary law on employee-shares was inaugurated in 1990–1991. Distributing shares to employees was not a subject of theoretical discussion any longer, but actually carried out for the first time. Employee ownership increased when preferences for employees were incorporated into the LIPSP programme that dealt with large enterprises in 1992. In the first round, 30 per cent of the shares in a given enterprise could be bought by the enterprise employees. Payment could be in either vouchers or cash. The price for employees was set at the 'initial price' which meant that they could get their part of the shares at a relatively low price. Because of only partial indexation of the price on the assets and on the value of the vouchers, the advantage of employees increased over time (Martinavicius, 1995). Employees were allowed to buy 50 per cent of the shares at a favourable price already in 1993. However, the 20 per cent extra shares reserved for employees did not have any voting rights, but later in the process it was made possible for the general meeting of the enterprises to convert these into normal voting shares.

The possibility of selling state-owned enterprises to foreigners was introduced in a programme as early as 1992. Yet, this programme was only implemented in a limited number of cases until 1995. Nor did restitution constitute an important alternative for the industrial enterprises. Consequently, employee ownership did become an important part of the privatisation process, especially the privatisation of large Lithuanian enterprises. Special preferences for employees in the small privatisation were not part of the LIPSP programme. Nonetheless, the group of insiders had probably also a relatively strong position in this part of the privatisation because of inside information and because of their access to resources for purchase in the form of vouchers. Although the small privatisation included around half of the 6000 enterprises to be privatised in the LIPSP programme, only a small percentage of the total assets and the total number of employees were found in the small enterprises.

A clear tendency can be found in the privatisation process and the spread of employee ownership. Data accessible in the database in the Department of Privatisation in the Ministry of Economy shows that the employees got a relatively small part of the shares in the first round of privatisation until the end of 1992. 67 per cent of the enterprises had no employee ownership after the initial privatisation. In 1993 and 1994 less than 5 per cent had no employee ownership after the first rounds of privatisation according to LIPSP. Furthermore, the percentage of enterprises where employees took over the majority of shares privatised according to LIPSP rose from 3 per cent in 1991–2, to 65 per cent in 1993, and further to 91–92 per cent in 1994–5.

In July 1994 responses from 357 industrial enterprises were received by the Lithuanian Department of Statistics as a result of the PFPB-ownership survey. These responses confirm that a considerable extension of employee ownership is actually prevalent in large enterprises in Lithuania. Only 1 per cent of these enterprises had no employee ownership by July 1994. 31–50 per cent employee ownership was found in 29 per cent of the enterprises, while 27 per cent of the enterprises had majority employee ownership. There is no correlation between the degree of employee-ownership in July 1994 and the time of the enterprise privatisation. The difference in relation to the distribution of ownership at the time of privatisation is probably the result of two tendencies. First is the gradual employee take-over through enterprise reserves and profits. Secondly, a certain amount of employee shares have been sold with the strongest effect in enterprises where the employees owned a high proportion of the shares.

The managers own more than the rest of employees in only 13 per cent of the cases with some insider ownership. An clear difference from the Estonian data is indicated by these data since Estonian managers owned more than the other employees in most cases. It is worth noting is also that on average, 87 per cent of the management staff and 73 per cent of the employees are owners.

Summarising these data, Lithuania has much more employee ownership than its northern neighbours. Nearly all enterprises have an element of employee ownership and the broad group of employees has a stronger position than management. Only few employees do not own shares in Lithuania.

CONCLUSIONS

What are the determining conditions behind the development of employee ownership in the privatisation process in the Baltic Countries? Some links are identified when the dynamic process of transition from plan to market, from dictatorship to democracy, from Soviet occupation to independence is analysed. The political process is the main link between these background conditions and the specific change in the institutional system. In particular, the differences in ethnic composition within the value system has had an important influence on the political development.

The differences between the three countries and the change in the development over time indicates that the following factors in the four subsystems have been determining factors for the establishing of employee ownership in the privatisation process:

The *value system* and the *social system* have determined the political climate and the political process which in turn determined the change of the institutional system. The two systems have a decisive role when new legislation, choice of privatisation models, and the actual implementation of the privatisation process are carried out. In the lack of substantial evidence, no solid conclusions can be drawn about the influence of cultural values. Collective and egalitarian values might be stronger in the catholic Lithuania than in the other two, more individualistically oriented countries. The cultural difference probably influenced the greater emphasis on vouchers and employee ownership in Lithuania. This tendency is, however, difficult to distinguish from the ethnic factor. Lithuania has the more homogenous population with the same culture, same ethnic and religious background, compared to the split between the Russian oriented population and the titular population in Estonia and Latvia. This is a good example of the close connection between the social system and value system. The cultural split has meant that the broad group of employees were weakened in the process of independence and further economic and political transition. This is the basic explanation behind the change in policy which limited the advantages for employees in Estonia and Latvia. Such a change did not happen in Lithuania. Here was no 'national question' to distract the political debate from the economic problems of transition, and the workers was not weakened by an ethnic split. Therefore, there was a reaction at the election. The labour party went into government and the conditions for further support for employee ownership were improved.

The transition from plan to market means an especially important change in the *institutional system*. It includes the privatisation process and the legal framework for the start and development of employee owner-ship. In the Baltic countries we have identified the following elements in the legislation which have given the most important favourable conditions for employees:

Discounts on the purchase price. Employees have been able to buy shares for the initial price which was normally below the market deter-mined price paid by other buyers. This system was used in the initial stages of small privatisation in Estonia and Latvia, and in large privatisa-tion in Lithuania.

The *leasing systems,* dominant in the initial stage in all three countries and also in the later stage in Latvia, have also often included a preferential price for the employees.

Vouchers distributed to the broad population to be used for the purchase of enterprises. This system was important for Lithuania in the period analysed. It was not important before from 1995 in the two other coun-tries, but at a stage where especially in Estonia most of the enterprises had already been privatised.

The actual implementation of the legislation is much dependent on the role and power of different agents. This is determined by the interaction between the institutional and the social system. The organisation of pri-vatisation through decentralised systems gave the insiders/management a quite strong position. They could use their existing networks to access local municipalities or branch ministries. This was especially the case in Latvia in the period before 1994. However, local municipalities had a role in small privatisation in all three countries. The centralisation of power in the Privatisation Agency, which first took place in Estonia, diminished the power of insiders.

The possibilities for other buyers including foreign capital are also very important for the scope for insider take-overs. The legislation and its implementation, combined with the distribution of capital in the society, are determinants of the strength of other buyers. This includes both the actual legal conditions for foreign capital and their evaluation of these conditions – the general legislative framework and the economic situation in general. In this respect Estonia put most emphasis on foreign capital, and foreigners have given a favourable evaluation of the economic con-ditions in Estonia by investing quite substantial amounts. Foreign capital has here been a strong competitor to domestic capital and insiders. This development can also be taken as an indication of the importance of the influence from the *surrounding world,* which should also be included in a model showing the complex interaction between different subsystems in a society in transition (see Mygind, 1994).

Note

1. The material for this chapter was collected in a research project on Privatisation and Financial Participation (PFPB) undertaken by ACE-PHASE 1992. A deeper theoretical analysis and additional documentation of the results presented can be found in the report from the project (Mygind 1996b, c and d).

REFERENCES

Arkadie, B.V. and Karlson, M. 1992, *Economic Survey of the Baltic Republics* (Stockholm; Pinters Publishers).
Cicinskas, J. (1994) 'The Economic Development Lithuania after Independence', in J. Å. Dellenbrant, and O. Nørgaard (eds) in *The Politics of Transition in the Baltic States: Democratisation and Economic Reform Policies*, Research Report 2, (Umeå Universitet).
Dellenbrant, J. Å. (1992) 'Estonia's Economic Development 1940–1990 in Comparison with Finland's', Chapter 10 in Åslund A. (ed.), *Market Socialism or the Restoration of Capitalism* (Cambridge: Cambridge University Press).
Frydman F., Rapaczynski A. and Earle J.S. (1993) *The Privatisation Process in Russia, Ukraine and the Baltic States*, CEU Privatisation Reports, Vol. II, (Budapest and New York: Central European University Press).
Hanson, P. (1990) *The Baltic States*, The Economist Intelligence Unit briefing (London: Economist Publications).
Jemeljanovs, O. (1996) 'Privatisation in Latvia in Figures', in N. Mygind (1996a).
Jones, D. and Mygind, N. (1996) *Employee Ownership and the Effects on Productive Efficiency and Employment: Evidence from the Baltics*, working paper of the PFPB-project, CEES/Copenhagen Business School and Hamilton College, Clinton, New York, US.
Kein, A. and Tali, V. (1994) 'The Process of Ownership Reform and Privatisation', paper for Institute of Economics, Estonian Academy of Sciences.
Martinavicius, J. (1995) 'Privatisation in Lithuania: The Legislative and Political Environment and the Results Achieved' in N. Mygind (1996a).
Mygind, N. (1994) *Omvæltning i Øst* (Copenhagen: Samfundslitteratur) Translated in, *Societies in Transition* (Copenhagen: Copenhagen Business School).
Mygind, N. (ed.) (1996a), *Privatisation and Financial Participation in the Baltic Countries* CEES/CBS.
Mygind, N. (1996b), 'The Baltic Countries in Transition: A Comparative Analysis', in N. Mygind (1996a).
Mygind, N. (1996c) 'Privatisation and Employee Ownership in the Baltic Countries: A Comparative Analysis of Conditions and Development', in N. Mygind (1996a).

Mygind, N. (1996d) 'The Economic Performance of Employee Owned Enterprises in the Baltic Countries', in N. Mygind (1996a).

Shteinbuka, I. (1996) 'Privatisation in Latvia and the Role of Employee Ownership', in N. Mygind (1996a).

Terk, E. (1996) 'Employee Ownership and the Political Debate in Estonia 1987–1994', in N. Mygind (1996a).

Vojevoda, L. and Rumpis, L. (1993) 'Small Privatisation in Latvia', paper for Institute of Economics, Latvian Academy of Sciences.

8 Growth in the Hidden Economy: The Case of Estonia

Garri Raagmaa

INTRODUCTION

In order to study the growth of the hidden economy, two different approaches could be adopted. First it would be possible to draw on the experience of other states, former socialist states in particular, to try to define the role of the shadow economy by deploying statistical methods and opinion polling. Alternatively, the focus could be on the social background of the phenomenon and on the factors that facilitate the spread of the hidden economy. This study has adopted the latter approach as cognitively more important. It therefore does not set out to determine the specific scope of the shadow economy but to describe the potential reasons for its emergence in Estonian economic life. Being aware of the aspects of life and the economic spheres which are most exposed to hidden activities, it is possible to advise on policies aimed at curbing illegal activity.

TERMINOLOGY

The subject of this research is denoted by various terms, each of which assumes a specific meaning attached to it by the author who deploys it. In addition to reference to the shadow or informal economy, other terms used include the black or grey economy; the unofficial, hidden and illegal economy; the parallel and underground economy, and so on.

Earlier classifications

According to the classification by Rose (1983), the economy is divided into three main groups:

(i) The official economy is measured by the flow of money through government departments, especially tax offices. National and local budgets are drawn up and economic development is planned on the basis of the official economy.

(ii) The unofficial economy can be measured in money terms as well but since this is an economic sector which involves mainly cash transactions and is operating illegally, it is difficult to measure by the methods of the official economy.

(iii) The domestic economy is not recordable in monetary terms and covers most of the goods (food grown for one's own consumption) or services needed by households (families) daily (cooking, driving a car, child care), periodically (laundry) or episodically (car or property repairs).

Cassel (1982) divides the national economy into two main groups, namely the public and the shadow economy (Schattenwirtschaft: secondary, unofficial, unregistered economy). The former, in turn, is divided into public and private economies while the latter is divided into underground (Untergrundwirtschaft) and self-supplying economies (Selbstversorgungwirtschaft).

Within either of these classifications, the hidden economy is characterised by its unrecordability by statistical means. Hence the definition that the hidden (informal) economy involves unregulated income while analogous income is regulated by the state (Castells and Portes, 1989; Feige, 1990). According to this definition, the hidden economy embraces only the illegal activity. On the other hand, the whole social activity that remains outside the official sector is classified as the shadow economy. The shadow sector is defined as all productive and distributive income earning activities which take place outside the scope of public regulation on the macro-societal level (Portes, 1994). Some authors, however, do not directly regard criminal activity such as drug trafficking as within the shadow economy (Roberts, 1994), although most authors still classify criminal activities (OECD, 1982; Cassel; Rose, 1983) under the shadow economy.

Under socialism, even the national economy of the Eastern bloc was divided into two, namely the primary or centrally planned economy which was regulated through government plans, and the unsocialised secondary or private initiative-based economy which was regulated by market mechanisms (Gabor, 1979; Raig, 1988). The secondary sector mainly involved the domestic economy and enterprises that produced officially on the basis of households. In the capitalist system the latter belongs to the official economy. According to several Eastern authors, the hidden economy (in Russian *tenevaya ekonomika*) also belonged to the secondary sector (Zaslavskaya, 1980; Gabor, 1979). According to the earlier classifications by socialist scholars, the concept 'shadow economy' was used only to describe illegal activities. In socialist countries or economies in transition, the so-called third economy has been identified, namely that incorporating the relations between the corrupt part of the state bureaucracy and the secondary or shadow economy(Gabor, 1991). This sector has also been called parasitic since it exploits national resources while the profit is taken by third persons (Rose, 1992).

System of concepts

In this particular chapter, the national economy is regarded as falling into two parts: the official and shadow economy (secondary, unofficial, unregistered economy). The principal factor that distinguishes between them is their being reflected in the official statistics and/or public budgets. State institutions and enterprises, officially registered private entrepreneurs and employees report to the public through their financial statements and income-tax returns. The official economy in turn is divided into public (state) and private economies. Officially registered enterprises declare their income and pay taxes to the state and/or local governments which thus collect the resources necessary for their own operations.

The shadow economy is the sort of production or distribution that takes place beyond public regulation. The public authorities, with their limited facilities, can neither objectively reflect the shadow economy in statistics nor can they regulate it. The shadow economy in turn is divided into two, namely the hidden and domestic economies. The domestic economy (household economy, family business) involves mostly domestic economic activities, the most typical examples of which are the daily household chores: cooking, cleaning, child care; do-it-yourself activities; repairs, growing food, picking mushrooms, preserving; helping neighbours, various barter transactions, and so on. The domestic economy involves non-cash activities aimed at the reduction of family expenditure. The GDP includes production activity and barter transactions, while it ignores the daily household chores. Therefore it would prove expedient to divide the domestic economy into domestic production which is reflected in the GDP, and domestic service which is not reflected in the GDP.

The hidden (informal) economy violates the existing laws. For instance, the goods produced in the domestic economy are sold either in the market or to acquaintances, or certain services are performed for money while the income is not declared. For the most part, the hidden economy has grown out of domestic economic activities and it is therefore difficult to distinguish between these two. For example, grandma first knits cardigans for her grandchildren but later makes them for sale. The main criterion for inclusion in the hidden economy is the existence of an unofficial cash flow and where the sole aim of the activity is to increase the income of those participating in it.

The hidden economy can be divided into grey or legal, and black or illegal, hidden economies (Table 8.1). The former does not directly endanger anyone and is rather overt, for example, in market trade, undeclared work, 'moonlighting' using the firm's resources, and so on. It mostly involves the concealment of income and the resulting tax evasion. The black or illegal hidden economy involves services that are either directly prohibited by law, are immoral (prostitution), or involve (illegal) trade (that of alcohol, drugs or weapons), or direct physical and moral violence (slave trade, extortion and other criminal acts). As an exception, the production of strong alcohol or narcotics for one's own consumption, together with contraband meant for supplying oneself and one's acquaintances, (petty) theft and other unorganised crime are classified as being within the illegal hidden economy since these are also non-cash activities. The hidden economy could also be divided into illegal activities of individuals (family business) and legal persons (enterprises). In the latter case, this involves economic crime while in the former case, the cheating of the state and its tax officials.

In post-socialist countries where the scale of public sector involvement in production is very extensive, the so-called parasitic economy is a borderline case between the public and private economies and deserves specific mention. During the transformation period, its role rapidly expanded due to the weakened political control, poorly developed legislation, and corruption.

CHANGES IN THE ROLE OF THE SHADOW ECONOMY

Economic change

This century, following social and economic development, the amount of work undertaken in domestic economies decreased considerably because of the growing role of large industrial and public sectors. The role of agriculture and small industry weakened, production and social structures

152

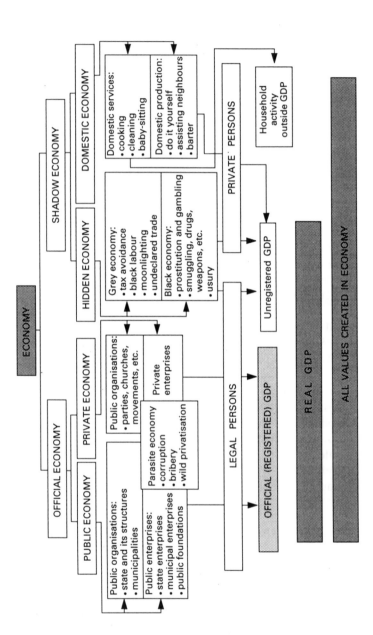

Figure 8.1   System of concepts

Table 8.1   Branches of economy and illegal transactions carried out in them

Branch of economy	Opportunity	Grey economy	Black economy
1 Agriculture, fishery and forestry	***	Sale of production straight to consumer, use of black labour	Illegal fishing, timber theft
2 Industry	*	Use of black labour in labour-intensive industry (sewing, timber processing)	Production of illegal drugs and alcohol, theft of materials
3 Construction	***	Labour-intensive operations	Theft of materials
4 Wholesale and retail	**	Sales machinations of mainly small shops, unreported sales	Drugs, smuggling
5 Hotels, restaurants, catering	**	Tips, unreported sales	Theft of food stuffs
6 Transport	**	'Black transport', unreported sales	Smuggling and slave trade
7 Financial and business services	*	Unreported income of private contractors	Forbidden transactions, fraud
8 Public sector, health care, education	*	Manipulation with repairs and building costs, costs shown bigger than they actually are	Corruption (bribery, leakage of confidential information)
9 Other personal services	***	Unreported income, use of black labour	Illegal gambling, prostitution

Source: OECD Economic Outlook (1982), *Occasional Studies.*

quickly concentrated into large concerns and nationally guaranteed services (Stöhr, 1990). As a result of this the opportunities for unregistered activities diminished substantially. Allegedly, working in the official economy became a social norm in the West.

Since the 1973 economic recession, the world economy has taken a turn towards decentralisation. As a result of the globalisation of industry and trade, unemployment has grown in developed states, the role of large-scale industry as an employer has diminished, and the size of economic units has been reduced again, encouraging the rebirth of small-scale entrepreneurship. The role of manufacturing industry has weakened while the number of jobs in the service sector has grown (Camagni and Capellin, 1981). Consecutive economic recessions, unemployment and inflation have combined to reduce real incomes and forced some people to seek additional earnings.

Most Western authors consider the shadow economy as the valve that regulates the restructuring hardships of the official economy. For example, a large bureaucratic state or a corporation needs time for readjustment, while people cannot afford to wait because of unemployment and reduced income. Hence they try to improve their living conditions. Therefore the increasing role of shadow economy is a direct indicator of economic hardships: the smaller the growth in the official sector, the bigger the growth in the unofficial sector, and vice versa (Cassel, 1984; Raig, 1988).

Taxes, inflation and the hidden economy

In the same way as the improvement or deterioration in the economic situation has its effect on the role of the hidden economy, so does the rise or fall of the tax burden. Taxes can be raised painlessly only under strong economic growth, otherwise people and enterprises tend to react with tax evasion (Rose, 1992). The lowering of taxes, on the contrary, will create an environment of less extensive tax evasion, but will not immediately reduce it. If the society has a habit of evading taxes, the practice will continue out of inertia. Inflation and the consequent fall of real incomes has an analogous effect.

Legislation and supervisory bodies

Laws play a very important role in the illegal hidden economy, especially as far as the explicitness of their interpretation and the simplicity of their application are concerned. A complicated interpretation makes it difficult to understand the law and allows legal manoeuvring. An application process enforced without consideration, on the other hand, inhibits control and does not allow efficient tax collection.

The efficiency of the work of the Revenue Office, the police and other organs of law enforcement play a critical role in restraining the hidden economy. Most of the people allegedly pay taxes only because they are afraid of getting into trouble otherwise. The work of law enforcement organs is important in reducing the role of the black economy, in areas such as smuggling, drug trafficking, illicit alcohol sale, and so on.

Economic structure

In the hidden economy, not all the enterprises or individuals enjoy equal opportunities. The opportunities are considerably better in certain fields which have a limited technological content or else are difficult to control for various reasons (Rose, 1989). This concerns mainly the primary sector including agriculture and fishery. In industry, illegal activity is relatively rare and inefficient, and mainly involves the use of illegal labour, particularly in such labour intensive spheres as the sewing industry (Roberts, 1994). However, as social development takes place, the hidden economy will increasingly shift into the services sector, such as in simple, elementary construction work, communal and business services, and so on.

The changes in social structure have led to the growth of the hidden economy in the West. Due to the increasing role of small entrepreneurship and private entrepreneurs, tax evasion appears to be expanding. Major corporations may influence price setting and reduce costs by automation and/or by transferring production to other countries with cheaper labour. In contrast, a small businessman can, in order to achieve cost reduction, resort only to tax evasion as well as undertake more intensive work for himself and his family (Cassel, 1984).

Due to the changing social structure and general economic pressures, Western countries have thus been forced to liberalise their taxation policies and attempt to reduce the sum total of centrally redistributed resources. Self-help strategies are ever more extensively propagated on the belief that they should replace the services and various aid packages guaranteed by the state (Stöhr, 1990).

Local government

In connection with the above, Western countries are trying to pay more attention to the decentralisation of power and to transferring the functions, from the state to the local government level, and shift the tax burden accordingly (Stöhr, 1990). The consequent increasing importance of local authorities should take the relations between the excessively bureaucratic and discredited (welfare) state and an entrepreneur to the local government level. If people and entrepreneurs had a better understanding regarding the use of the tax revenues which they paid, unreported income might presumably diminish as well.

THE PECULIARITIES OF SOCIETIES IN TRANSITION

The transition economies of former socialist states represent a special type of capitalism which is strongly influenced by the earlier social arrangements and which is much more unstable than the Western societies owing to political (the action of neo-communists and radical nationalists) as well as socio-economic problems, including the stress caused by rapid changes, unemployment, accelerating material stratification and so on. As a result, one indicator of instability and crisis is the spread of hidden and illegal activities during the transition period.

According to Šik (1994), the East European transition economies display some parallels with Latin American states: namely having a significant or dominant role of the state and/or foreign capital, the presence of a semi-peripheral economy, and being relatively poor, though not comparable to the third world. By way of contrast, Rose (1992), claims that East European states are analogous to the new industrial countries (NICs) of Asia with their large primary sector and a substantial rural population, important semi-legal and illegal sectors, the absence of a routine tax-paying tradition, and new state structures.

The major economic processes of the transition

The most important structural shifts accompanying the transformation processes include the following:

- In transition economies, private ownership prevails instead of the earlier state ownership. Various organisations and parties start defending the rights of private owners.
- Laws change quickly and frequently, rendering it impossible to follow and consider, let alone observe all the new laws.
- Both the spontaneous (wild) as well as centralised privatisations reduce the relative importance of state property. The weakness of leg-

islative and supervisory organs does not enable spontaneous privatisation to be kept under control.

- The small-scale privatisation and reprivatisation schemes create a wide circle of 'poor owners' who are unable to invest, and are not competent to draw up well-motivated business plans for getting bank loans or find collateral for the loans they apply for.
- Unemployment is accepted as government policy and as a phenomenon inevitably accompanying restructuring and privatisation. The lack of previous experience of unemployment together with the fall in living standards causes the extreme, and in places overdramatised, growth of social problems – a social shock (Šik, 1994; Kornai, 1990, 1992).

As these processes work through the system, the transformation results in the following major problems:

- Economic recession
- Inflation
- Unemployment
- The fall of real incomes
- The impossibility of collecting taxes because of changes in the taxation system
- The break-off of former economic ties

Many of the problems accompanying transformation that are listed above also act to enhance the relative importance of the hidden economy in the West. The post-socialist countries are thus no exception as far as these general economic problems are concerned. At the same time, Eastern Europe suffers from the distinctive legacy of the so-called secondary economy of the socialist period, which has had a major effect on the growth of the hidden economy.

The secondary economy: a peculiarity of the post-socialist economy

Under socialism, the secondary economy came into being and, in addition to the domestic and hidden economies, it also included the private sector. The primary sector involved state-owned productive enterprises and institutions of the non-productive type. The secondary economy did not harmonise with the ruling Marxist ideology in which human activity was to be channelled into the public sector as much as possible and therefore the domestic economy (let alone private entrepreneurship) was reduced to a minimum. For example, the forced building and subsidising of canteens and kindergartens served this purpose and was designed to reduce the amount of household chores. The hidden economy, which was also classified under the secondary economy, was a clearly criminal activity (Raig, 1988), embracing first and foremost the black and parasitic economies, according to the terminology used earlier in this chapter.

The secondary economy and deficit compensation

The weaknesses of the command economy and the self-reproductive deficit forced the authorities to allow the people to utilise their small plots of land, and later resort to small-scale production. Towards the end of the socialist period, many urban families, because of the rampant deficit as well as their wish to compensate for the ever-widening gap between Western and local living standards, took up productive activities in their home environment. The growing of food was a particular example of this.

The areas to develop most of all were plant growing and horticulture. On the one hand, the products of these activities were in short supply and production could in general remain less mechanised. On the other hand, because of Estonia's specialisation in cattle breeding, the official sector (particularly in Northern Estonia) displaced private cattle breeding due to high wages as well as to achieve the full utilisation of land. Although the rural population kept falling until the beginning of the 1980s, the number of those using the land was steadily growing, from 243 000 in 1966 to 284 000 in 1983. The growing shortage of foodstuffs in towns forced the residents of apartment houses to start growing their own food. For example, in 1966, 5 698 Estonian families belonged to horticultural co-operatives, while their number had risen to 40 189 by 1984 (Raig, 1987).

The secondary economy and the Soviet public sector

The operation of ancillary farms was regulated by law. For example, the use of paid labour was prohibited and participation in production was required. The earnings could, through the tacit consent of authorities, be kept at a low reported level and thus be concealed. As a result, such income grew much more rapidly than that from official industry.

The spread of the secondary economy was evidently one of the factors that accelerated the collapse of the socialist economies. People paid more and more attention to their own kitchen garden or workshop while neglecting their basic jobs and therefore quality suffered. Both the state sector and large-scale industry lost efficiency, technology was not modernised while the people earnestly devoted themselves to work with inefficient technology. The unstable environment of coercive measures and tolerance created many niches for corruption; hampered the emergence of normal market relations, entrepreneurs and meaningful labour relations; and ruled out long-term planning and investment. Until the transition period, the secondary economy had no difficulty in achieving production due to the general shortage of goods and the national procurement system subsidised by the state. Neither marketing nor public relations were necessary, quality was unimportant (Šik, 1994). Society was split into the state sector and pseudo-private sectors, where people tried to take advantage of the benefits of the public sector as much as possible. Theft from the state was not considered a crime.

The secondary economy and illegal networks

The reckless attitude towards work described above caused disorder in supplying enterprises and generated the need to buy up raw materials 'just in case and at the first opportunity'. This, in turn, aggravated the shortage of these materials. Personal relations and acquaintances began to play an ever bigger role in procuring technology and raw materials, at the same time creating fertile soil for various manifestations of corruption. Directors and collective farm leaders who wished to successfully lead their enterprises and cope with planned tasks were unavoidably forced to use semi-illegal means to acquire funds and circumvent limits.

Illegal transactions and hidden private work were also widespread at an individual level and grew during the Soviet stagnation period. According to polls in the mid-1980s about 100 000 people in Estonia were engaged in offering illegal services. The shortage of consumer goods and the poor quality of services offered by state firms caused a boom in both under-the-counter trade and speculation. One study showed that this was especially marked in procuring spare parts for cars (17 per cent of respondents), footwear and clothes (13 per cent) and building and repairs materials (10 per cent) (Raig, 1987). A wide supply network based on personal relations developed, through which passed a large proportion of imported goods which were in short supply. Thus, people wore fashionable clothes, owned cars and colour TV sets but it was virtually impossible to buy anything at a shop.

The hidden economy during the transition period

Links between the secondary and hidden economies

In the present transition period one important issue is whether the households and enterprises who have so far operated semi-legally will opt for illegal or legal operations. The question is dual: how will the transition affect the secondary economy? And how will the secondary economy affect the transition? Some of these interfaces can be hypothesised from Table 8.2.

During the transition, some branches of the secondary economy such as small-scale production, private entrepreneurship, currency transactions and individual work, are likely to become part of the official economy. Some enterprises and domestic economies will continue their earlier illegal activity and this may even considerably expand under weaker control. Due to the reduced importance of the public sector and major budget restrictions, the role of parasitic phenomena typical of the socialist economy will diminish but the scale of corruption is likely to increase.

Post-privatisation enterprise problems

Privatisation alters the conditions within which enterprises exist and the earlier weak budget restrictions and limited resources are replaced by strong budget restrictions and limited market demand. In addition, the privatised sector is faced with unfavourable conditions due to a shrinking domestic market, and the difficulty in penetrating international markets because of low technological standards and scarce marketing skills. Moreover, the owners of the (re)privatised resources are, as a rule, poor and cannot develop production because of the general shortage of capital. Thus profits cannot be readily increased by the rapid build-up of mass production, by penetration into new markets, or by implementing new technologies (Kornai, 1980). Only two alternatives remain for enterprises to increase their profits in the short term in order to survive, namely, cutting costs and raising prices.

In consequence, employees are exploited more intensively or else they get paid less. This is possible where there is large-scale unemployment and weak trade unions. Such strategies can be used in small enterprises in particular. Another alternative is the use of domestic, part-time or subcontracting labour which helps reduce local costs and protect against additional costs concurrent with possible layoffs. A method frequently used in the transition period is the evasion of salary and wage-related taxes, including the concealment of wages fund contributions and hence the evasion of social and income taxes, or the use of 'black labour'. In Estonia, it is fairly common that in spite of being an active operation, a small enterprise employs not a single paid worker, or else employees are officially paid the minimum wages in addition to which they get unofficial pay. The latter can be several times bigger than their official salary. In the

Table 8.2   Transformation of the secondary economy: the hypothetical increase or decrease of illegal activities

	Enterprises (public sector)		Individuals (autonomous)	
	Legal	Illegal	Legal	Illegal
Labour and pay	1 Petty (agricultural) production: intrapreneurship (*part of official economy*)	2 Tip, 'black labour', 'moonlighting' with the resources of the enterprise (*'moonlighting' and tips decrease, the use of illegal labour, including that of immigrants, increases*)	3 Subsistence, self-service (*the exploitation of family members and relatives increases*)	4 'Black labour' (*illegal working and concealment of additional wages, working abroad increases*)
Positional and network capital (acquaintances)	5 Interfirm barter, barter between individuals (*the role of personal networks in buying goods decreases; the use of private structures as business develops*)	6 Corruption, theft (*theft and bribery in buying goods decreases; the use of investments through personal networks, bribery in selling goods, buying of political power and business information increase*)	7 Interhousehold barter (*the use of former ties, joint activity increase*) increase	8 Blackmailing threats (*clan ties, hence blackmailing and threats due to competition*)
Financial capital	9 Entrepreneurship (small state firms, co-operatives) (*part of official economy*)	10 Tax evasion, money laundering (*the concealment of wages fund, showing costs bigger than they are, the use of suspicious finances increases*)	11 Private entrepreneurship (*part of official economy*)	12 Usury, smuggling, black currency, drug trafficking, slave trade, prostitution (increase)

Source: Adapted from Šik, E. (1994).

context of weak control by the Revenue Office, enterprises can evade taxes by claiming that other production costs (such as raw material, fuel, equipment) as being larger than they actually are. This in turn enables the enterprise to show a smaller profit, break-even, or loss in order to disguise the liability to pay corporate tax.

Economic recession and domestic economies

The transition period, the termination of former relations with the Commonwealth of Independent States, and the price rise of raw materials and goods, resulted in deep economic recession and a fall of real incomes in all East European states. Since only one third of East European families think that their salaries are enough to buy necessities, it is evident that people are forced to seek extra income for subsistence (Rose, 1992).

The hardships of domestic economies may push people into overtly illegal activity, such as smuggling, theft and participation in criminal groupings. The relative stability and openness of Eastern Europe, which is accompanied by uncontrollability and the lawbreaking of relevant officials (such as border guards and customs) leads to growth in the consumption of smuggled commodities. This is statistically confirmed through the rise of criminal activity. While in 1987, 11 465 crimes were registered in Estonia, the figure rose to 41 254 in 1992 (Remmel, 1994).

Unemployment and poverty, in border areas in particular, may thus combine to increase the number of people earning their living this way. On the other hand, selling contraband has become an important source of income for many townspeople who earlier used to sell their belongings in the market or in the street. Moreover, there are certain known locations where numerous groups of people buy goods either for resale or for personal use.

The genesis of entrepreneurs

A positive side-effect of the forced situation and hidden activity outlined above is the emergence of many new entrepreneurs. People who are jobless or dissatisfied with their income will develop their domestic economy or additional job to the level that they are able to officially regis-ter it. At the early stages they will try to keep their record books in the manner typical of family businesses, by showing break-even despite the actual situation, using as much black labour as possible and paying them the so-called additional wages. But as the firms get stronger they should start legalising a growing part of their activity. One of the most wide-spread areas of illegal activity on the part of new entrepreneurs is in trade, involving the transporting of goods across borders in order to gain from price differentials. According to Remmel (1994), Estonian businessmen also engage in the smuggling and sale of ordinary food stuffs in order to avoid VAT.

New entrepreneurs experience major hardships at the beginning and therefore attempt to make use of all the skills and opportunities applied in the second economy. Their biggest problem is getting credit while they are short of both material resources and guarantees. Therefore, the beginner firms try to economise wherever possible. Here it is especially important to use existing and developing personal networks through which the private sector, as it struggles to develop, creates pressure for further corruption (Šik, 1994). It is also possible that new entrepreneurs experiencing hardships accept loans which are offered by the underworld as part of its money laundering. Thus some new entrepreneurs will inevitably acquire the mentality of those who offer the loans, if not their methods.

Due to the decreasing effective demand and the liberalisation of imports, there is no longer a general shortage of consumer goods in Estonia. While bribes and the use of personal networks to buy goods in short supply are becoming rarer, bribery and corruption in the sale of goods are both gaining importance (Šik, 1994). This happens in particular in the public and local governments sectors, for example in the use of the services of private firms in construction projects or in the supplying of state institutions.

Business and politics

In view of the confusion regarding laws and their application, the growing uncertainty of economic policy and because of the opening up of the whole society, excellent business opportunities do emerge. Thus active and adventurous businessmen can seize the moment and increase their wealth, market position and power on the economic as well as the political arena within a very short time period. As a result, corruption of civil servants is likely to substantially increase. Simultaneously, large multinational corporations and small (often émigré businessmen of local origin) players have appeared on the scene, both trying to steer the political system and thus economic policies in a direction which is beneficial to them (Šik, 1994).

The taxation system

During the transition period, the taxation system is also thoroughly changed. Together with new tax laws, the direct and visible tax burden grows, whereas it was previously covered by the profit appropriations of state-owned enterprises. This particularly concerns personal income tax and the social taxes collected from the enterprises' wages funds. In the opinion of new entrepreneurs and ordinary people who lack the experience of the Western taxpaying routine, these taxes are lost money. At the same time, neither the work of the Revenue Office nor the activities of corrupt officials make it possible to properly collect these taxes. The new tax laws are often drawn up according to Western models and do not consider the local realities (Rose, 1992). Tax laws should clearly not encourage criminalisation. The state should thus avoid imposing progressive taxes which encourage large money-makers to keep their earnings in foreign bank accounts. Also a budget deficit should be avoided and social expenditure should be contained, otherwise people will resort to further developing their domestic economy. Equally, it is more sensible to use taxes which are difficult to evade (Rose, 1992).

In summary, and as Table 8.2 shows, part of the legal branches of the second economy have either become part of the official economy (fields 1, 9 and 11), or become illegal. Since most of the illegal activities of the second economy, especially within enterprises, have received a boost and acquired new niches, it can be assumed that during the transformation the number of illegal activities increases.

The hidden economy and inequality

One of the important pressures on hidden economic behaviour is the Western standard of living which the local people can observe. Thus people try to obtain comparable goods or follow the lifestyle associated with that standard of living. Wage levels and the movable stock of money, however, cannot sustain these ambitions which in turn motivates people to resort to illegal methods. The development of market relations and the expansion of the hidden economy have given rise to both new opportunities and material inequality; the ever deepening pauperisation of the representatives of certain spheres of life and certain social groups, and the rapid enrichment of others (Annus and Noorkõiv, 1994). The growth of inequality is intensified by the disappearance of the earlier double strategies where people used to have a low-paid but secure job in the primary economy and an uncontrolled earning opportunity in the secondary economy.

Of the other forces emerging, the most important is internationalisation, which again involves mostly full-time work. Inequality is increased by the influx of foreign capital which relies on the narrow local elite whose salaries and benefits drastically differ from local income levels. Also, the income differentials are increased by corruption because bribery is offered to a very narrow circle of officials (Sik, 1994).

Full-time illegal activities promise larger incomes but also require additional expenses to compensate for the risk. These include transaction costs, such as bribery and Mafia taxes and conspicuous consumption which could guarantee success in certain circles through the growth of prestige or popularity. Finally, inflation helps to increase inequality. The ability to avoid loss resultant from the rise in prices is clearly correlated with income level. Moreover, hyper-inflation is useful for certain types of speculative trading activity (Annus and Noorkõiv, 1994).

Inequality is rapidly rising on the centre–periphery (country and town/city) line, causing a disproportionate regional effect. Transformation occurs more rapidly in the innovative city environment, since both foreign and local capital primarily flows into major centres. The crisis in the primary branches of the economy, and agriculture in particular, exerts a negative influence on the economy of rural regions. As regards the breakdown of regions, the so-called 'Western orientation' is clearly observable in most of the East European states (for example, Hungary, Poland, Estonia). But the western regions have been considerably more active in creating new entrepreneurship and attracting foreign investment (Farago, 1993; Ciesnocinska, 1993; Raagmaa, 1995). In westernmost regions, the general tax evasion and capital concentration is higher. In consequence, the material differentiation is more obvious than in most easterly areas.

The parasitic economy

The command economy with its large state sector could only successfully function under strict political or legal control. The weakening of this system quickly led to society becoming corrupt and to the decay of ethical principles and morals. This in turn has led to the proliferation of a parasitic economy where a narrow clique gets rich at the cost of national property. Rose (1992) compiled a matrix of the market and command economies (civil and uncivil economies) and their legality (see Table 8.3). This approach, however, is slightly simplistic because market relations worked both under socialism and under the present anarchy. Several wild privatisation cases have been carried out quite legally, although national property has been transferred to single individuals.

According to the State Audit Office in Estonia, the number of violations concerning the use of state property has grown (Riigikontroll, 1994). Post-

Table 8.3   Systems

Legal	Market	
	Yes	*No*
Yes	Civil	Command
No	Uncivil	Parasitic

Source: Rose (1992).

socialist states with economies in transition are thus, as a result of the weakening of control, the best hotbed for the openly parasitic sector. The controversial nature of many laws contributes to this. Even ministries and other government offices try to conceal their intra-departmental income from the state budget, not to speak of the inexpedient usage of budget resources.

Even under the strictest control, the so-called parasitic economy existed within central planning systems, exploiting national resources while the profit was reaped by third parties. Such activities were rather risky. Falling out with the boss or getting caught by random inspection could result in a prison sentence or at least in 'relegation to another job'. Greed was also limited by social control, in that it was impossible to buy a limousine and/or build a large villa without arousing suspicion. Therefore the parasitic sector in Estonia did not grow very large (Raig, 1988). On the other hand, the strict controls forced people to skilfully arrange their illegal activity, including an elaborate system of bribery and mechanisms for working upon superiors and subjects. The stress caused by social and legal control was supposed to generate a so-called compensation complex, which might therefore lead to an increase of violations as soon as control becomes less effective.

Thus, due to controversial and deficient laws plus weaker control in post-socialist economies in transition, there are many opportunities for the spread of the earlier covert and limited corruption and for the growth of the parasitic sector. Another factor is the low salaries of civil servants and those holding elected offices, both of which facilitate corruption. In other parts of the world, corruption is exemplified in contexts such as Southern Italy and Latin America where public figures are often connected with or even directly controlled by criminal organisations which direct public life in ways which are useful to certain interest groups (Mingione, 1994). Some authors have described the Russian Mafia as having originated from the earlier parasitic sector (Rose, 1992).

Socialist entrepreneurs

One of the most characteristic and complicated problems in East European countries is that of the 'socialist entrepreneur', who balances his activities between the public and private sectors. It has been argued that the success of transition processes depends on how the state is able to protect and support private entrepreneurship, control the public sector with an iron hand and create, at the contact area between these two, strong legal measures and moral codes which would ensure both legality as well as morale in this corruption-sensitive zone (Kornai, 1992).

A distinction must be made between ordinary people, private entrepreneurs and people working in a state office, including directors and other managers of state-owned enterprises. The director or department head of a state-owned enterprise is not an entrepreneur, he is the same type of wage-earner as is a library director or schoolteacher (Kornai, 1992). A private entrepreneur can do whatever he likes with his money while a director who is hired to administer state property must do his job as well as possible and his earnings depend on the efficiency of his work. The director of a state-owned enterprise has no right to pay himself additional wages or waste the taxpayers' money entrusted to him. If he is caught red-handed, he should, logically, compensate for the damage, and be punished (Kornai, 1992). If the director of a state-owned enterprise buys a luxurious car at excessive cost, squanders money wantonly and on top of everything, using state resources, to set up a shareholding venture with himself sitting on the board and pumping money out of the state-owned enterprise until it goes bankrupt, such behaviour cannot be ethically justified. Some authors, in order to stress the dual nature of such half-officials, half-entrepreneurs, have called them 'socialist entrepreneurs' (Gabor, 1991).

The state and the hidden economy

If the state is not respected by ordinary citizens who conceal their income because otherwise they will not be able to make both ends meet; or by private entrepreneurs, who evade taxes or establish an off-shore firm because the state cannot guarantee them legal or physical security; or by civil servants in their practice of legal violations, a vicious circle may ensue. The reduced confidence in the state and its officials will lower the self-esteem of civil servants and lead them to either violate the laws or to behave in a negligent way. Such civil servants in turn reduce the confidence of the people in the state, the income from public and private sectors drops and the state thus has fewer resources to call its officials and citizens to order. Entrepreneurs and ordinary citizens have openly said that they are not sure whether the state uses the money collected in the form of taxes in an expedient way. Therefore they either try to conceal their income or channel their taxes directly to local governments through sponsorship.

As far as Estonia is concerned, the past decades of alien ideology and government have added to the distrust of the state. The regaining of independence enhanced confidence in the state and its leaders, but the enthusiasm quickly abated, The Soviet era passiveness has thus been replaced by relatively overt dissatisfaction. If the state is unable to guarantee law enforcement, raise the qualifications and reliability of its officials and thus improve its reputation, Estonia and other East European countries will be doomed to the fate of Columbia where one third or more of the GDP comes from the hidden economy.

THE IMPACT OF TRANSITION PROCESSES ON THE GROWTH OF THE HIDDEN ECONOMY: MACRO-ECONOMIC SHIFTS

Over the past decade, drastic changes have taken place both in the Estonian economy and in Estonian statehood. Virtually all facets of social life have changed with the newly-found political independence and during the transition from a closed social order and centrally planned economy to an open market economy. Legislation and the economic structures that regulate the society and underlie its functioning have undergone especially rapid changes. Inevitably, such changes are accompanied by confusion and the spread of many unwanted phenomena. One of these is the hidden economy.

Changes in GDP

The GDP of Estonia kept falling until the spring of 1993 and began to grow again in the third quarter. According to the estimates of the World Bank, the GDP grew by 5 per cent in 1994, while in the opinion of the Estonian Ministry of Economy it grew by a mere 3.5 per cent. According to alternative calculations by the Estonian Statistics Department, the GDP was still falling in 1994. The calculation of the scale of the shadow economy within the GDP causes problems. According to the estimates of the Estonian Statistics Department, the share of the hidden economy was 13.1 per cent of GDP in 1993.

In 1991, Estonian GDP fell by 14 per cent, in 1992 by 14.2 per cent. Large-scale industry went through a particularly rapid fall with production dropping by 73.4 per cent compared to 1991. In agriculture, the numbers of cattle fell by 34 per cent in 1992–4. According to the official statistics, agriculture experienced the fastest relative fall, its share in the GDP fell from 18.0 per cent in 1991 to 9.6 per cent in the first quarter of 1993. It will be evident that state enterprises and state co-operative agriculture which together used to dominate the Estonian economy have been suffering a severe crisis.

Growth has, however, taken place in some branches of economy, particularly in labour intensive export-oriented industry (timber, furniture, sewing industry, etc.), in raw materials extraction (timber, metal, peat), and also in the service sector aimed at both the local market and foreign tourists.

Legislative basis for new forms of enterprises

One of the signs of the *perestroyka* which started in the Soviet Union in 1985 was the lifting of the ban on small state entrepreneurship from 1986 onwards. The continuing liberalisation in the Soviet economy in 1987 led to a freedom to establish co-operatives based on joint leadership, work and capital. These organisations were relatively free from state control. The same year, a legislative basis was created for the establishing of joint ventures with foreign shareholders.

In 1988, the IME (Independently Managing Estonia) project was initiated, which fixed the principles of Estonian-centred development. While until 1989 Estonia's economic laws drew upon those of the Soviet Union, from 1990 on, Estonia began to work out independent legislation. In January 1990, the Estonian Supreme Council adopted the Entrepreneurship Law and in July 1990, the Ownership Law. In 1990, the number of small enterprises, mainly shareholding ventures based on private capital, began to rapidly grow. In 1991 the small privatisation of shops and service firms began all over Estonia, and in 1992, the first stage of large-scale privatisation started.

The boom in the creation of co-operative ventures started after the passing of the relevant law in 1987 and lasted until the adoption of the Entrepreneurship Law in 1990. Thus, the first wave of the active formation of new enterprises began in 1988. In 1991, more flexible types of enterprises, namely shareholding companies and private firms, began to take shape. The period from the second half of 1991 could thus be regarded as the second, much higher wave of enterprise formation.

In the existing public sector very few completely new enterprises have been established. The new units that have emerged in the 1990s are mainly affiliate firms which are now independent, and state-owned small enterprises which have been reorganised into state-owned shareholding ventures since 1991. Municipal companies have also been formed on the basis of former state-owned communal and heating enterprises whose property was handed over to local governments. The rapid emergence in 1992 of companies fully based on foreign capital was aided by Estonia's newly-found independence and the currency reform which introduced the kroon.

Decline of large-scale enterprises

In 1990–93, large-scale enterprises rapidly dissolved into independent units. During the past few years, the numbers of people working in large-scale enterprises has fallen. For example, from 1 September 1991 to 1 February 1993, nearly 80 000 jobs were lost in such enterprises in Estonia. Their collapse has had its impact on the explosive proliferation of small enterprises, which attract the more active managers and skilled workers with a flair for entrepreneurship who have felt confined in large-scale enterprises. Also, it is only logical that the unemployed are forced to find a better standard of living than that derived from unemployment benefit and to set up firms of their own. Against the background of unemployment and the hardships of large-scale enterprises (such as low wages, unpaid holidays, shutdowns, potential dismissal), the new enterprises had therefore a chance to hire the best labour available. Another important fact to be taken into account is the rise of the role of micro-enterprises in Estonia, namely that with four workers and under. The levels of these enterprises are higher than the respective indicators for Germany and Finland. This can be put down to the 1991–3 entrepreneurship boom during which a large number of new units were created which have not yet managed to expand their activity.

It is evident that large-scale industry in Estonia is in for a further reduction in its labour force. At the same time it is clear that, given the low labour costs, a substantial number of large plants will persist. Due to decades of life under socialism, the enterprising spirit of Estonian people, and of non-Estonians in particular, is lower than that in the West. An immediate rise of entrepreneurial activity to the Western level is not therefore to be expected.

CONCLUSIONS

As regards the impact of the shifts in economic structures in Estonia, there have been three main effects. Firstly, under the Soviet occupation,

Estonian enterprises grew substantially. The main reason for that lay in the Soviet industrial ideology which proceeded from the principle of the concentration of production (the so-called socialist fordism) as the only factor which raised productivity and lowered prime cost. No attention was paid to the intensification of production, to automation or to the development of information technology. The enterprises set up during the post-war period were mainly industrial and were meant to satisfy the needs of the whole economic space of the Soviet Union. They were therefore too large for the needs of Estonia alone. Nevertheless, some of these large-scale enterprises have a better chance of penetrating Western markets than they did 70 years ago because the cheapness of Estonian labour. Consequently, within a certain period the large firms which manufacture at low cost though labour-intensive mass production as, for example, in the sewing and furniture industries, may prove successful.

Secondly, by comparing the relative importance of workers employed by Estonian enterprises in the three main sectors of the economy with comparable indicators of highly developed Germany and Finland, it is evident that the role of the primary sector is much bigger in Estonia. However, behind such differences there is substantially lower productivity and, due to lesser and poorer technology inputs, there is also more inefficient production. Further, exports to eastern markets still play a significant role in this sector. Given the instability of these export prospects due to political factors and the higher efficiency of production owing to privatisation, the amount of labour necessary in agriculture will be further reduced. Thus, Estonia will, having reached the level of Finland, lose about half of the primary sector jobs it had in 1991 – nearly 6 per cent of the total employment – and, having reached the level of Germany, lose about 8–9 per cent of all jobs and therefore 70–80 per cent of agricultural jobs. In rural areas where agriculture has so far been the principal employer and where it continues to prove difficult to create jobs in the secondary or tertiary sector, this will mean massive unemployment and the resultant increase in the role of forced hidden activity.

Thirdly, there is the question the of scale of enterprises. The biggest difference between the average enterprise size in the different branches of Estonian and Western economies becomes manifest in the service and processing industries. Such a discrepancy has emerged on the basis of 'uneconomical' affiliate firms (particularly from rural areas and small centres) which were first nationalised, then concentrated under one large-scale enterprise and eventually liquidated. So, enterprising people who lost their jobs in large-scale agriculture or industry do have a chance to respond to some of these opportunities. As this occurs, it will alleviate the unemployment, enrich service potential and improve the poor service culture. In principle, it should also enable Estonians to apply their biggest resource, namely, relatively cheap labour in light industry, including the establishment of small sewing workshops, and so on. However, there is another aspect to it. Incompetence in book-keeping, competition and the shortage of new ideas, together with the uncontrollability stemming from the large number of enterprises and the inexperience of the supervisory bodies, will lead to the emergence of an extensive network of illegal relations. Thus it is essential that the state should organise appropriate training to introduce standards of legal behaviour and offset the spontaneously disseminating 'know-how' about illegality in the business sphere.

STAGES IN THE DEVELOPMENT OF THE HIDDEN ECONOMY

Following the impact of economic recession on the economic behaviour, six stages can be identified in the development of the hidden economy in Estonia.

The growth of the secondary economy in 1980–89

In this period, a crisis situation developed and a large part of economic activity became informal. The temporal aspect was important because the protracted crisis shaped certain stereotypes and a way of living that was to persist. In Estonia, the so-called secondary economy worked for years and grew into a way of life which in some aspects became a fertile soil for illegal behaviour. The economic stagnation of the Soviet Union served as an important background factor in this period.

The collapse of economy in 1990–1992

This directly influenced the speed of change. While the small size of Estonia is a relative advantage, the scarcity of local investors, the shortage of resources and the long-time integration of the economy with a large economic system is a disadvantage. The economic crisis was aggravated by the transformation of several principles of social life after Estonia regained independence, and the concurrent instability. The changes in the principles of tax collection, the privatisation of state property, the explosive growth of new entrepreneurship generated confusion. Moreover, the new structures in areas such as customs, border defence, police and the Revenue Office were not in place and the old ones, such as the KGB and the office for combating the theft of socialist property were not operating. All these were factors creating opportunities for corrupt and illegal activity.

The beginning of reforms in 1992–93

These reforms became inevitable after an economic collapse. The monetary reform in the summer of 1992 and the full liberalisation of foreign trade early in 1993 resulted in shock therapy aimed at rapid changes. The functioning of the economy was guaranteed only with necessary laws in place and the non-interference of the government. This enabled both local and foreign entrepreneurs to profit, invest the proceeds or export them from Estonia.

Among the side-effects of rapid reorientation was the inability to control crime, the emergence of social inequality and other negative phenomena. The sectors that were more closely connected with the secondary sector, such as agriculture and large industry, suffered major setbacks. The more active workers went to the private sector on a full-time basis where, mainly due to the lack of experience, the business culture of these enterprises remains weak. A national privatisation programme was launched while simultaneously active wild privatisation was continuing and state property was transferred to private ownership with the help of semi-legal devices. The less active people became jobless, trying to resort to the domestic economy and barter for their survival.

The provisional stabilisation of the macro-economic situation in 1993–95

The provisional stabilisation took place within a couple of years when the economic growth could be really felt. But since the growth was bigger in the hidden sector than in the official one, it was not reflected in the official statistics. A few people became rich very quickly while most of the people grew poorer. Politically, the danger of turning to the left emerged.

Simultaneously, a cadre of entrepreneurs began to emerge. The existing enterprises became stronger and began to pay more attention to their reputation, so the tax-paying culture improved and investment began to grow. Unfortunately, the Taxation Law adopted in December 1993 and enforced in 1994 assumed honesty. For example, the patentee system was abolished and replaced by the system of income tax returns. Income tax incentives for investments were abolished. These measures intensified pressure on tax evasion, the more so when the Revenue Office was still unable to control the situation. At the same time, the illegal privatisation ceased since this method could not be applied to the remaining large-scale enterprises under the surveillance of both the government and the media.

The planned period of rapid economic growth in 1995–97

If the liberal economic policies and stability continues, the businessmen who gained during the period of rapid changes and confusion will invest their capital. This capital used to circulate in trade and in foreign banks, thus creating well-paid jobs and raising the living standards of a large part of the population. Since it is impossible to manage or finance large integrated enterprises with the 'coffer bank' method, most of the activities, including those concerning relations with customers and contractors in particular, will have to be legalised. Economic growth will manifest itself in the official sector as well. Presumably, by that time politicians will have already realised the mistakes made, part of the laws will have been amended and the Revenue Office will operate more efficiently.

The (prospective) period of stable economic development after 1997

About four to five years after the beginning of reforms the growth of the official sector is likely to exceed that of the hidden sector and the whole economy may stabilise. If this happens, Estonia will become more like a European country in its business culture and practices.

To date, Estonia has reached a period where the official economy is growing slowly while the hidden sector is growing fast. In the near future both will grow rapidly until the capital concentration and the attitudes of businessmen have reached the level where the growth rate of the official sector exceeds that of the unofficial sector. Unless the state takes any extreme leftist steps which force capital owners to conceal their income again and if the state's watchdog role in guaranteeing security and blocking illegal activities is enhanced, we can expect the role of the hidden economy to diminish.

CONCLUSIONS AND POLICY RECOMMENDATIONS

The transition economy of former socialist states, including Estonia, is a special type of capitalism which is strongly influenced by the earlier secondary or pseudo-private sector. The instability and crisis prevailing during the transition period find their expression in, and are amplified by, the spread of hidden and illegal activities.

The impact of the secondary economy on a society in transition

During the transition period both the earlier habits as well as the personal networks persist. The decades-long practices of the secondary economy were shaped into a subculture immersed with personal networks which socialised their participants and which still shapes their relations. Such a subculture will not disintegrate rapidly because every social formation is inert. However, the legacy of the secondary economy is not wholly negative. Inside it there emerged a large petit bourgeois elite of workers. Moreover, it has acted to support the real standard of living, due to a culture of conservatism and self-supply. To that extent, the official statistics exaggerate the economic decline.

The growth of the hidden activity in enterprises

In Estonia, the most important factors affecting the expansion of the hidden sector are the crises resulting from the altered economic space and the new terms of existence for enterprises. Drawing upon the above there are several factors which have played a crucial role in the evolution of the Estonian hidden economy and in the development of the illegal behaviour of entrepreneurs. Among these is the general crisis of the Estonian economy and the major hardships of several sectors within it. It is even more important to point out the institutional and legal vacuum and the activities of certain interest groups in influencing the shaping of Estonian legislation with the aim of extending the period of uncertainty. The problem lies in the inexperience of lawmakers and the executive due to poor skills and low wages, and in places unnecessary haste. Laws and decrees adopted do not consider the real situation, facilitating the spread of informal activities. The corruption cases which are made public blemish the state's reputation which in turn gives some taxpayers enough reason to justify their illegal activities.

The spread of illegal activities is also directly facilitated by the extremely rapid changes in the economic structure ensuing from economic difficulties. Above all it is the multiplication of the number of enterprises as a result of which thousands of workers and specialists without any previous managerial experience and with no idea of business ethics, have become entrepreneurs. This detracts from a Western style business culture and creates a general atmosphere of negligence. Simultaneously, the dissolution of large enterprises creates a free labour force ready to participate in the 'black' labour market. As noted previously, the shifts that have taken place in different sectors are also rather important. In this context the intertwining of global trends as well as changes inherent in all post-socialist states came together to generate a fertile soil for the spread of hidden activities.

The differential effect of economic growth as a result of various factors, of which the most important is the development of entrepreneurship, has given rise to the increase of material inequality between different social groups and different regions of Estonia. Former company managers and deputy managers, having reoriented themselves, acquire good positions in the privatisation process. Also a generation of young businessmen has emerged. It is mainly elderly, unskilled and now jobless workers, young families with children and pensioners who have problems. Regional differences have also been aggravated. These take various forms, such as the centre–periphery divide and East–West lines; with the areas of major cities distinctive as islands of development and north-eastern Estonia at the other extreme.

The reaction of domestic economies to economic recession

Under an economic crisis, part of the domestic economies resort to a defensive strategy according to which families live more sparingly. This in turn results in the fall of domestic demand and causes problems for enterprises. On the other hand, families try to augment their income in various ways. On most occasions, the wages earned in public service or in privatised large-scale enterprises are insufficient to support a family. People are therefore forced to seek additional income to be able to manage better. In such cases, the most typical solution is to take on additional work, either in one's own profession or outside it. What is often styled as 'labour tourism' also occurs as people look for unskilled work in wealthier regions. On the other hand these hardships in domestic economies may induce people to resort to illegal activities.

Recommendations for constraining the hidden economy

Against the background of the above-described economic, legal and social context, the situation of the central subject of the economic life, namely the entrepreneur, acquires a special significance. The most efficient means of reducing the role of the hidden economy is in promoting honest entrepreneurship through, for example, assistance in official formalities in customs and in the Revenue Office, in executing the right of property, and so on. The official execution of transactions should be simplified and the costs related to their official confirmation cut because the hidden economy does not pay these taxes. It is also helpful to create public credit guarantees for small entrepreneurs who are unable to offer surety to banks when starting their own business; to support prospective branches of entrepreneurship from foreign competition; and promote exports. More attention should also be paid to the economic activity of minorities within the country.

The constant reviewing of laws and decrees should be abolished. Even before the submission of a draft law or project its impact on the economy and its different sectors should be analysed. If any obstacles to the official economy can be anticipated, measures should be worked out to prevent the hidden economy from taking advantage of the temporary hardships of the official economy. In order to efficiently combat the hidden economy, its causes should be ascertained and eliminated. Frequent alterations of taxation laws have a particularly harmful effect. A taxation system that prefers the honest economy to the hidden should be introduced. This might involve, for example, real estate and land tax depending on the location of the property and its market value, the reduction of income tax and sales tax, while social tax should be pegged to pensions and other benefits. The taxation system should be altered to consider the normal functioning of economy. For example, sales tax could be paid after incomings, since in seasonal industries, expenses in certain periods are larger than income. Equally, depreciation costs should be maintained at the current level.

The participation of government officials, managers and specialists within state-owned companies in entrepreneurship and their political parties' membership should be strictly regulated. The relevant activities must be transparent since this would reduce the chances of becoming tied to the hidden economy. Political parties should be obliged to declare their sources of income and relevant sanctions for concealing officially unreported income should be imposed. The national system of security services should be developed. Were that to happen, entrepreneurs would not need to hire bodyguards or use security firms, whether legal, semi-legal or criminal, many of which are not interested in paying national taxes.

The possibilities for out of court settlement of disputes should be expanded. Legal proceedings are so expensive and time-consuming that part of the demands are made through the hidden economy. The operation of monopolies and cartel agreements should be restricted. This would help to deprive the hidden economy of the opportunities to blackmail those who get monopoly profit and to operate illegally in the spheres where demand exceeds supply due to the absence of free competition. Non-cash transactions should be stimulated, and here the state could help develop the corresponding infrastructure.

Benefits ensuing from the public sector, such as education, health care, pension and security, must be differentiated reflecting the contribution to the upkeep of the public sector. Were this to happen, entrepreneurs and employees would be more interested in paying taxes on their real income. The spheres that are directly connected with the hidden economy, such as prostitution and drug addiction, should be regulated. Equally, if a house is built to be a home but is actually used for economic activity, the land and real estate taxes should follow the actual utilisation of the building and the owner should be fined if it is not used for the prescribed activity. Attention should be focused on the spheres where the hidden economy is already evident, including markets, alcohol and tobacco products, weapons, and so on. The market administration should be responsible for security and the preservation of goods and other property without the assistance of national structures. Overall it makes sense to prohibit only such activities that can be controlled, with the rest being legalised.

Of all the recommendations made, the following are perhaps the most immediate, namely, preferential training and credits for entrepreneurs; focus on the quality of laws including more resources to analyse their likely effects; establish a social system where every resident is interested in paying relevant taxes; glorify honest taxpayers; and minimise corruption and restore confidence in state supervisory structures.

REFERENCES

Annus, T. and Noorkõiv, R. (1994) *Eesti teel turumajandusele* Estonian path to the market economy, (Tallinn: Ministry Social Affairs).

Camagni, R. and Capellin, R. (1981) 'Policies for full employment and more efficient utilisation of resources and new trends in European regional development', *Lo Spectorale Internazionale*, 2, 99–135.

Cassel, D. (1982) 'Shattenwirtschaft – eine Wachtumbranche?' *List Forum*, 11 (6).

Cassel, D. (1984) 'The Growing Shadow Economy: Implications for Stabilisation Policy', *Inter Economics*, 5, 220.

Castells, M. and Portes, A. (1989) 'World Underneath: The Origins, Dynamics and Effects of the Informal Economy', in A. Portes, M. Castells, and L.A. Benton, (eds), *The Informal Economy* (Baltimore: Johns Hopkins University Press).

Ciesnocinska, M. (1993) 'The Polish Baltic Regions under Transition Process', paper presented at the European Summer Institute in Regional Science, Joensuu.

Estonian Economic Survey (1994) Ministry of Economic Affairs of the Republic of Estonia, Tallinn.

Farago, L. (1993) 'Regional Disparities and Regional Development Endeavours in Hungary under Transition', paper presented at the European Summer Institute in Regional Science, Joensuu.

Feige, E.L. (1990) 'Defining and Estimating Underground and Informal Economies: The New Institutional Economic Approach', *World Development*, 18 (7), 989–1002.

Gabor, I.R., (1979) 'The second economy', *Acta Oeconomica*, 22 (3–4), 263–300.

Gabor, I.R. (1991) 'Prospects and limits to the second economy', *Acta Oeconomica*, 43 (3–4) 1991, 349–52.

Kornai, J. (1980) *The Economics of Shortage* (Amsterdam: North Holland).

Kornai, J. (1992) *Tee vabasse majandusse* Path to the free economy (Tallinn: Eesti Entsüklabeediakirjastus).

Kornai, J. (1992) *Vastuolud ja dilemmad* Contradictions and dilemmas (Tallinn: Olion).

Mingione, E. (1994) 'Life Strategies and Social Economies in the post-fordist age', *International Journal of Urban and Regional Research*, 18 (1), 23–44.

OECD Economoc Outlook (1982) *Occasional Studies* (Paris: OECD).

Portes, A. (1994) 'Paradoxes of the Informal Economy: The Social Basis of Unregulated Entrepreneurship', in N.J. Smelser and R. Swedberg, (eds), *The Handbook of Economic Sociology* (Russell Sage Foundation and Princeton University Press).

Raagmaa, G. (1995) 'New Enterprises and Regional Development in Estonia', in M. Tykkyläinen (ed.), *Local and Regional Development During the 1990s Transition in Eastern Europe*, (Aldershot, Hants: Avebury).

Raig, I. (1987) *Teie pere majapidamine* The household of your family (Tallinn: Valgus).

Raig, I. (1988) *Teisene majandus,* Secondary economy (Tallinn: Valgus).

Riigikontroll, 1994 1993 tööaruanne, (Tallinn: Riigikontroll).

Remmel, M. (1994) *Kuritegu ja majandus, kuritegu kui tehing* Crime and economy, crime as a deal, Rahva Hääl, May 30 and 31.

Roberts, B. (1994) 'Informal Economy and Family Strategies', *International Journal of Urban and Regional Research*, 18 (1), 6–23.

Rose, R. (1983) *Getting by in Three Economies: The Resources of the Official, Unofficial and Domestic Economies* (Glasgow: Centre for the Study of Public Policy).

Rose, R. (1992) *Ordinary people in Public Policy* (London: Sage).

Rose, R. and Maley, W. (1994) *Nationalities in the Baltic States, A Survey Study* (Glasgow: University of Strathclyde).

Šik, E. (1994) 'From the Multicoloured to the Black and White Economy: The Hungarian Second Economy and the Transformation', *International Journal of Urban and Regional Research*, 18 (1), 46–69.

Stöhr, W. (1990) 'Synthesis', in W. Stöhr, (ed.), *Global challenge and Local Response* (London and New York: United Nations University).

Zaslavskaya, T.I. (1980) 'Economisheskoe povedenie i economisheskoe razvitie', Serija Ekonomitsheskaja 3, 15–33.

9 Accounting and Audit in Latvia

Igors Ludborzs

GENERAL SITUATION

Since 1 January 1993 the accounting system in Latvia has experienced a radical transition from the so called 'soviet accounting system' to European and worldwide accepted accounting practice. Since then two laws regulating the accounting system in the Republic of Latvia have been adopted and enforced; namely 'On Accounting' and 'On Company Annual Reports'. Both laws are based on the EU Directives 4 and 7, as well as other EU Directives. The motive for adopting the laws has been to facilitate the integration of Latvia into the EU, for which harmonisation of legislation with the EU has to be accomplished.

The two approaches to the regulation of accounting in the EU can be summarised as follows:

> *Germany, France, Italy* The State regulates accounting and the preparation of financial statements
> *England, Holland, Denmark* Professional associations regulate the activity of their members, as well as accounting and the preparation of statements, by developing and publishing national standards

The comparative position in Latvia is set out in Table 9.1.

There are two methods which have been adopted for the harmonisation of the national accounting and audit standards within the European Community. Firstly, during the 1970s, the development of directives began to regulate accounting and audit procedures in the member countries of the EU. Secondly, at the beginning of 1990s, the member countries of the EU started discussions about the application of the International Accounting and Audit Standards for national accounting and audit purposes.

In 1995 the EU made a decision to refrain from further activity related to accounting and audit regulation through the publication of directives,

Table 9.1   Two approaches to the regulation of accounting

Background	
English law	Roman law*
Large, old, strong profession	Younger, weaker profession*
Large stock exchange	Smaller stock exchange*
General accounting features	
Fair*	Legal
Shareholder-orientation*	Creditor-orientation
Disclosure*	Secrecy
Tax rules separate*	Tax-dominated
Substance over form*	Form over substance
Professional standards	Government rules*
Specific accounting features	
Percentage of completion method	Completed contract method
Depreciation over useful lives*	Depreciation by tax rules
No legal reserves	Legal reserves*
Financial leases capitalised*	No lease capitalisation
Cash or funds statements	No cash or funds statements*
Earnings per share disclosed	No earnings per share disclosure*
No secret reserves*	Secret reserves
Few tax-induced provisions*	Tax-induced provisions
Preliminary expenses expensed	Preliminary expenses capitalisable*
Taking gains on unsettled foreign* currency monetary items*	Deferring gains on unsettled foreign currency monetary items
Some examples of countries	
United Kingdom, Ireland, United States of America, Canada, Australia, New Zealand, Hong Kong, Singapore, Denmark, The Netherlands	France, Germany, Austria, Switzerland, Spain, Italy, Portugal, Japan, Belgium, Greece

Note:
* denotes the approach in the Republic of Latvia.
Source: Adapted from Nobes, C. (1994), Table 3, p. 7.

but only to co-ordinate and improve the opportunities of the member countries to use the International Accounting and Audit Standards for national accounting and audit. The International Accounting Standards have been developed by the International Accounting Standards Committee, which includes professional associations not only in Europe but also in America, Australia, Asia and Africa. To a large extent these standards are based on the national standards of the USA and the UK. The approach of the USA and the UK in the development of standards strictly separates financial accounting from tax accounting. This approach was also used, for example, when developing legislation in Denmark in the 1970s and 1980s.

Regarding this approach as also acceptable in Latvia, on 14 October 1992 the 'umbrella' Law 'On Accounting' was passed which is now applicable to accounting in all Latvian companies registered with the Company Register. At the same time the Law 'On Company Annual Reports' was passed, separating financial accounting from tax calculations as strictly as in the Danish case. The Law 'On Accounting' applies to all enterprises registered with the Company Register of the Republic of Latvia, without any exceptions. This Law specifies the accounting methods to be followed by enterprises, as well as identifying the accounting authorities. The law 'On Company Annual Reports' applies to all enterprises except banks, other credit institutions, insurance companies, as well as specific enterprises and entrepreneurial associations. This law regulates the procedure for the preparation of the annual reports of these enterprises. The Annual Report is an entity consisting of the Balance Sheet, Profit & Loss Statement, relevant Notes and Director's Report. It should be noted that besides the above laws, the accounting system and preparation of the Annual Reports of enterprises are regulated by other laws of the Republic of Latvia, particularly those on entrepreneurial activity (including the laws 'On Entrepreneurship', 'On Limited Liability Companies', 'On Joint Stock Companies').

According to current legislation, the government is entitled to adopt special decrees on most important accounting issues, as well as to determine the authorities of government institutions in the sphere of accounting methodology requirements. According to the legislation the government has established a special Accounting Methodological Council. This institution has broad authority in the development and implementation of appropriate accounting practices; development and evaluation of draft laws and other legal requirements; preparing recommendations and advising on issues related to the training of accountants as well as licensing certified auditors.

The accounting practices and methods applied in enterprises are strongly influenced by such state institutions as the Ministry of Finance and the State Revenue Service (former State Financial Inspection). Within their sphere of competence these institutions publish various instructions, manuals, resolutions and other requirements related not only to accounting practice and methods, but also to the disclosure of information for taxation purposes. Among many other documents, one of the most important is the Ministry of Finance Executive Order No. 63, 'On Uniform Chart of Accounts for Enterprises and Entrepreneurial Associations', which was approved 13 May 1993. This provides the uniform chart of accounts to be used starting from 1 January 1994 as the basis for the development of the individual chart of accounts in enterprises.

Accounting practice is currently indirectly, but nevertheless significantly, influenced by tax legislation which to a great extent regulates the preparation of accounts and accounting methods. In addition to this, it should be noted that frequent amendments and additions to tax legislation create difficulties in the understanding and implementation of these laws for the preparation of accounts. The situation is made worse because both the State Revenue Service and the Accounting Methodology Council are under the control of the Ministry of Finance. As result there is a conflict of interest between the problems related to tax calculation and the payments made to the state and the budgets of municipalities on the one hand, and problems related to the development and application of the financial accounting principles in the enterprises on the other hand. Currently the conflict is most often resolved in favour of increased tax payments, accordingly leading to the decrease of the state budget deficit.

An example of the above can be illustrated by the regulations recently adopted by the government regarding 'Regulations on maintaining records of cash transactions' and 'Regulations on usage and issuance of goods delivery notes–invoices'. These regulations have been introduced with the aim of increasing the state budget income by imposing additional requirements on enterprise accounting procedures. Unfortunately the regulations attempt to solve the consequences and not the reasons that create the problem. The source and resolution of the problem should be found in a true and fair tax policy based on consensus between businessmen and the government, the more effective use of resources available, and so on.

After the laws 'On Accounting' and 'On Company Annual Reports' had been passed, no logical continuation followed to provide for the development of national accounting and audit standards. As a result, the current situation is that the Accounting Council, State Revenue Service, Ministry of Finance, Bank of Latvia and other organisations started to develop several unco-ordinated and incomplete regulating acts and to require their compulsory application by Latvian companies. These requirements, when applied to financial accounting, distort annual reports in many cases so that they do not give a true and fair view of the assets, liabilities and financial position of a company at the end of the reporting year, nor do they truly reflect the profit or loss of the company for the reporting year.

It should be noted that there are the some deficiencies in the adopted Laws 'On Accounting' and 'On Company Annual Reports', which to a certain extent reduce their effect, especially in relation to preparation of annual reports. These can be summarised as follows:

1. Disclosure in the balance sheet of the transactions with the affiliated undertakings have been limited to the transactions with subsidiaries and associates, leaving out the transactions with the parent company and the parent's other subsidiaries.
2. The Ministry of Finance is authorised to require unaudited quarterly financial reports, which involves additional costs both for the businesses affected and for the Ministry of Finance. Yet there is no clear and understandable concept of how such reports would be used by the Ministry of Finance.
3. Statutory requirements regarding, consolidation principles and procedures set out in the EU Directive No. 7 have either been partly included in the law, or have not been included at all, which means that the production of consolidated annual reports is practically impossible.
4. The format of the unqualified auditor's opinion provided in the law actually leaves no possibility to issue an unqualified opinion, because in this case the auditor would undertake an unreasonable risk by giving his opinion on the company's annual report.
5. In accordance with the above regulations the annual report of the company (approved by its shareholders) should be submitted to the State Revenue Service not later than four months after the end of the accounting period. Such a procedure creates unnecessary pressure in auditing large companies, provides the possibility for the State Revenue Service to interfere in the sphere of financial accounting and reports, and effectively disallows the concentration of all publicly available information in one place.

It should be noted that after these laws were passed, the Ministry of Finance and the Accounting Council did not start work on training programmes for certified auditors, as stipulated by the Regulations 'On Accounting Council' and Regulations of the Ministry of Finance. From the passing of the law in October 1992 up until spring 1995, neither the Ministry of Finance nor the Accounting Methodology Council have developed and implemented accounting or audit standards.

As concerns accounting practice and methods in banks and other credit institutions, in addition to the above-mentioned laws, other requirements including the law 'On Banks', and the Cabinet of Minister's Regulations and the Bank of Latvia Regulations and Instructions have to be followed. Unfortunately, there is not always sufficient co-ordination among the various institutions whose role it is to regulate the accounting practice and methods to be applied in commercial banks and credit institutions. Due to this situation, various problems frequently arise in the preparation of accounting documentation for commercial banks.

Despite the above stated problems, accounting in the commercial banks might be regarded as the most developed in Latvia. In accordance with the current legislation, the Bank of Latvia regulations on accounting should be in line with the International Accounting Standards. In addition, starting with 1 January 1994 the annual reports of credit institutions have been audited mostly by the international accounting firms. As result there is no ground for the view that one of the reasons for the crisis among the commercial banks was the lack of accounting principles in that industry. It would be more appropriate to regard the improper or incorrect use of these accounting principles as the reason for the crisis.

Insurance companies have to undertake their accounting and prepare annual reports in accordance with the laws of the Republic of Latvia and the Instructions and Regulations issued by State Insurance Supervision Department of the Ministry of Finance. In practice this means that the balance sheet and profit and loss account formats provided in the Law 'On Company Annual Reports' have been widely used, slightly amended to include the specific characteristics of insurance business. Without any doubt the best solution to the problem described would be the adoption of regulations based on the EU directive on the annual and consolidated accounts of insurance undertakings.

In accordance with legislation, all Annual Accounts and Statements have to be examined by auditors. Such an audit should be carried out either by the internal audit committee of the enterprise, or by specially appointed certified auditors, depending on the total balance, net turnover and average number of employees per year. Anyone can be appointed as the member of the internal audit committee, while in accordance with the Cabinet of Minister's Regulations No. 14 'On Certified Auditors' (until 15 April 1995 the Law 'On Certified Auditors') a certified auditor can only be a person who has passed a special qualification test and obtained a licence issued by the Accounting Methodology Board. The first certified auditors in Latvia started their activities in 1994 and currently their number is close to one hundred. In Latvia audit services are currently provided by such world renowned companies as Arthur Andersen, Coopers & Lybrand, Price Waterhouse and other international audit firms of the so called 'big six', as well as local audit firms.

The main problem is that due to the lack of audit standards it is impossible to assess the quality of the performance of auditors or audit firms. There are also no minimum requirements that should be followed by auditors for the audit to be considered sufficient to express an auditor's opinion. This could be due to the fact that the Ministry of Finance and the Accounting Methodology Council have insufficient resources to accomplish these assignments. In 1994, the Latvian Certified Auditors' Association was established, one of the main purposes of which is the development of audit and accounting standards. Currently the Association has approximately 90 members (of 100 certified auditors). The Association has established its organisational structure on the basis of experience of European countries (including the UK, Sweden, Denmark) and has members (professionals) already trying to accomplish the above assignments partly within the existing system. However, in the circumstances where the certified auditors are not authorised to manage their professional activities as in many countries in the world, there is a vague hope that the development of accounting, and especially audit, in Latvia will reach the level of the EU. In the situation when the accelerated privatisation process of state enterprises is expected in Latvia, the importance of accounting statements will increase. As a result the independent auditors' opinions on the true and fair view of the annual reports of these companies will become more important.

During the recent meeting of the members of the Certified Auditors' Association with the Management of the International Accounting Standards Committee, as well as Managers of the Professional Accountants Association of Great Britain, opportunities were discussed for the Latvian Certified Auditors' Association to become a member of the above international accounting and audit organisations, as well as to receive technical assistance from professional associations. Moreover, besides the Accounting Methodology Board in Latvia there are also other professional associations, such as the Latvian Association of Certified Auditors and Association of Latvian Accountants that carry out activities in the sphere of accounting and auditing methodology. However, work related to the development of national accounting and audit standards is at a very initial stage.

COMPARISON OF ACCOUNTING AND AUDIT DEVELOPMENT WITH THE OTHER BALTIC STATES

Comparing the development of accounting and audit in Latvia with the situation in Estonia and Lithuania it is possible to draw the conclusion that it follows the progress made in one or another country. Thus, Estonia has the leading position among the Baltic States in the process of transition to the market economy and also takes the first place in implementation of changes in accounting. This is illustrated in the following:

1. Estonia was the first to adopt legislation on accounting in 1991 while in Latvia and Lithuania it happened only in 1992.
2. Estonia was the first to adopt a law envisaging the implementation of International Accounting Standards. Other Baltic States so far are only planning to do this in the future.
3. Problems related to the development of the cost and management accounting in Estonia have been regarded as most important ones, while in the neighbour countries the top issues are problems relating to financial accounting.

However, assessing the current situation in the Baltic States in the development of audit, it has to be noted that the situation is approximately the same everywhere. The problems experienced by the profession in Latvia are similar to those which exist both in Lithuania and Estonia.

CONCLUSIONS: PROGRESS AND PROBLEMS IN ACCOUNTING

In Accounting

On the basis of the foregoing analysis, the following positive aspects of Latvian accounting today can be identified. There has been a transition from 'soviet-style accounting' to 'western style (financial) accounting". The Latvian Association of Certified Auditors has been established and the 'big six' and other international accounting firms operate in Latvia. At the same time the problems in this sphere should be noted. They include the activities of tax authorities in regulating financial accounting and the lack of generally accepted Latvian accounting principles (GAAP). There is also an evident lack of knowledge in the sphere of financial accounting among practising accountants; and accounting in credit institutions and insurance companies is not sufficiently covered by legislation and regulation.

In audit

Summarising the development of audit in Latvia it is possible to pick out the following progressive elements. The legal environment for the development of audit profession has been created and the Latvian Association of Certified Auditors established. Moreover, the 'big six' and other international accounting firms are now operating in Latvia. There are, however, some problems not yet resolved in this field. They include the lack of self-regulation; the lack of Latvian generally accepted auditing standards (GAS); and lack of knowledge among practising auditors of how to perform high-quality audits.

REFERENCES

Ernst & Young, 'Danish Companies' Accounts Act' (1994) Regulations on Danish Companies' Annual Account, Copenhagen.
IASC, (1995) 'Target 1999: Global Approval', *IASC Insight* (London: International Accounting Standards Committee).
Lasis, J. (1995) 'Razmischlenia prisjaynogo revidenta', *Biznes & Baltija* (Latvian Business Daily), 13.12.95.
Nobes, C. (1994) 'A Study of the International Accounting Standards Committee', (London: Coopers & Lybrand International).
Skuja, V. (1996) 'Zvèrinâtie revidentí kopø pagâjuøâ gada strâdâ savâ profesionâlâ asociâcijâ', *Dienas bizness* (Latvian Business Daily), 26.1.96.

10 Latvia's Emerging Capital Markets[1]

Gregory Jedrzejczak and Alex Fleming

SUMMARY

The growth of the Latvian capital markets over the next few years will be driven by supply-side developments. The main source of supply will likely be shares of privatised companies. A second source will be the government's own financing needs which will lead to an increasing supply of government securities. Growing difficulties in financing budgetary deficits and the phasing-out of direct lending from the central bank will require the government to tap a wider range of market sources.

On the demand side, the successful stabilisation programme has provided a sound basis for savings and investment. However, Latvian investors have been exposed to events which severely undermined their confidence in financial institutions. The introduction of the proposed reform of the pension system – involving the development of a funded pension pillar – would have a significant impact on securities markets in the longer term.

It is likely that the Riga Stock Exchange (RSE) will be the only licensed trading system in Latvia. Openness of the RSE to all brokerage houses eligible and willing to participate is critical and should be secured by appropriate regulation. The Central Depository for Securities (LCD) should be strictly supervised by the Securities Commission.

Latvian commercial banks will play an important role in the development of the capital market. Their lending/deposit activities should be separated from their capital market activities.

Poor enforcement of the law is likely to be a problem. The most appropriate solution may be to create an independent commission covering institutions offering and dealing in all non bank long-term financial instruments offered to the public at large. A strong role should be envisaged for self-regulation of market participants.

The involvement of investment funds, insurance companies and pension funds in the more active corporate governance of companies in which they invest should be allowed once markets are liquid enough to provide a valuation of portfolios, and once the necessary skills are developed in portfolio management and in administrative supervision of financial institutions.

To succeed as a capital market centre Latvia has to become an open economy, which would include permitting the free flow of foreign portfolio investment. This could help Latvia find its niche in the provision of capital market services to neighbouring countries. To achieve these goals, Latvia would have to establish its competitive advantage *vis-à-vis* other well-established European market centres as well as the new centres in Central Europe.

INTRODUCTION

Experience from Central and Eastern Europe, as well as Russia, shows that in most countries the regulatory and institutional infrastructure for capital markets was developed too late to accommodate the emerging needs of the transition process. The regulatory standards and institutions of capital markets have to be established simultaneously with the implementation of the privatisation programme if the latter is to evolve in the optimum way. The Latvian privatisation programme and capital market development are at an early stage of development. While this rudimentary development of the market can be a constraint in itself it also provides an opportunity to immediately introduce modern solutions in the areas of market technology and regulation. It also offers the opportunity for the government to synchronise strategies and policies adopted in different segments of capital markets with more general policies relating to the transition to a private market economy. There is not a ready-made pattern for Latvia to follow. Market regulation and architecture have to be country-specific, with the experience of mature and emerging markets – including those from the Central and Eastern European economies – serving as a reference point (see Pohl *et al.* 1995).

The chapter is structured as follows: (1) it identifies the major driving forces and impediments to capital market development; and (2) it addresses the most critical policy questions facing Latvia today and proposes answers to these. The capital markets are defined in this chapter to comprise the markets for enterprise equities and bonds as well as the market for various forms of government securities.

DRIVING FORCES AND IMPEDIMENTS

There are four forces which will have a major impact on the development of the capital markets in Latvia:

- supply of securities emerging from the privatisation process;
- supply of securities resulting from the new funding requirements of government and enterprises;
- demand for securities (as investments) from individuals and institutions; and
- business opportunities – vested interests of people who have linked their financial and professional future to the development of the securities industry.

Supply side: privatisation

Even the best designed and implemented institutions and regulations are of little use if there are not enough attractive securities to trade. Today the supply of securities and their diversification is limited. In March 1995 the Latvian capital markets dealt in the long-term products of 12 enterprise issuers. These included common shares, preferential shares, fund participation units, and trust contracts. There were no corporate bonds available. Most of the issuers offered a broad variety of classes of shares, mostly trying to sustain corporate control by diversification of property rights attached to different classes. Shares of three financial institutions are quoted and traded in a more regular way: Bonus Inc (financial conglomerate), Riga Commercial Bank, Aizkraukles Bank. These securities are traded on an unregulated over-the-counter (OTC) market, operated by unlicensed broker/dealers. In January 1996 shares of the largest Latvian bank – Unibank – began trading. There are approximately ten informal financial intermediaries and investment companies in Latvia. Prices of securities are stagnant and slightly above their face values with broad bid/offer spreads around 25 per cent. Securities are traded in negligible amounts, sometimes no bigger than Ls100 (US$200) per month per security. Shares of six Russian companies are also offered but there is a little trading reported.

Trading in privatisation certificates is the dominant activity. Transitional by its nature, it acts as a check on market capacity and the behaviour of market participants. About 2.4 million inhabitants received 103 million privatisation certificates with an aggregate nominal value of 2880 million Ls (US$5670 million). Certificates may be used for the redemption of land, the purchase of presently occupied public apartments, and direct privatisation. It can also be used for the purchase of shares of privatised companies through open auctions. Transfers of privatisation certificates have been allowed as direct contracts between individuals or as intermediated by licensed broker/dealers. In total, as of 1 April 1995, about 16 per cent of privatisation certificates have been disposed of by their original holders, of which 10.2 million have been transferred through licensed intermediaries. Privatisation certificates are traded on an OTC market – operated by licensed broker/dealers – and the Latvian Universal Exchange. At present 315 broker/dealers are licensed by the Ministry of Economy. These include employees of banks and financial conglomerates as well as independent intermediaries. About 10 per cent of overall trade is intermediated by the Latvia Universal Exchange. The exchange provides facilities for retail and block trading. The sessions, held daily, are open out-cry auctions. In block trading, the exchange matches offers on a daily basis. The market prices of privatisation certificates oscillate between 5 and 20 per cent of their nominal value. Prices are very sensitive to political developments, especially regarding expected legislation on the privatisation of apartments with the use of privatisation certificates. The market is fairly transparent. Prices and volumes of trades are reported to the Ministry of Economy and disseminated by the media. The system of dematerialised privatisation certificates is a trial for a proposed system of dematerialised securities. The results are not uniformly positive. There was, for example, an attempted fraud that was not identified early enough to avoid investor loses. Usually, it takes as long as 2–3 weeks to complete transfers of ownership.

In the near future the main source of supply of securities will most likely be shares of privatised companies. Latvia *de facto* has implemented case-by-case privatisation which has meant a limited supply of shares available for capital market trading rather than a massive and rapid divestiture of shares to the public. In April 1995 the shares of the first three companies were offered to the public.[2] All three companies have strategic investors holding majority blocks of shares. There was a public auction for the reminder of the shares in which 700 bids were collected in total. The shares of these companies are traded on the Riga Stock Exchange (RSE). However, due to the small number of public shareholders and the small size of the companies, they have to be considered more as a pilot for the trading and depository systems than as the basis of a significant market offer. The real take-off in trading is expected to happen when the next waves of public privatisation are completed, including companies more suitable for stock exchange trading and broader public interest in shareholding. In total, shares of about 20 companies were offered to the public by the end of 1995. Some companies – with large enough public shareholding and capitalisation – will be a good starting point for secondary trading on the RSE. The most promising at this moment seems to be the Unibank – noted above – which has begun the process of privatisation. Also, a limited number of private financial institutions contemplate raising capital through the public offering of their shares but these plans have not materialised yet.

Supply side: the need for financing

The government's central budget is potentially a major source of demand for available financial resources. Government financing activities may have several consequences for emerging capital markets: first, as the most direct consequence, it may crowd out corporate instruments by offering more attractive investment alternatives; second, it may provide much needed support to market intermediaries and institutions by adding a new source of revenues; and, third, it may make markets more liquid and risk-diversified, thereby making investments in enterprise securities more palatable. The existing primary and secondary markets for government securities are still in their nascent stage. Short-term Treasury bills (T-bills) are offered mostly to the banks.[3] The current liquidity problems of commercial banks and the very high denomination of T-bills are the major obstacles to the government being a more active player and therefore influencing capital market development for the time being. During the first half of 1995, the government was not prepared to see the yield on its T-bills rise to levels that would attract greater demand. Subsequently rates were permitted to find their own levels.

Growing difficulties in financing budgetary spending, and the phasing out of direct financing from the National Bank of Latvia will require the government to use market sources more broadly. This may mean looking for direct access to savings of local individuals (households) and businesses as well as foreign financial markets. With regard to local markets it is important that the government target a wider range of non-bank investors. Savings bonds may be an appropriate investment for individuals. As institutional investors, such as insurance companies and pension funds, gradually emerge they will have a preference for longer term government bonds. Accordingly, an attempt should be made to move out gradually along the maturity spectrum. This would take the pressure off having to roll over increasing volumes of short-term T-bills as funding requirements grow.

One positive aspect of the current banking crisis is that some banks – perceived to be the safer ones in the system – are likely to gain significant liquidity at the expense of the weaker banks as depositors flee to quality. At the same time, the current uncertainties may decrease the demand for credit and thereby create a pool of bank funds that could be invested in the T-bill market. The only longer-term bonds that the government has issued are those which have been placed on the balance sheets of the Savings Bank and the Unibank in replacement of non-performing loans. These, however, are non-negotiable. The government's refusal to set and maintain a determinate bond coupon and, at the same time, service these securities in a timely fashion creates a bad precedent for its fund-raising efforts over the longer term.

There are no known plans of municipalities to finance their activities by issuing long-term securities. Municipalities mostly finance their activities from taxes and to a lesser extent from selling real estate. Also, commercial banks are willing to lend money to municipalities because the banks perceive them as riskfree clients which would be bailed-out by the government in a case of financial difficulty. The existing system of allocation of tax revenues from the rich municipalities to poor ones also alleviates the pressure to find new sources of financing and, therefore, may be a disincentive for issuing securities.

With the exception of the Mortgage Bank that has made a limited issuance of ECU-linked mortgage backed bonds, commercial banks have made no significant attempts to increase the maturity of their liabilities by issuing longer term certificates of deposit or bonds. This is only likely to take place when the banking system has stabilised following the current crisis and when confidence returns to the system. One international institution did contemplate an issue of Lat denominated bonds in the local market to mobilise long-term Lat resources that would be on lent to banks in the form of a credit line for investment. On balance this could be a positive development for the local capital market although in the current phase of budget difficulty there is some danger of a crowding out of Government financing or, alternatively, of increasing costs of servicing of the public debt.

As is the case for most companies in Central and Eastern Europe, Latvian companies need very badly an injection of long-term financing, especially risk-sharing equity financing. Until now, the ability of companies in other countries of the region to attract long-term capital from capital markets has been very limited. Raising capital by issuing shares and/or corporate bonds has only happened when the secondary market becomes more liquid. It has also required a period of (risk-adjusted) return on publicly traded securities to be visibly higher than on bank deposits and Treasury securities. Looking at the experience of other economies in transition, this may happen in Latvia after a year or two of more substantial trading, especially if there is a positive impact of capital gains resulting from privatisation.

Demand side: a need for investment opportunities

There are a number of forces working towards high savings rates in Latvia, with the potential this brings for investment in securities on the part of households or institutions that handle their longer term savings. Culture and tradition in Latvia militates in favour of high savings. Successful stabilisation and the introduction of a strong local currency provide a sound basis for savings and investment. However, Latvian investors have been exposed to events which have severely undermined their confidence in the local financial institutions. First, pre-independence savings were virtually wiped-out by hyper-inflation following the break up of the Soviet Union. Later, a number of investment companies promising high returns on collective investment collapsed. The low market value of privatisation certificates in relation to their face value has also raised questions about the benefits promised by the government and politicians. The current banking crisis compounds the negative experience of the past. As the transition proceeds and economic growth resumes, income and financial saving will increase. The resulting investment in securities, particularly through collective vehicles, may provide new impetus to capital market development.

The introduction of the proposed reform of the pension system – involving the development of a funded pension pillar managed privately – would have a positive impact on securities markets. Mandatory and voluntary pension funds will play a critical role as a stable source of demand in a long run. It is estimated that total funds in the pension system may reach one billion lats (or US$2 billion) by 2010.

Foreign portfolio investment – that would provide an independent impetus to capital market development – usually follows on direct investments and foreign exchange investments (hedge funds). Latvia is only now beginning to attract direct investment (World Bank, 1995). There is anecdotal evidence, however, of hedge funds' interest in Latvian currency and government securities.

Business opportunities: securities industry

A rudimentary capital market infrastructure already exists and a small community of broker/dealers, collective investment vehicles (investment funds, investment companies and trust companies) and so-called universal exchanges trade available financial instruments. The buying and selling of vouchers and the establishment of voucher investment funds are significant sources of income for some market operators. The two banks designated to open privatisation accounts, Sakaru and Saving Bank, made a substantial part of their profits for 1994 from trading privatisation certificates. Sakaru Bank earned 400 000 Ls from trading in vouchers in 1994; the Saving Bank earned more than 700 000 Ls.

The concentration of privatisation certificates – and therefore the role of voucher investment funds – is expected to be smaller than in other countries which have implemented voucher schemes. Of the 100 million vouchers issued, it is expected that a maximum 15 per cent of the vouchers will be invested through investment funds.[4] As of March 1995, there were three investment funds which had obtained licenses from the Ministry of Economy. One had collected 100 000 Ls (US$200 000) equivalent of vouchers and the other two were in the process of being set up. The main reasons for the relatively slow growth of investment funds may be the temporary and partial regulations, ambiguous characteristics of privatisation certificates, and the slow privatisation process.

Local commercial banks, including the shareholders of the RSE, have had a relatively modest involvement in securities markets activities. Few of them are buying privatisation vouchers for their own account for investment and/or future profit. Banks do have a general interest in operating in the capital markets in the future but typically have no clear strategic vision about how to do it. This is in part a function of the unusually profitable environment for banks over the past three years – commercial banks were 'spoiled' by easy profits from trade activities and have not yet adopted strategies for operating in the current, more difficult environment. Financial conglomerates appear to be the most dynamic participants in the markets. Usually they are holding companies – combining the functions of broker/dealer, investment fund, quasi banking services, a variety of insurance services and sometimes pension funds and commodity trading. The largest insurance companies expressed an interest in enlarging their holdings of corporate shares and T-bills as the market grows and becomes more liquid.

A new, more regulated and technologically advanced system of trading in securities is being introduced. It is based on three pillars: a single national stock exchange, a central depository for dematerialised securities, and an independent securities commission.

The *Riga Stock Exchange* acts as a single trading place for publicly issued securities. It was established as a non-profit institution in

December 1993 and is owned by the 16 largest Latvian banks and two financial conglomerates. The Securities Law does not exclude a variety of trading systems; however the central position of the RSE seems to be secured by two factors: (1) the Latvian Privatisation Agency (LPA) has chosen the RSE as its agent for the public offering of shares of privatised companies; and (2) the RSE is the only exchange now ready to fulfil license requirements. The RSE uses an order driven trading system that consolidates all buy and sell orders registered at the opening of the session, setting a single price per session and maximising the turnover of concluded transactions. The number of sessions will gradually grow from one to five per week.

The *Latvian Central Depository for Securities (LCD)* was established in January 1995 by the RSE (48 per cent of shares), the LPA (33 per cent), and the Saving Bank (19 per cent). The LCD is part of a two tier depository system. The LCD itself keeps aggregate accounts of brokers, while the brokers themselves maintain accounts for investors. The LCD settles transactions – transferring dematerialised securities between accounts of brokers participating in transactions, and preparing the necessary documentation for settlement of payments. Besides settlement, the LCD also provides auxiliary services as registrar for publicly traded companies – keeping track of the shareholders and making sure that no more than the authorised amount of stock is in circulation.

The *Securities Commission* will be independent but supervised by the Finance Ministry. The law gives the legislative responsibilities of the Commission to a Council composed of seven members. The executive responsibilities of the Commission would be handled by a Board of five members, appointed by the Council. The precise boundary between the responsibilities of these two bodies is not clear, but could be resolved by decisions of the Council. In addition, the Commission would have employees, answering to both the Board and the Council.

MAIN POLICY OPTIONS

There are a number of issues, the resolution of which will decide the immediate future of the capital markets in Latvia. The most important of these issues are: (1) the nature of capital market institutions, (2) the nature of capital market supervision, (3) the impact of market participants on corporate governance of publicly traded companies, and (4) the ability of Latvia to attract foreign portfolio investors.

Institutions I: Is the Riga Stock Exchange enough?

Latvia faces the same problem as all countries of Central and Eastern Europe: a trade-off between market consolidation and its competitiveness. The simplest answer to the threat of potential market fragmentation would be to license only one trading system. The simplest answer to monopoly threat would be to set liberal rules and to allow all qualified trading systems to compete. In Latvia policy choices may be even more difficult than in other countries of the region. On the one hand, the expected small size of the Latvian market over the next few years suggests that there will be barely enough trading activity for one marketplace. On the other hand, the RSE, which is most likely to be a single market, is owned by a group of market participants which may have a vested interest in limiting the access of others to the trading facilities. A number of measures should be undertaken to balance these two tendencies and to create a consolidated and – at the same time – competitive market place:

It is likely that RSE will be the only licensed trading system available for some time. Therefore openness of the Exchange to all brokerage houses eligible and willing to participate in trade is critical and should be secured by proper regulation and supervision. For example, if a new member is required to buy shares of the RSE, this requirement should not be used by existing shareholders to prevent the entry of new members (for example, by establishing an unreasonably high level of shareholding for new members). In the operation of the RSE, a distinction should be made between the corporate governance function and the self-regulatory function. The first function should be executed by owners according to their voting power (shareholding). Owners would elect a Management Board responsible for the operation of the RSE as a not-for-profit joint stock company. The second, self-regulatory function, would be executed by members of the RSE with each member having equal (one) vote. That would eliminate a potential basis for discrimination against smaller, mostly non-bank, brokerage houses. Members would adopt rules and regulations of trade, codes of conduct, listing requirements, listing and delisting of particular securities, fees (in agreement with the Management Board). Members of the RSE might elect an RSE Board to fulfil these functions. While at this stage of building the RSE the corporate governance function dominates, the self-regulation function will be more and more important once the system matures. Self-regulation may create its own problems as it may lead to a trading monopoly with negative consequences for customers (investors). To avoid this, thorough supervision by an independent Securities Commission must be exercised.

The above comments are also valid for the LCD, particularly as the LCD is supposed to serve all licensed trading systems and has a monopolistic position secured by the Securities Law. The LCD rules and practices should be 'trade neutral'. An effort should be made to permit 'user friendly' transfers of shares for OTC transactions. It should be a legal requirement that prices of all concluded transactions be reported to the LCD, which would disseminate them through the media. The functioning of the LCD should be strictly supervised by the Securities Commission. Consideration should also be given to the appointment of a Supervisory Board of the LCD including persons with high authority and perceived as 'public trustees'.

Institutions II: What should the role of commercial banks be in the securities markets?

Latvian commercial banks are better capitalised, with access to financing through deposits, and to some extent money markets, which gives them greater access to funding than existing and potential securities firms. That will make them strong competitors to the brokerage companies in the securities markets. Furthermore, the banks can control large financial and political power through interlocking ownership over the enterprises that will be the issuers of the securities in the markets. The two major issues relating to the role of banks in capital market development in Latvia are: (1) the potential domination of the securities industry by banks, and (2) the type of commercial banking Latvia will follow with the evolution of the money and capital markets.

Under the present regulatory framework, the commercial banks in Latvia are permitted a broad range of direct and indirect participation in the capital markets. They can:

- become broker/dealers either through setting up a separate department or through a subsidiary,
- trade securities for their own account without obtaining a license,
- become custodian banks of the mutual investment companies/funds,
- become owners of investment companies with 25 per cent ownership, or up to 15 per cent of the bank's own equity whatever is less,
- become custodian banks for private pension funds and shareholders of the management companies of these funds up to 15 per cent of the bank's own equity,
- manage the distribution and trading of their own shares, and

- consolidate into financial holding companies through interlocking ownership with other credit and financial institutions.

Although the present regulatory structure for the banking industry is in the process of evolution, it is clear that the authorities have opted for the universal banking model, but not allowing direct long-term investment and control of non-financial institutions (as for example in Germany). The present framework allows the Latvian banks to invest in equity and exercise corporate control either through subsidiaries or under a holding company structure. The regulatory framework and the system of supervision of the banks need to be refined to take into consideration the potential formation of bank/financial conglomerates or holding companies in future, therefore risks from these activities.

The growing importance of banks in the area of corporate governance is not free of controversy. Banks have better access to information and can react more quickly to managerial shortcomings but, in contrast to stock market-based systems, are more conservative and tend to provide less financing to new entrepreneurial firms. There are also serious potential conflicts of interest between the role of banks as lenders to and owners of an enterprise on the one hand, and managers of public deposits and investments, on the other hand. For example, in the Czech and Slovak Republics, there are concerns about banks controlling the large voucher funds that in turn are major shareholders of enterprises and banks. In Russia, there is concern about 'circular ownership' in which enterprises own the banks and then banks own the enterprises.

The potential advantages of universal banks as capital markets participants may only emerge when a number of conditions are fulfilled. First, banks should be subject to appropriate prudential standards and fiduciary rules. Second, lending/deposit activities should be separated from securities markets activities in a way protecting bank deposits from inappropriate securities market risk. Third, the system should be open to competition from non banking market operators. Existing and new operators not related to the banks should be encouraged to enter the markets to fill niches likely to emerge as a result of privatisation.

Market supervision: Should Latvia have an independent securities commission?

Latvia has adopted one of the best Securities Laws in Central and Eastern Europe. However, as in most countries of the region, poor enforcement of existing laws is likely to be a problem. Enacting modern laws is of little value if the laws are not enforced. Enforcement may be poor because of inefficient administration, lack of self-regulation and/or a weak court system. It may also be in the interest of some managers of privatised companies and market operators to keep regulation vague and unenforceable. A law was adopted to create a Securities Commission that will enforce the law and oversee the self-regulatory organisations.

The first issue for Latvia to consider is whether to create a separate securities commission. There are many countries, including the Czech Republic, Japan and the Slovak Republic, where the Ministry of Finance is responsible for regulating banking, securities and insurance. Keeping all these responsibilities within the Latvian Ministry of Finance would arguably improve co-ordination; issues could be addressed within one organisation rather than across organisations. Keeping all responsibility in the Ministry of Finance would also arguably improve accountability; if there was a failure in securities regulation, the Minister of Finance, and ultimately the government, would be answerable. There are also, however, many countries in both the developed and developing world that have separate securities or financial commissions. France, Germany, Italy and the United States all have separate securities commissions. In Scandinavia, Norway has a Banking, Insurance and Securities Commission, and Sweden has a Financial Supervisory Authority. In Eastern Europe, Hungary and Poland have opted to create separate securities commissions. A separate commission is able to focus more closely on the securities industry and the issues for which it is responsible. A separate commission may also have a degree of political independence that is deemed desirable. And a separate commission may find it easier to recruit and retain securities or financial specialists. This is in part a question of money, but also a question of prestige; working for a securities commission is often thought to be more important and interesting than working for a government ministry.

A second issue for Latvia to consider, if it decides to create a separate financial commission, is how broad its responsibilities should be. At one extreme, the commission could be responsible only for securities regulation, like the Securities and Exchange Commission in the United States.[5] At the other extreme, the commission could be responsible for securities, banking, and insurance issues, like the Commission in Norway. A narrower commission can focus more closely on 'its' issues; a commission with broader responsibilities can perhaps eliminate some co-ordination problems and duplication of personnel. In a relatively small country, like Latvia, it may not make sense to have separate regulatory agencies, each with its own commissioners and general staff, responsible for each of the various financial industries. In considering these structural issues, it is important to recognise that there is no one correct answer. As the foregoing makes clear, different countries have adopted different approaches, appropriate for their own situations. It is also important to bear in mind that devising a structure is a means to the end of effective financial regulation.

From the perspective of a securities regulator, what is particularly critical is to have enough people – and people of sufficient talent – both to handle the routine work of processing disclosure documents and license applications, and to handle the more difficult work of detecting and prosecuting securities fraud. To attract and retain talented securities professionals, it is necessary to pay them reasonably well. If creating a separate financial or securities commission, funded in part by industry fees, would allow for higher salaries than those currently paid to the employees of the Securities Division, this factor alone would argue strongly in favour of some form of separate financial regulatory commission. There are also some more 'technical' issues that need to be considered in creating a financial or securities commission. The structure at present proposed by the Government for the securities commission, with a council responsible for 'legislative' matters, and a board responsible for 'executive' issues, is an unusual one. Most securities commissions around the world unite these responsibilities in one body, such as the commissioners of the US Securities and Exchange Commission. One argument for uniting these responsibilities is that it allows the commissioners to bring enforcement experience to bear in writing rules and vice versa. Another argument, particularly important if the commission is to be relatively small, is to avoid having too many 'seniors' and not enough 'juniors' in the organisation. Another issue is the possibility of conflicts for the council members between their responsibilities at the Commission and their 'other positions', perhaps positions in the securities industry.

In the Latvian context the most appropriate solution may be to create an independent commission covering institutions offering and dealing in all non-bank (non-deposit) long-term financial instruments. This would include both securities (serial products) and contractual products – pension plans, insurance polices, trust contracts, participation contracts, etc. – offered to the public at large.

The present market architecture – a single trading system vis-à-vis an administrative regulation – leaves too little space for self-regulation of market participants. A more diversified structure would be recommended. The strengthening of the self-regulatory functions of the RSE may be considered as one alternative. The Latvian Association of Securities Markets

Operators may be another alternative. The government may also consider the establishment of a mandatory self-regulatory organisation of brokers (individuals) and/or brokerage houses.

Corporate governance: Should the government encourage institutional investors to be active in the governance of companies?

One of the critical challenges of a successful transition to a market economy is to install effective owners of enterprises. Privatisation is only a first step on this road. In particular, the role of the commercial banks, investment funds, pension funds and insurance companies in the capacity of an owner has been discussed from the early stage of the transition of post-socialist economies.

The *voucher investment funds* are perceived as the primary candidates for this function. It is necessary to set a proper balance between interests of fund holders (mostly unsophisticated investors) and active corporate governance functions. The present regulation (Governmental Decree) on the investment funds tries to balance protection of unsophisticated investors using collective investment vehicles and the more active behaviour of funds vis-à-vis enterprises. Its provisions try to minimise undesirable fund behaviours like mismanagement and self dealing of the management company. However, it does not establish enough clear and accountable measures of investors' protection, for example, preventing funds managers from investing in securities with a higher risk than would be proper for a given type of investor. A legal base for the operation of investment funds is not adopted yet.

The privatisation voucher funds are structured as closed-end investment funds expiring on 31 December 1999. These funds are not incorporated but are contractual arrangements under the Civil Code of Latvia. Due to constraints of the Civil Code, the planned private pension funds are not to be incorporated either. This legal structure gives the participants in the funds little control over the activities of the management company and the performance of the fund. Given the importance of investment funds to the corporate governance of Latvian enterprises, consideration should be given to making amendments to the Civil Code allowing funds to be incorporated. The general consensus – based on experience to date in East and Central Europe – has been that in developing capital markets, and especially in those with large voucher privatisation programmes, funds should be established initially as closed-end, with the legal structure of an open joint stock company. The Latvian authorities are working on a separate draft law on investment companies and funds. The following areas of regulation need to be taken into consideration: the promotion of competition among funds and fund managers, the creation of proper information disclosure for the benefit of fund participants and shareholders, the creation of proper governance rights over the fund management for the participants/shareholders, the limitation and control of self dealing, conflicts of interest, fraud and other undesirable behaviour of the funds and their managers, and limitations on investments the funds can make.

Insurance companies and pension funds are potentially a significant group of institutional investors. This sector is still in its embryonic stage despite the large number of registered providers of these services. The policy regarding their possibly more active role in the corporate governance of companies should be carefully developed and conditioned on the following:

Clarification of ownership. Existing insurance companies and pension funds are typically a part of financial conglomerates with intermingled and opaque ownership structures. The structure of ownership should be made transparent. Presently only founding shareholders are registered in company registrars, since there is no requirement to register subsequent changes in ownership.

More precise definition of products offered. Providers of insurance and pension services often structure the products they offer in an innovative but non-transparent way. Partly this reflects the particular needs of local markets (for example, one insurance company offers a fixed payment to cover funeral expenses). Partly it reflects the low level of professional skills of the providers of services in an unregulated market. A number of the pension plans currently being offered on the market are good examples of these.

Better definition of permitted investment portfolios. Although the Law on Insurance stipulates that the portfolio of insurance companies should be sound, diversified and liquid, the actual operations of insurance companies are not, in practice, in accord with these principles. The insurers appear to keep most of their resources on deposit in related banks. Moreover insurance companies are not subject to the same supervisory oversight that banks are. In fact, some insurance providers are performing many of the functions of banks – accepting deposits and offering short-term loans. In addition, some insurance companies are tightly tied up with the banking sector as they provide credit insurance services. This means that they put both policy holders' and depositors' funds at significant risk. It also represents a potentially serious shifting of credit risk to a sector beyond the reach of bank regulators.

It would be advisable to start with strengthening institutional investors (investment funds, insurance companies and pension funds) in their capacity to act as passive portfolio investors. This could be achieved in steps – by starting with limited risk exposure and restricted portfolio composition, and gradually increasing the proportion of risky assets (including shares) that they keep. The involvement of institutional investors in more active corporate governance functions of companies in which they invest should be allowed once markets are liquid enough to provide a proper valuation of portfolios, and once the necessary skills are developed in portfolio management and in administrative supervision of financial institutions.

Long-term perspective: Can Latvia attract foreign portfolio investors?

A capital market is only as good as investors, particularly foreign, believe it is. In Latvia the perspective of foreign portfolio investors may be even more relevant than in some other Central and Eastern European countries. For Latvia to thrive it has to become an open economy, which means permitting the free flow of foreign portfolio investments. Latvia may also try to find its niche in capital market services offered to the neighbouring countries, for example, facilitating trade between the FSU and Scandinavia, the Baltics, etc. To achieve these goals, Latvia would have to establish its competitive advantage in comparison with well-established sophisticated and highly efficient markets in London, Frankfurt, etc., as well as the new markets in Central and Eastern Europe.

Foreign investors expect that trading of securities to be safe, and efficient. This requires, in particular, the availability of efficient services of a depository for securities, a clearance and settlement system, a custodian agent, and an information dissemination system. Given the special nature of modern capital markets – an elimination of physical flows of securities and money, and their reliance on technology and communication – localisation of trading systems is of much lesser importance.

Clearing and settlement

International investors are extremely sensitive to settlement safety and speed. While they will take other risks, they are not willing to assume the risk that settlement may fail. The system of dematerialised securities with the two-tier Central Depository seems to suit well Latvian conditions and responds to expectations of an international community. In this context, the objections of some local market participants that the dematerialisation of securities and centralised depository may result in settlement delays and a biased treatment of some market participants must be taken seriously. The concern that the LCD will prefer the RSE transactions and its members at the expense of other market participant should be alleviated by precise procedures guaranteeing equal access to the depository for all legitimate market participants and its strict supervision. Some concerns may however reflect a desire to trade securities outside regulated (unlicensed) markets. This should be clearly rejected as one of the main functions of the Central Depository is to consolidate the market in terms of information flow and dissemination. An effort should be made to explain to the public at large, and potential foreign investors, the consequences of dematerialisation and measures adopted to make the system safe.

Custodian agent

A shortage of reliable custodian services seems to be the most acute institutional bottleneck to attracting foreign investors to Central and Eastern European markets in general. Investors appoint custodian banks for a variety of reasons including confidentiality of transactions, limiting exposure to credit risk, asset protection, gathering information, acting on behalf of an investor during the clearing and settlement process, and communication with the depository. This is particularly true for institutional investors such as mutual or pension funds that often have strict internal audit rules requiring high-standard custodian services. Internationally recognised custodian banks move into countries with emerging stock markets based on a long-term strategic decision to establish a market presence and to deliver custodian services to their international clients. There is an important role for the government in limiting sovereign risk of share ownership and extending risk-related guarantee facilities.

Information availability

The information available to foreign investors regarding specific investment opportunities, market practices, services, foreign exchange, and taxes was traditionally limited and not reliable in the FSU. Information may not be available or reliable because it is not presented in internationally accepted formats, it is not actively marketed to foreign investors, or internationally recognised rating agencies do not rate investments in the country. The promotion of portfolio investment opportunities is not only the responsibility of exchanges and brokerage houses but also of governmental agencies.

CONCLUSIONS – EMERGING CAPITAL MARKETS AS PART OF THE TRANSITION PROCESS

Latvia has entered its fifth year of transition to a market economy. The economy has stabilised but other aspects of its performance remain unsatisfactory; in 1995 the decline of GDP was reversed but GDP is still no more than half of 1990 level. The situation in manufacturing has been particularly severe and its decline has continued. In 1994 output reached only 38 per cent of the 1991 level. The contraction has not been uniform across all branches of industry – the food industry, wood industry, and metallurgy have rebounded well; the largest falls in production have come in light industry and the engineering industry.

The transformation of the economy has been slower than political liberalisation, and progressed differently in particular areas. The country succeeded in fast privatisation of almost all small units mostly in municipal jurisdiction – shops, cafés and restaurants, services were sold or leased. Privatisation of medium and large state enterprises was much slower. Latvia adopted a privatisation approach which requires case-by-case deliberation of each privatisation, no matter how big or small. The adopted policy that each privatisation starts with a strategic investor slows down public offering of shares. Public offering of shares has been originally considered as a way for mass privatisation, using privatisation certificates on the demand side. In reality, there have been only three auctions of shares for certificates, involving in total only 21 companies. These were medium-size companies, not very suitable for being publicly owned, and not very attractive for small investors. There is a serious risk that the supply side of privatisation is becoming a bottleneck of transition.

It appears that Latvia is moving towards a bank-led, control-oriented financial system. The commercial banks, or their subsidiaries, may become major controllers of enterprises and financial institutions. With substantial equity and debt exposure, banks may exert a significant monitoring role, including representation on the boards of directors of companies. Bank control over corporations may not be limited to shareholding alone – banks can control by exercising voting rights on behalf of small investors. This would leave a smaller but still important role for capital markets. Capital markets – as markets for ownership and control rights over firms and assets – will play an essential role in facilitating the restructuring process. Latvia, as in all transition economies, has inherited large companies and organisations in nearly every line of economic activity. In market economies, by contrast, large firms can only survive where technological or other scale economies outweigh the monitoring and control problems inherent in managing them. Privatisation of existing state-owned enterprises is only a first step in the transition; if market reforms are to be successful, privatised enterprises must be profoundly transformed. For example, they must stop production of unprofitable products; adopt better design, production, and marketing techniques; spin off non-essential activities into separate firms; and invest in new products and production facilities. The present universe of several thousand companies will eventually be replaced by a more diversified, but smaller, set of companies.

Notes

1. This chapter is based on a World Bank study prepared by the World Bank staff Gregory Jedrzejczak (Task Manager) and Alex Fleming, in collaboration with Esen Ulgenerk and Eeva Leskinen (World Bank). Walter B. Stahr (Assistant General Counsel, US Securities and Exchange Commission) also contributed to the study. Paul Siegelbaum (World Bank) and Carlis Cerbulis (President of the Riga Stock Exchange) made valuable comments on the final version.
2. This included a canned fish factory (book value of 2 730 000 Ls.) – 25 per cent of shares offered to the public; a transportation company (book value of 2 382 000 Ls.) – 23 per cent offered to the public; an oil storage facility (book value 424 000 Ls.) – 30 per cent of shares offered to the public.
3. Only banks can participate directly in auctions. Non-bank investors may participate through the banks but at end-April 1995 their share was only 6 per cent of outstanding T-bills.
4. A public opinion survey in August 1994 had found that only 2 per cent of the voucher holders were interested in putting their vouchers into investment funds. It was an unfortunate decision that privatisation certificates may be used for many purposes, mainly for buying apartments and for buying shares. In addition, the decision regarding usage of certificates for buying apartments has been postponed, introducing even more confusion into individual decisions of Latvian citizens.
5. Even in the United States, there is now debate about whether the SEC should be combined with the Commodity Futures Trading Commission, the agency responsible for futures regulation.

REFERENCES

FIAS IFC/World Bank (1995) *Latvia – Improving the Business Climate for Strategic and Export Oriented Investors*, April, draft.

Fleming, A. and Talley, S. (1996) *The Latvian Banking Crisis: Lessons Learned*, World Bank Policy Research Paper, (No, 1590) (Washington: World Bank).

Pohl, G., Jedrzejczak, G. and Anderson, R. (1995) *Creating Capital Markets in Central and Eastern Europe*, World Bank Technical Paper No. 295 (Washington DC: World Bank).

11 Enterprise Exit in Lithuania
Gediminas Rainys

INTRODUCTION

Until 1991 Lithuania followed the same economic trajectory as the Soviet Union. The integration into the Soviet networks of production remained the dominant factor of industrial organisation. The final collapse of Soviet central planning, a systemic shock, caused widespread disruption in both trade and financial links, which in turn led to shortages of goods and raw materials, loss of export markets, disfunctioning of payments and monetary arrangements, and a 'wait-and-see' attitude among enterprise managers.

Lithuania, like other former Soviet republics, is plagued by large industrial complexes, effectively multifunctional units that operated in a non-monetary environment. Such complexes cannot be viable in a monetary framework and require not only the transfer of ownership, but also fundamental restructuring. Many companies have internal structural drawbacks, together with equipment and technologies which are both obsolete. In the new monetary framework enterprises started downsizing production capacities and the exit process had begun.

Business exit, from an overall point of view, can be defined as a reduction in the volume of activities, which can be expressed in terms of sales output and by the reduction of employment. From the enterprise point of view, two separate forms of exit can be distinguished, namely gradual or radical. The gradual form of exit is defined here as a process of downsizing; while the radical form of exit is defined as a process of bankruptcy.

This chapter aims to shed some light on the nature and efficiency of both forms of enterprise exit process in Lithuania. Other scholars have examined these issues in Central Europe in the recent past (Belka, 1995; Lainepa and Sutela, 1994; Samonis, 1995). The analysis of both exit forms in this study is based on empirical evidence. Informal exit was analysed from a sample of 71 companies, representing six main branches of industry. About one third of the total of industrial employees in the country are employed in those enterprises and they account for about one third of industrial production. Furthermore, these companies were not split up during the process of privatisation and their data therefore is comparable. The formal exit evidence is based on a sample of 22 bankrupt enterprises. This was the total number of major bankrupt enterprises in Lithuania at the time of research and all of them were included in the study.

As regards the relationship between formal and informal exit, this was one of the research themes pursued. Equally, it was important to explain the large numbers involved in informal exit, whereas formal exits were less evident.

INFORMAL EXIT

The process of gradual exit started at the beginning of the transition. The point of departure in Lithuania's case was 1990, later than in Vysegrad countries. The transitional period in Lithuania actually started in 1991. It is quite difficult to evaluate the general decline in Lithuanian industry during the period since then. Even official statistics do not provide comparable data about the longer-term trends of industrial production. There are several reasons for that, including changes in methodology and the reclassification of industrial sectors, together with the influence of recent hyper-inflation which affects the comparability of indicators. Finally, there were three currency units in Lithuania during the period analysed, which also complicates the evaluation of the trends.

The indices of industrial output changes are shown in Table 11.1. In 1994, Lithuanian industry produced only one fifth in comparison to the output volume of four years before. This is an unexpectedly large drop. In order to set this in the context of large scale enterprise exit, Table 11.2 shows the exit volumes for the 71 sample enterprises in the largest Lithuanian industry branches. In Table 11.2 the data concerning employees is comparable for both 1990 and 1994. However, when analysing the

Table 11.1   The indices of industrial output

	1991	*1992*	*1993*	*1994*
The decline in Lithuanian industrial output				
(previous year = 100)	–4.90	–51.60	–46.00	–20.00
1990 = 100	95.10	46.10	25.00	20.00

Table 11.2   The exit volumes in the largest industry branches

		Number of employees		Sales output Thousand LTL	
Branch	Enterprises	1990	1994	1990	1994
Food production	14	16,663	12,336	891,338	691,434
Light industry	15	34,441	23,091	993,976	463,493
Timber processing	8	12,137	6,649	292,403	139,663
Chemical industry	5	8,936	5,790	248,207	406,332
Construction materials	9	9,301	6,078	168,734	181,934
Machinery and equipment production	20	57,548	32,122	1,106,698	529,775
Total	71	139,026	86,066	3,701,356	2,412,631

trends in sales output, it is important to take into consideration two factors, namely hyper-inflation and currency reform. The data about sales output and employee numbers in selected branches, after eliminating the influence of above mentioned factors, is given in Table 11.3.

It is evident that 1994 sales output volumes for the companies analysed constituted only 26 per cent of the 1990 level. This number is similar to the estimated general decline in industrial output, namely about 20 per cent of 1990 level. Volumes of industrial production during the time of transition declined and the current level of production constitutes only one fourth of the level when Lithuanian industry commenced the transition process. These numbers characterise the environmental context of the exit process. It is clear, however, that the picture is quite different when the exit process is evaluated in terms of the changes in the number of employees which fell by about one third and constituted 62 per cent of the 1990 employment level. A survey of incumbent managers shows that the number of people employed exceeds the necessary level in all industrial companies. On the evidence of Table 11.3, there is still a considerable volume of labour shedding to occur.

FORMAL EXIT

During 1995, either by the decision of a court or of creditors, bankruptcy proceedings were initiated for 62 Lithuanian enterprises. Because the formal bankruptcy process only started in 1994, it was only really beginning to gain momentum in 1995. There were more cases of bankruptcy in

Table 11.3 Sales output and indices of employee numbers
in selected industry branches in 1994

Branch	1994 Employees (1990 = 100)	1994 Sales output (1990 = 100)
Food production	74	31
Light industry	67	19
Timber processing	55	19
Chemical industry	65	65
Construction materials	65	43
Machinery and equipment production	56	20
Overall	62	26

Lithuania although the majority of them were company bankruptcies. The range of activities represented in the sample is very broad and includes food processing, construction materials, machinery production, trade, and services. At that stage, no particular industry can be singled out as especially prone to bankruptcy. However, an analysis of the main markets for the enterprises shows that 14 out of 29 analysed product groups were mainly exported to former Soviet Union countries (FSU). Of this number six product groups were sold to FSU markets solely and they caused most severe problems due to trade disruption and the overall instability in the East.

In surveying the enterprises, no fewer than eighteen factors were mentioned as the main causes of financial difficulties, but four of them were regarded as the most important when measured by frequency of incidence in the sample, namely

● Inconvertible currencies of the FSU countries: 20.4 per cent
● Decreased purchasing power of local consumers: 16.7 per cent
● Decreased demand in the East: 15.7 per cent
● High costs of credits: 13.0 per cent
● Other reasons (taxes, energy prices, etc.): 34.2 per cent

As indicated above, the two main causes of business distress and subsequent insolvency are problems with FSU partners. This is not surprising in the light of the high level of distorted, Soviet-type integration which was inherited by Lithuania after the collapse of the USSR. It should be noted that the problem of currency convertibility in the newly independent countries of the FSU was separately mentioned. Recent years have witnessed the emergence of the commercial banking system. In 1992 monetary shock was particularly severe because annual inflation was more than 1,000 per cent. Every day by which accounts settlements were delayed brought further large financial losses. In the majority of enterprises studied, the severe financial difficulties started in 1992. Among the other reasons given, tax policy, ineffective business partners, growing energy prices and other reasons were mentioned. These reasons were those cited by the managers and administrators of the enterprises and therefore have their personal bias built in to them. In contrast, among the causes of bankruptcy, creditors more often claim that the incompetence of the former managers is a major factor.

Turning to the financial position of these enterprises, the total debts (excluding wage arrears) to outside creditors remained almost unchanged at the end of 1994 as compared with beginning of the year and respectively constituted 90.8 and 88.4 million LTL. This static situation can be explained in several ways. First of all, after the initiation of bankruptcy proceedings, fines were no longer added to the current loans to the company. Second, the implementation of re-organisation projects approved by either the creditors or by the courts often achieve positive results in stabilising the company's finances. Third, the liquidation procedure is not applied to the majority of bankrupt enterprises and as a result the quantity of debt decreases significantly. The total debts of the sample enterprises to outside creditors was distributed as follows:

- Commercial banks (principal debt): 35.7 per cent
- Suppliers: 29.1 per cent
- State budget and social security (principal debt): 18.3 per cent
- Delayed interest payments and fines: 16.9 per cent

The majority of the enterprises had liabilities to a number of creditors, including banks, suppliers, state, employees. Asked the question as to what debts had triggered the bankruptcy proceedings, the incidence of responses was as follows:

- Late salary payment: 38 per cent
- Delay in paying back debt to banks: 22 per cent
- Delay in paying interest and fines to banks: 19 per cent
- Delayed payments to suppliers: 12 per cent
- Failure to fulfil liabilities to the state: 9 per cent

As indicated, salary payments emerge as a dominant factor as company employees are keen to be paid the salaries they have earned. Tax inspectors and social security institutions have tended to play a rather passive role in the initiation of bankruptcy proceedings even though these institutions have the same legal right to get back at least part of their debts during the bankruptcy process.

Bankruptcy law in Lithuania foresees the possibility of implementing bankruptcy proceedings in either a judicial or an extra-judicial manner. The extra-judicial procedure was in fact implemented in two-thirds of bankruptcy cases studied. One of the reasons for this is the poor preparation of the courts and the fact that the processing capacity of courts is also very low. However, it is probable that the role of the courts in bankruptcy proceedings will increase in the future.

In the majority of cases analysed (12), managers were changed after the initiation of bankruptcy proceedings. The same general manager stayed in three cases, but in eight others general managers were changed. The rest of the enterprises (9) had not yet made their final decision concerning bankruptcy proceedings when the study was completed. Enterprise bankruptcy law in Lithuania is rather flexible in the application of various bankruptcy proceedings. For example, of the 13 cases where decisions had been made to implement specific bankruptcy proceedings, re-organisation plans were approved for eight enterprises; decisions to liquidate were made for three; and a rehabilitation decision was approved for one. However, upon unsuccessful completion, one type of bankruptcy processes can revert to another as a result of a decision of court or as the outcome of a meeting of creditors.

None of the enterprises examined was sold as an integral unit. There were some evident reasons for this. Firstly, there are no growing industries in Lithuania and therefore there is no need for new production facilities and little demand for them. Moreover, recovering industrial enterprises use their reserves to expand production rather than acquire new enterprises. Secondly, the amounts of foreign direct investment are small, and there is little demand for the production facilities offered from that source. Two enterprises indicated that all their assets were sold out in pieces. When this occurs it usually means that fewer financial resources are recovered to satisfy the claims of creditors. Two of the enterprises indicated that they utilised more than 90 per cent of their production capacity and one enterprise utilised 60 per cent. All the others used less than 20 per cent of their production capacities. These ratios indicate that many enterprises have major structural problems and it is entirely possible that not all of them will be able to prepare and implement viable reorganisation projects. Some enterprises will simply have to be liquidated.

Only one of the enterprises succeeded in attracting large, additional investment, whereas two received credits after the approval of their re-organisation plans. It is frequently not possible to reorganise activity without additional external financing and one of the most important and difficult tasks of any administrator is to prove to outside investors the via-bility of a re-organisation plan in these circumstances. None of the enter-prises with approved re-organisation plans foresaw any increase in their numbers employed. Despite the fact that all the enterprises had already significantly reduced the number of employees, they all planned to reduce it even further by 10 per cent and 40 per cent. This gives further evidence that there is a high level of hidden unemployment in Lithuania and that the problems of the labour market will become even more severe.

The interests of various groups in the bankruptcy process are multi-dimensional and, in part, contradictory. There are possibilities for com-mercial banks to recover at least part of the debts owed to them. But during the bankruptcy process interest no longer accumulates and fines are stopped. When the implementation of re-organisation plans is successful, the owners are able to pay back the enterprise's debts, and the business survives. But if the case reverts to liquidation they lose everything. Employees are declared redundant as a result of liquidation, and many of them are usually laid off during reorganisation. Employees who lose their jobs evaluate the bankruptcy process in a negative way. But those who are retained and get their salaries in time see the rationale behind it. In inter-views, several administrators mentioned their moral satisfaction with the job well done, not least because it raised their professional prestige.

Enterprise bankruptcy proceedings in countries operating in a market economy are an inevitable feature of structural change. The comparison of the situation in Lithuania with practice in Central European countries shows that the restructuring process in the majority of enterprises is just starting. Bankruptcy proceedings will be one of the most radical forms of enterprise restructuring and will probably be adopted for a significantly larger number of economic subjects in the future.

CASE STUDIES

Case A

This fuel equipment enterprise located in Vilnius provides a good illustra-tion of downsizing in the Lithuanian machinery and equipment sector. The company produces fuel pumps for the Minsk Engine Plant, fuel injectors for the Charkov Engine Plant and brake cylinders for the VAZ plant. The integration level into the FSU economy is still very high (see Table 11.4). The level of downsizing which has occurred is evident from the decline in employment and sales.

The company has serious structural flaws, obsolete equipment and technological stock. Due to the low relative share of labour in total production costs it is virtually impossible to compete on the basis of low labour costs alone. There is a need for very substantial investment for the introduction of new technologies. Meanwhile, the financial situation of customers in the FSU remains very difficult and so barter trade agreements are deployed to set up transactions with customers in the FSU. The low level of contacts with Western markets has not enabled the management to learn marketing, modern management techniques, and so on. In effect, due to differences in technological processes Case A company types are constrained both technologically and geographically.

Table 11.4   Case A

(1) Product destinations (%)

Markets	1991	1992	1993	1994	1995
Lithuania	11.4	5.2	5.3	4.0	5.0
CIS	87.1	94.1	94.5	95.5	93.0
Others	1.5	0.7	0.2	0.5	2.0

(2) Employees

	1991	1992	1993	1994	1995
Employees	6,537	6,322	5,334	4,500	3,600

(3) Product Mix

Products	1991	1992	1993	1994	1995
Fuel pumps ('000)	306.4	272.9	222.8	120.0	120.0
Fuel injectors ('000)	1,371.7	1,110.7	829.9	630.6	700.0
Precision steel castings (in tonnes)	1,679.0	1,222.0	1,009.0	600.0	590.0

Case B

This case illustrates a formal exit in the food sector. In 1994 a bankruptcy case was initiated against Alytus Food, a 47 per cent state owned food processing enterprise employing about 800 people. The total value of the assets of the enterprise amounted to LTL 18.3 million while the total debt was some LTL 14 million. In this instance, it was not the stock but the flow measure which was used to trigger bankruptcy. The value of mortgaged assets was about LTL 15 million and more than half of the debt was owed to the Agricultural Bank. LTL 4.2 million were owed to some 2,600 (predominantly) small farmers. By 1995 two meetings of creditors had taken place. The main creditors, the social security fund, heat suppliers, an investment company Dzukijos Maistas, considered that only by the continuation of production, rather than liquidation, could the situation be retrieved.

The enterprise had three main divisions. Plans were initiated to sell the commercial complex, including a hotel and public house, for LTL 2 million and a buyer was sought for the administrative building. The sale of nonessential assets brought LTL 800 000. In order to release funds owed, Alytus Food initiated bankruptcy cases against its debtors, which owed LTL 5 million. The former director of Alytus Food believes that its assets, though valued at only LTL 18.3 million, were really worth about LTL 33 million. In his opinion, the financial distress was caused by payment problems between enterprises (especially those in the CIS); the unstable exchange rate of Litas against convertible currencies; and the credit policies of the Lithuanian banks. In the opinion of the appointed administrator, bankruptcy had its internal causes as well and as causes of the bankruptcy were investigated, some unexpected events happened, including the arrest of the former general manager by the economic police. For example, the police had found about 80 tonnes of spoilt meat products which, according to contract, had been transferred to other enterprises which were not able to sell it. The investigation showed that many similar contracts had brought losses to Alytus Food. As a result of these scandals, the enterprise lost confidence in the eyes of its partners and, consequently, lost its markets.

There is evidence that elements of fraud can also be observed in many other Lithuanian bankruptcy cases. The following appear to be among the most common examples:

- Private businessmen take credits from commercial banks secured on the enterprise's assets. When the loans are not paid back in time, the banks have claims on industrial enterprise which provided the security.

- Incumbent managers of enterprises establish their personal companies and thus engage in double business. In some cases, the main point of such activity has been to channel profit into a personal company while ascribing expenditures and losses to the main enterprise. In some other cases, such managers transferred valuable assets to their private firms.
- Due to the inconvertibility of FSU currencies, enterprises holding them try to use barter trade with those countries or even undertake transactions which do not make a profit but rather are designed to convert Eastern currencies. However, in many cases, while the money was paid to Eastern partners, nothing was received in turn.
- Enterprises take high-interest bank credits and mortgage their assets but they do not have effective plans to use those credits. Thus, when the time comes to repay the loans it becomes clear that there is no money and an enterprise gets into debts.

In the opinion of experts, creditors complain about the legal basis not being strong enough to gain access to hidden assets. The current situation shows that in many cases of bankruptcy, owners or managers of enterprises often try to separate valuable assets from the claims of creditors in order to use them for their own purposes.

THE ROLE OF COMMERCIAL BANKS

The major problems of the Lithuanian banking system are closely linked to industrial restructuring. The large quantities of debt within enterprises, together with those owed to the state (municipal) budget and the social security fund, leave no possibilities for the effective re-organisation and modernisation of most enterprises. Although Lithuanian commercial banks have become more cautious in providing loans for loss-making enterprises, the amount of bad debt carried forward from earlier years is very considerable.

On the one hand, the financial system constraints inhibit enterprise growth, leading to their possible collapse, especially those recently privatised. On the other hand, further borrowing by enterprises which are already non-viable creates bad loans and thus spurs insolvency in the banking system. Bankruptcies and liquidations of some newly established commercial banks gives evidence to this. However, in most cases the evidence suggests that the larger commercial banks have greater prospects for survival, while many industrial enterprises are already on the verge of collapse.

Following the decline in interest rates on bank loans and the emergence of new investment opportunities, commercial banks are beginning to define their strategies as universal banks, by choosing sectors and enterprises for investment and selecting reliable clients with whom they can co-operate over the longer term. Most often banks use both re-negotiation and the roll-over of credits in their relations with debtors. Efforts have been made to ensure the disclosure of the asset and liability positions of banks using new methods of commercial bank regulation. For example, a new classification system has been introduced whereby bad and doubtful loans are very precisely defined and it is required that over a three-year period commercial banks must form reserves from profit in order to cover bad loans.

Since the new law for commercial banks was passed in November 1994, they have been allowed to invest up to 10 per cent of their authorised capital in new and already functioning enterprises. Thus, legislation has given banks an opportunity to control debtor enterprises, to be involved in their management and in the preparation of re-organisation plans. Among other issues, this had created opportunities for debt-equity swaps.

Commercial banks are not interested in precipitating bankruptcy procedures. There are several main reasons for this, including the absence of capital markets, the impossibility of selling company assets, legal concerns relating to the market value of assets taken as collateral, and the lack of the experienced lawyers, judges, and administrators in bankruptcy procedures. In general commercial banks avoid triggering bankruptcy by prolonging the terms of loans. However, with the new stricter regulations it is not possible for banks to prolong these beyond 180 days, since afterwards a loan is to be judged as a bad loan. Not surprisingly therefore, a common practise is the re-negotiation and roll-over of credits.

CONCLUSIONS: THE RELATIONSHIP BETWEEN FORMAL AND INFORMAL EXIT

As noted, downsizing of enterprises can be considered as occurring as a direct result of the transformation processes in the economy. Both a legal framework and incentives have to be available in order to turn informal exit into a formal bankruptcy process. In the Lithuanian case, declining production levels have often resulted in informal exit. According to official data, there had only been 62 cases of formal exit in the industrial sector by mid-1995. The question then arises as to why there have not been more formal exits. There are several reasons for this.

The first is the low demand of bankrupt enterprises' assets due to the absence of growth in the industrial sector, and the underdevelopment of capital market. Recovering industrial enterprises use their reserves to increase present capacity. The low volume of foreign capital investment is also a factor and as a result the supply of assets (especially production buildings) exceeds demand. The continuation of voucher privatisation has also played a part. There are two main ways to acquire fixed assets; namely their privatisation or purchase (including from bankrupt enterprises). On the whole it is better to purchase privatised assets because the price is usually much lower. There has been no evidence of bankrupt state enterprises being privatised. The second set of reasons relates to both human factors and institutional capacity. For example, the qualifications of judges and administrators is below the required level. Moreover, as a consequence of distributional privatisation, managers of enterprises are often their owners as well. In the case of formal bankruptcy, the assets of the enterprises would be transferred to new owners and therefore taken away from the managers. This is one of the key reasons why managers are not enthusiastic about the initiation of formal bankruptcy proceedings.

The third issue concerns the passive role of creditors. The government, as a major creditor, is afraid of the social crisis which could happen following a large number of bankruptcy proceedings. It also feels the pressure of various interest groups representing industrialists. These factors result in soft budgetary constraints and the postponement of debt payments to the budget and social security fund. It should be mentioned that state employees which represent state interests are also rather passive. For example, in the case of state enterprises collecting debts, there is the view in some quarters that it is not worth much effort because 'money moves from one pocket of the state jacket to the other'.

As far as commercial banks are concerned, they are often not concerned with the initiation of formal bankruptcy proceedings even though they often give mortgaged credits and actually control the situation. Several factors explain bank behaviour. First of all, it is difficult to sell assets and recover money. Secondly, if banks want to get mortgaged assets it is not necessary to initiate bankruptcy proceedings as this can be achieved by following other laws. Thirdly, bad loans damage the bank's financial indicators, hence their preference for the use roll-over credits rather than the write-off of bad debts to losses. Turning to the debts owed to suppliers, it has to be noted that Lithuania is small country and very often the suppliers of raw materials or goods and the buyers of production are legal persons from other countries, most often from the CIS. This fact in itself can complicate debt settlements.

In an early stage of economic transformation there is actually no difference between formal and informal (unconventional) exit. This statement is illustrated by the comparison of two Lithuanian electronics sector enterprises: Tauras and Venta. The Venta case is a typical example of formal exit, while the Tauras case is a characteristic example of informal exit. The various problems of the enterprises' activities are compared below.

Output decline: both enterprises have experienced significantly reduced output. No signs of recovery are yet visible.

Management: the former deputy general manager was appointed as administrator of the bankrupt Venta. He actually acts as the general manager. The managers of Tauras remained unchanged. The net situation in both enterprises is very much the same.

Debt relief: Venta bankruptcy proceedings resulted in a temporary relief from debt service. Tauras was relieved by the government via a decree postponing the payment of debts to both the state budget and the social security fund.

New investment: both enterprises are negotiating with potential foreign partners.

Organisational structure: Venta has not changed its organisational structure. Tauras started the implementation of a so-called 'management reform', which mainly resulted in spinning off 18 smaller units. Tauras itself turned into a holding company which owns stock representing from 20 to 80 per cent of equity in all 18 enterprises. All the debts were dumped onto the holding company, and the new enterprises were made debt-free. If Tauras had gone bankrupt before the 'management reform', it would have been responsible for its debts with its total assets. In the situation which now prevails it can only be held responsible for the percentage of its equity holding company in the 18 enterprises. All the creditors knew that the debts were dumped onto the holding company but they were passive and did not have any alternative proposals. Currently there is a probability that not all of the Tauras enterprise will become formally bankrupt, but several of the new enterprises might.

Ownership structure: both enterprises are joint stock corporations with a share of state capital smaller than 50 per cent.

Multifunctionality of enterprises: both enterprises own many supplementary productional capacities, and social assets which can be sold. Venta has sold the employees' canteen facilities and established a trading centre. The success of the deal was caused by the convenient location of the building for trade. Stocks of both companies are not yet publicly traded.

These examples suggest that in this initial stage of economic transformation there is actually no difference between formal and informal exit. And due to above mentioned reasons the agents involved are often not very interested in the initiation of bankruptcy proceedings or movement from informal to formal exit.

REFERENCES

Belka, M. *et al.* (1995), Enterprise Adjustment in Poland: Evidence from a Survey of 200 Private, Privatized and State-owned firms, CEPR Discussion Paper 233.

Lainepa, S. and Sutela, P. (1994) The Baltic Economies in Transition, (Helsinki, Bank of Finland).

Samonis, V. (1995) Transforming the Lithuanian Economy: From Moscow to Vilnius and From Plan to Market, Centre for Social and Economic Research (Warsaw).

SECTION THREE

SECTORAL EXAMPLES

12 Problems Facing the Development of Small and Medium-sized Manufacturing Firms in the Baltic States[1]

David Smallbone, Urve Venesaar, Laimonis Rumpis and Danute Budreikate

INTRODUCTION

One of the issues facing Central and East European (C&EE) countries in the transformation from centrally planned into market-based economies is the need to develop a small and medium-sized enterprise (SME) sector. The potential role of SMEs includes generating employment and thus contributing to absorbing any labour surpluses which result from economic restructuring; using privatised property for production; contributing to the development of a diversified economic structure (including their role as suppliers to larger companies); and, in some cases, as a source of innovation (for a more detailed discussion see Smallbone, 1995). Moreover, it can be argued that the development of *manufacturing* SMEs is of particular significance in the transformation process because it is manufacturing (together with some parts of the service sector) that constitutes the economic base[2] thus emphasising the potential role of the sector in generating external income and thereby contributing to the growth of the economy (Gudgin, 1982). In addition, the multiplier benefits of a given expansion in the manufacturing sector is likely to be greater than a similar growth in service sector activity. In the Baltic States there are additional factors which justify paying particular attention to manufacturing SMEs in policy terms. This is because of the need to modernise and re-orientate the manufacturing sector of the economy as part of a wider process of restructuring

227

that involves a closure of some activities on the one hand, and the development of new activities on the other.

During the 1990s the share of GDP represented by mining and manufacturing has declined in all three countries: in Estonia from 25 per cent in 1992 to 19 per cent in 1994, in Latvia from 26 per cent to 20 per cent and in Lithuania from 37 per cent to 20 per cent. This structural shift is also reflected in the changing structure of employment so that between 1992 and 1994 the share of employment in manufacturing decreased from 31 per cent to 27 per cent in Estonia; 24 per cent to 19 per cent in Latvia; 27 per cent to 20 per cent in Lithuania (Central Statistical Bureau of Latvia, 1995; Lithuanian Department of Statistics, 1995a; Eesti Bank, 1995). At the same time the share of economic activity (in terms of both GDP and employment) represented by the trade, financial, social and personal services sectors increased in all three countries (Venesaar and Hachey, 1995; Latvijas, 1995; Lithuanian Department of Statistics, 1995b). Although the orientation towards manufacturing under the centrally planned system means that a relative shift between manufacturing and services is to be expected as transformation to a market based system develops, it is clear that in some sectors (e.g. textiles; leather and footwear; wood products; paper products) a decline in output has occurred since 1991 which reflects a decline in competitiveness as well as the effects of losing ties with the former Soviet Union.

The problem for the manufacturing sector in the Baltic States is to adjust from a highly concentrated structure based on mass production methods and relatively inflexible production processes, to a more flexible production system. During the socialist period, manufacturing in the Baltic States was integrated into a technological chain and locked into markets in the former Soviet Union which resulted in a high level of military orientated production at the expense of consumer goods. As a consequence, there is now a need to radically restructure the manufacturing base in order to develop a more flexible system of production which is responsive to changes in consumer demand and the forces of market competition. Clearly within such a context, the potential role of SMEs is considerable because of their inherent flexibility, although to fulfil such a role in practice will almost certainly require more than a 'laissez-faire' response on the part of government. The loss of traditional markets, the effects of recession on demand conditions in the domestic market, together with the effects of trade liberalisation on the level of foreign competition, combine to produce a relatively hostile external environment for enterprise development. This is exacerbated by the competitive disadvantage which results from the underdeveloped nature of the producer services sector so that whilst there are undoubtedly new opportunities for manufacturing SMEs in the Baltic States, the external environment also contains many threats which are contributing to considerable turbulence within the sector.

Transforming a centrally planned, socialist society into a liberal, democratic, market-based system involves fundamental social change as well as economic restructuring, which SMEs can also contribute to. The creation of an entrepreneurial class is part of that process as the Lithuanian government has explicitly recognised in the stated aims of its programme for SME development, one of which is: 'the development of a new category of businessman in society' (Lithuanian Ministry of Economic Affairs, 1994). SME development can also contribute to the process of privatisation and/or the restitution of property. Thus the role of SMEs in the transformation process, and thus the case for policy support, extends beyond a purely economic rationale.

However, it is clear that if the contribution of SMEs to the development of the Baltic economies (and other economies in transition) is to be maximised, it will be necessary to take steps to improve small business survival rates and also to increase the growth performance of those firms that are able to survive. Raising new firm formation rates may be a first step in the process of transition but the longer-term development of competitive economies in Eastern Europe will be affected by the number of new firms which survive and grow. In Poland there is evidence that the initial explosion of entrepreneurial activity has been followed by a period in which new firm formation rates have fallen and there has also been an increase in the failure rates of existing firms (Piasecki and Rogut, 1993). The birth rate of enterprises has also fallen in the Baltic States: in Estonia from 13 enterprises per 1000 inhabitants in 1993 to 9 enterprises per 1000 inhabitants in 1994; in Lithuania from 10 enterprises per 1000 inhabitants in 1992 to 7 enterprises in 1993 and 1994, although in Latvia the birth rate of enterprises has remained stable (12–13 enterprises per 1000 inhabitants) during the last three years. Referring specifically to Estonia, Lumiste (1993) has described the high proportion of enterprises facing bankruptcy, stressing that future economic development depends on being able to identify SMEs with growth potential and then providing policy support to enable them to exploit opportunities for growth. It is this that provides the policy context for the study with which this chapter is concerned.

This chapter is based on a study of the factors influencing the survival and growth of manufacturing SMEs in Poland and the Baltic States, funded under the EU's Phare (ACE94) Programme. The project includes a survey of 300 SME owners and managers in the Baltic States (100 each in each country) that was completed in 1995. However, this particular contribution is focused on an analysis of the external environment in which SME development is taking place in Baltic countries, highlighting those elements that have particular implications for the nature and pace of SME development; empirical evidence is only used where it helps to clarify the distinctiveness of SME development in Baltic countries.

The rest of the chapter is divided into three sections: firstly, a summary description of the main characteristics of SME development in the Baltic States to date; secondly by a discussion of the key elements in the external environment affecting SME development; finally, an attempt to identify the main policy issues raised by the analysis.

CHARACTERISTICS OF SME DEVELOPMENT IN THE BALTIC STATES

As in other C&EE economies, the 1990s has seen a rapid increase in the number of SMEs in the Baltic States and also in their contribution to the economy. In all three Baltic countries, the total number of registered enterprises has increased in the early 1990s, reflecting a marked increase in the number of private businesses, most of which are small. For example, in Estonia new firm birth rates rose from 3 per 1000 in 1990 to 10–13 per 1000 in 1992[3] although, as mentioned previously, these rates have subsequently fallen. According to the Business Registers at the beginning of 1995, about 55 000 businesses were registered in Estonia, 86 000 in Latvia and 120 000 in Lithuania. Almost 90 per cent of the businesses were privately owned in all three countries although there are differences in the size distribution of privately owned firms: for example, in Estonia in 1994 more than 80 per cent of the total number of enterprises are micro-enterprises (1–9 employees), whereas in Latvia and Lithuania comparable estimates are 50 per cent and 60 per cent respectively (Venesaar and Hachey, 1995).

Although gaps in the statistics mean that it is not possible to determine the share of economic activity or employment contributed by SMEs precisely, available estimates confirm the continuous expansion of the SME sector in the Baltic States during the transition period. As a result, the number of registered enterprises has reached 39 per 1000 inhabitants in Estonia, 34 in Latvia and 32 in Lithuania, compared with an EU average of 45 (EIM, 1995). Whilst this describes a rapid pace of change and the growth in the number of registered businesses undoubtedly does reflect a sharp increase in private sector business activity in all three countries, the figures do exaggerate the extent of the convergence with western economies because of the number of registered enterprises that are not actually trading. Nevertheless, the share of total employment in SMEs is undoubtedly growing. For example, in Estonia it has been estimated that by the end of 1994 small private firms employing less than 100 persons, accounted for 40.6 per cent of total employment compared with 25.8 per cent in 1992 (HLT, 1995). By contrast in the EU in 1990, firms employing less than 100 represented 99.5 per cent of the total number of enterprises, accounting for 56.7 per cent of total employment and 49.2 per cent of total output by value (EIM, 1994). Although firms employing less than 100 dominate in all sectors, as in western economies it is the trade and services sectors where the proportion is the highest.

In the case of Estonia, most registered firms are SMEs although their share of both total employment and output is considerably less than their numbers would suggest. Table 12.1 shows that whilst manufacturing firms employing less than 100 represent 97 per cent of all manufacturing enterprises, they account for just 31 per cent of total manufacturing employment and 29 per cent of total output. This compares with the 12 EU member states where 98 per cent of the total number of manufacturing enterprises account for 43 per cent of manufacturing employment. However, it should be noted that in the Estonian case, many of the large scale enterprises are still state owned which means that SMEs account for a higher proportion of output and employment generated from private sector activity than Table 12.1 suggests. Despite the fact that industrial production in Estonia declined considerably during the 1990–93 period, the number of manufacturing enterprises increased markedly to reach 8200 by 1994 compared with about 300 in 1987. Most of this increase is accounted for by an increase in the number of SMEs.

Table 12.1   Characteristics of manufacturing enterprises in Estonia by employment size groups (October 1994)

	0–9 %	*10–99* %	*100–499* %	*500+* %	*Total* %
No. of enterprises	81.20	15.70	2.50	0.60	100
No. of employees	5.50	25.70	30.00	38.80	100
Turnover	8.40	20.80	40.50	30.30	100
Cost of fixed assets	6.70	19.90	33.10	40.30	100

Source: Venesaar and Vitsur (1995).

At the same time, the survival rates of newly established firms tends to be low although even in a mature western economy, such as Britain, approximately 36 per cent of new firms do not survive the first three years after start-up (Stanworth and Gray, 1991). Nevertheless, in the Baltic economies the available evidence suggests that survival rates are a good deal lower than in western Europe. This can be illustrated with reference to Estonia and Lithuania, where only 25 per cent of firms on the Business Register in 1991/2 were still in business in 1995. Although a 'non-survival' rate of 75 per cent is significantly above that which is typical in mature western economies, it must be remembered that some of the businesses registered in 1991/2 will never have traded. Others will have re-registered because of changes that have been made to the legal requirements for registration (such as an increase in minimum capital requirements) which results in some existing enterprises re-registering under different legal forms. As a consequence, survival rates based on analysis of the business registers are not a reliable basis for estimating small business survival rates in the Baltic economies. Moreover, even if it could be demonstrated that the death rates of small firms are higher in the Baltic States than is typical in the West, this would not be altogether surprising in view of the fact that small private firms in these countries are almost all very young firms. In western economies such as Britain, it is the more mature SMEs that are the most resilient and the failure rate of businesses decreases rapidly following the first three years after start-up. Thus although a relatively hostile external environment may be contributing to higher rates of failure in Baltic economies, an additional factor is the age structure of firms since most of them have been founded since 1990. However, the real problem in this respect in the Baltic countries at present, is to obtain an accurate picture of what the rates of 'failure' actually are.

There are marked regional imbalances in the distribution of SMEs in Baltic countries although the spatially uneven nature of SME development is also a feature of most western economies (Mason, 1991; Reynolds, Storey and Westhead, 1994). In Estonia for example, a disproportionate share of SMEs is located in the Greater Tallinn region (Tallinn and surrounding counties) which in 1995 accounted for 54 per cent of all registered businesses but only 29 per cent of the total population. In June 1995, when there were about 40 registered enterprises per 1000 inhabitants at the national level, spatial variations ranged from 18 per 1000 inhabitants in Ida-Viru to 73 per 1000 inhabitants in Tallinn, which reflects a marked inter-regional and urban-rural contrast in the rates of new business formation. The situation is similar in Latvia, where more than half the total number of enterprises are registered in the capital Riga and its surrounding county. In Lithuania by contrast, enterprises are less heavily concentrated in the capital and its environs than in its Baltic neighbours: about 20 per cent of registered enterprises in Lithuania were in Vilnius and 16 per cent in Kaunas at the end of 1994. In fact, the number of registered firms per 1000 inhabitants in Vilnius is below the national average in Lithuania: 26 compared with about 32 enterprises per 1000 inhabitants nationally. In Lithuania, the highest rates are found in the resort regions (for example 117 enterprises in Neringa, 70 in Palanga).

Although in some respects the pattern of SME development in Baltic countries shows some similar features to that in western economies (such as its regional imbalance; high rates of non-survival among new and very young firms) in other respects the conditions experienced in the early stages of transformation make it more distinctive. In Lithuania for example, it has been found that many small firms do not have a single or clear product focus, which means that entrepreneurs are often engaged in several different activities, some of which may be based on individual trade deals (Segal *et al.,* 1995). Such a pattern can be explained in terms of the uncertainties that exist in the external environment and the need to generate a quick return on capital employed. Multiple ownership is another feature of the development of small private enterprises in the Baltic countries during transition. For example, in our survey of 300 manufacturing SMEs, 54 per cent of firms had three or more owners; 41 per cent had four or more; 17.5 per cent had ten or more. This compares with our parallel survey of SMEs in the same sectors in Poland where a longer tradition of private enterprise exists; in our Polish sample, only 20 per cent of firms had three or more owners. Finally, in comparison with mature market economies where apart from a small number of management buyouts, most SMEs are founded as completely new businesses, in economies in transition privatisation is also an important contributory factor to the process of business formation. On the basis of our survey evidence, a substantial number of surveyed firms were founded as a direct result of privatisation. There is also evidence to show that the actual form of privatisation used in a country can influence the pattern of SME ownership that develops. Although the median number of owners was 3.0 in all three Baltic countries, in Lithuania the voucher system that was used for privatisation contributed to a very high number of owners in a minority of firms surveyed; for example, in eight firms the number of owners were between 182 and 10 000.

KEY FEATURES OF THE EXTERNAL ENVIRONMENT
AFFECTING THE NATURE AND PACE OF SME DEVELOPMENT
IN THE BALTIC STATES

Macro-economic conditions

Low domestic purchasing power limits demand for goods and services
from a large part of the population. Low purchasing power means that
the structure of demand is characterised by a high percentage of income
being spent on basic goods such as food, housing, clothes: an estimated
60 per cent in the case of Estonia (Venesaar, 1995). Low average income
levels (US$ 190 per month in Estonia, US$ 150 in Latvia and US$ 110
in Lithuania in the first quarter of 1995) are a particular constraint on the
development of SMEs producing niche-focused consumer goods that are
a characteristic of mature western economies. Low average income
levels combined with the small domestic population of Baltic
economies, means that SMEs attempting to produce high value added
products, are faced with the need to look to export markets at a relatively early stage in their development. This can place heavy demands
on their limited resource base, particularly in terms of management and
financial resources.

Macro-economic conditions also act as a disincentive to entrepreneurs
to make long-term investments. Although macro-economic policy is not
normally sensitive to its effects on smaller firms, factors such as high
interest rates and a high rate of inflation can act as constraining influences
on SME development, particularly when the macro environment is relatively unstable. Experience in the West emphasises the sensitivity of
SMEs to relatively hostile macro-economic conditions which can affect
the ability of managers to plan; as well as their willingness to invest,
expand and commit themselves to long-term initiatives. In the Baltic
economies, the low level of savings, high inflation rates and high rates of
interest discourage entrepreneurs from making long-term investments,
encouraging them instead to engage in activities with high turnover and
relatively high profit margins (as well as low entry thresholds in terms of
the capital required); in other words in trade (such as retailing) rather than
manufacturing. It is such characteristics that contribute to a relatively
uncertain external environment which in turn contributes to turbulence in
the development of small business activity in the Baltic economies in
terms of high rates of non-survival and rapidly changing product/service
portfolios at the firm level.[4]

Legal frameworks

The types of legal form available to companies are a potentially important influence on the nature and pace of development of the SME sector in the economies in transition. Although the details vary between individual countries, entrepreneurs wishing to start a private business in the Baltic States are faced with a choice of legal form. As in the West, it is possible to register and trade as a private individual, or as a group of individuals (e.g. family members), without forming a limited company. In such cases, the property of the individual (or family) and that of the company are inseparable so that the owner(s) is/are personally liable for any debts incurred by the company. On the other hand, an individual (or group of individuals) may choose to form a limited liability company, which means that the shareholders are only liable for company debts up to the value of their shareholding. The company is fully liable for its obligations up to the value of its assets in these cases. A limited liability company may be a single owner or alternatively the capital may be divided into shares, although in this case the shares are not securities and cannot be bought and sold on a stock exchange; this makes this form of company similar to a private limited company in a country such as the UK. A joint stock company is essentially a limited liability company with a minimum number of shareholders; in this case the shares can be bought and sold on a stock exchange, which makes this type of company similar in this respect to a public limited company in Britain.

In the Baltic States hitherto, minimum legal and capital requirements have made it relatively easy to establish private enterprises but they have also enabled a large number of weak and non-operating companies to be set up. In Estonia and Latvia in particular, low minimum capital requirements have encouraged entrepreneurs wishing to start a business to establish joint stock or limited liability companies (accounting for 87 per cent of the total number of enterprises in Estonia and 48 per cent in Latvia). It has been estimated that nearly one third of all registered companies in Estonia are not currently trading (Estonian Ministry of Economic Affairs, 1994) although this situation should be changed with the introduction of the new Estonian Business Code from September 1995, which increases the minimum capital requirement for both limited liability and joint stock companies. The aim of the new business code is to regulate entrepreneurship by increasing the responsibilities of entrepreneurs and company shareholders in order to encourage banks to be more willing to lend to such enterprises. Although the problem is not confined to Estonia, it is less extreme in Latvia and Lithuania for the reasons already stated; in Lithuania for example, it is estimated that approximately 15 per cent of companies on the Business Register do not operate.

In Lithuania where capital requirements are higher, most private firms are without legal entity; in other words they are sole proprietorships or firms without limited liability. In fact, almost two thirds of the private firms in Lithuania and 18 per cent in Latvia are under joint ownership. The second most common legal form for private companies in Lithuania is the joint stock company, which accounts for about 20 per cent of private firms. More than 40 per cent of joint stock companies employ less than 100 employees, representing approximately 10 per cent of the total number of enterprises (Naujafif, 1995). If individual private companies are combined with private joint stock companies employing less than 100, then about two thirds of all registered enterprises would appear to be SMEs in Lithuania.

The minimum capital requirements required to establish joint stock and limited liability companies are shown in Table 12.2. To put the figures into context, in Estonia the capital required to establish a joint stock company was equivalent to one third of average wages in 1993 and one seventh in 1994. By contrast, in Latvia and Lithuania the minimum capital required is somewhat higher which helps to explain why Estonia has the highest proportion of enterprises with legal entity and Lithuania the lowest.

Table 12.2   Minimum capital requirement for limited liability and joint stock companies ($US)

	Limited liability companies	Joint stock companies
Estonia		
Up to 1994	–	23
Since September 1995	750	7,500
From September 1995	3,000	30,000
Latvia		
Up to 1994	180	910
Since 1995	3,650	9,100
Lithuania		
Up to July 1994	250	625
Since July 1995	2,500	25,000

Source: The Estonian Business Code; the legal acts of Latvia and Lithuania.

The supply of finance

The most critical issues facing SME development revealed by a survey of Estonian entrepreneurs in 1994, were the limited possibilities for raising external funds (particularly long term finance), and high interest rates (Klaamann, 1994), and the picture appears similar in both Latvia and Lithuania. Although average annual interest rates have been falling, they remain too high for most entrepreneurs: 20–30 per cent in Estonia; 31–44 per cent in Latvia; 43–44 per cent in Lithuania. As a consequence, loan finance typically plays a smaller role in the financing of SMEs than it does in many western countries. A number of problems contribute to a shortage of loan finance for SMEs in the Baltic States, and for manufacturing SMEs in particular.

One problem is the limited supply of domestic capital which is partly a structural problem since the capital stock of domestic banks is small and they have been mainly been refinanced by short term deposits. A second contributory factors is that private banks are said to be disinterested in supplying finance to small firms and to new firms in particular (HLT, 1995), although this is a problem that is not confined to economies in transition. One aspect is the higher perceived risk by the banks of lending to new firms because of their lack of a track record and a frequent shortage of collateral; another problem for the banks is the disproportionately high administration costs of dealing with small sums. As a consequence, to be successful a loan application from a small business is said to require proportionately more security and is required to pay a higher rate of interest than a loan to a larger firm.

The collateral issue is a problem for small firms in many western countries (including Britain) although there are additional constraints on the ability of small firms in Baltic economies to find sufficient collateral that stem from uncertainties over property ownership. In Latvia for example, the complicated process of consolidation of ownership rights together with various legal limitations on deals involving property, are contributory factors. In Estonia also, the limited nature of the legal framework for regulating property rights and mortgages has contributed to insufficient collateral being available for small business loans. However, the adoption of the Real Estate Rights Law in December 1993 which introduced a new property rights system, should assist the development of the credit market in this respect (Venesaar and Vitsur, 1995). Finally, where bank loans are available, they are typically short-rather than long-term, which is a particular constraint on the development of manufacturing SMEs that typically need to invest in modernising their production equipment if they are to be competitive at home and abroad. In Latvia for example, 78 per cent of all loans granted in the first half of 1994 were for periods of less than a year. Where medium-term loans have increased, this is mainly from foreign sources.

Although there have been some attempts to intervene in the market for SME finance funded by organisations such as the World Bank and EBRD, the financial resources devoted to funds offering loan facilities to SMEs appear limited so far. The small scale of funds, together with the apparent lack of co-ordination of foreign aid programmes and the underdeveloped nature of the business support infrastructure, reduces the likelihood of these initiatives having the maximum impact.

Labour market characteristics

It is apparent from our survey evidence that labour market conditions during the transition period are also creating problems for the development of manufacturing SMEs in the Baltic States (Smallbone *et al.*, 1996). Skills shortages (which were reported by 54.4 per cent of respondents in our survey) are related to the restructuring of the economy which tends to produce a mismatch between demand and supply in the labour market. A decline of employment in some sectors and a growth of employment in others clearly has implications for the demand for different types of labour skills. Our survey evidence supports the view that a skills mismatch exists in the labour market, and this will need to be addressed if unemployment is to be kept at a low level and constraints on the ability of businesses to develop are to be eased. Although the official unemployment rates in the Baltic States in 1995 were relatively low, the number of unemployed per vacancy has been rising. In addition, there are considerable regional variations in unemployment rates as a result of labour market segmentation.

Another constraint on SME development during the transition period has been a shortage of management and business skills which, although an internal characteristic of SMEs, reflects the orientation of the educational system and the lack of a recent tradition of private business activity. Estonian banks for example, have referred to the deficiencies in management and marketing competence on the part of entrepreneurs, as a factor contributing to the shortage of good business propositions they are presented with (HLT, 1995). Whilst it must be recognised that such a view almost certainly reflects a combination of supply and demand side 'failure' in the market for small business finance rather than simply being a result of management deficiencies within the firm, an upgrading the management resource base of SME is an important target for policy makers in the Baltic States in the mid 1990s.

Business support services

Although the first consulting firms were established in Estonia, Latvia and Lithuania when the first new private enterprises were being set up in the early stages of transition, the business support infrastructure is still under-developed. A number of organisations for entrepreneurs exist (such as the Small Business Associations and the Chambers of Commerce) which have initiated a number of co-operative projects with western partners and have offered short courses and advice to entrepreneurs. Nevertheless, their impact on the development of the SME sector to date appears limited. In addition, foreign projects such as the business centres established under the EU PHARE Programme in all Baltic States, or the Swedish sponsored NUTEK entrepreneurship centres are contributing to providing support for enterprise development. Nevertheless, the resources available appear modest in relation to the scale of the problem and the spatial coverage is limited.

Government policy

Although government policy with respect to SME development is often equated with direct support measures, it can be argued that the impact of the burden of taxation and of government regulations is a more fundamental influence on the nature and pace of small business development. In assessing the burden of taxation on companies, it is the total financial burden placed on firms by the state that needs to be considered which means that both taxation and social security payments must be included. Although there are a variety of policy considerations to take into account when establishing the extent of the taxation burden to be placed on the private business sector, it is important for government to recognise the effect of its taxation policies on the environment for developing enterprises. This can be a particular issue for small firms because of the additional pressures they face in managing cashflow compared with larger companies. Moreover, the direct costs which government imposes on business through taxation and employers social security contributions (or social taxes), are one of the main factors encouraging entrepreneurs to move into the informal sector or shadow economy. Although a large and growing informal sector may be seen as a target to be reduced through stronger policing and controls, it can also be argued that the level of the government imposed 'burdens' on small firms needs to be reviewed in such circumstances, in order to ensure that the level of taxation is compatible with the encouragement of enterprise in the formal economy and not placing too many burdens on emergent entrepreneurs.

In terms of the tax on company profits, it is only in Lithuania and Latvia where there is any current distinction made in the tax burden imposed on firms of different sizes. In Lithuania this is in the form of allowances that are partly offset by a higher rate of taxation compared with Estonia and Latvia. In Lithuania, the standard rate of profits tax is 29 per cent although since December 1991 allowances have been available for enterprises with less than 100 employees in which the main activity accounts for at least two thirds of total output. By comparison, in the UK there is a lower rate of 25 per cent Corporation Tax (tax on profits) which is imposed on firms with an annual profit of less than £250,000; larger firms pay 42 per cent. In Latvia, private sector businesses are currently liable to a 25 per cent tax rate on profits, which is below that for state enterprises (35 per cent) and also banks and wholesale firms (45 per cent). Small firms that meet at least two of the following criteria pay a lower rate (20 per cent): book value of fixed assets less than US$ 13,000; net turnover of less than US$ 370,000; less than 25 employees. As a consequence, it may be claimed that entrepreneurship and SME development is now being encouraged in Latvia. However, in Estonia the tax situation is less advantageous for smaller enterprises. In this case the uniform rate of taxation of 26 per cent has applied to all enterprises since 1994; the only allowances are for investment and for donations; these amount to 5 per cent and 10 per cent of operating profits respectively although the annual rate of depreciation of fixed assets is also deducted from taxable income: 8 per cent in the case of buildings and structural components; up to 40 per cent in the case of other fixed assets.

Rates of social taxation on employers vary between Baltic countries: 30 per cent in Lithuania, 33 per cent in Estonia and 37 per cent in Latvia. However, unlike most western countries employees either make no social security payments (Estonia) or only pay a very small proportion of their salary: 1 per cent in Latvia and Lithuania. This contrasts with the UK for example, where employers pay up to 10 per cent of an employee's salary costs and the employee a similar figure. These high social tax rates represent a substantial burden on private sector employers in the Baltic States which discourages firms from creating or increasing employment, at least in the formal sector of the economy. Moreover, they represent a disproportionate burden on smaller companies which tend to be more labour intensive than larger firms, thus increasing their liability for this aspect of taxation. Of course, one of the factors that contributes to these high social tax rates is the absence of a national insurance fund based on accumulation over an extended period of time. However, in the context of the need to establish an environment which encourages enterprise development and employment generation in the formal economy, the disincentive effect of a relatively high total tax burden on small business development does need to be recognised as a priority issue.

Until now, direct support measures to encourage SME development have not been prioritised by Baltic governments and the contribution of government to the development of the SME sector has been passive rather than active. At the same time, as the previous analysis of the tax environment suggests, some difference can be detected between countries: stronger support in Lithuania and Latvia than in Estonia. In Estonia a number of bills aimed at supporting SMEs have been over-ruled by Parliament and those support measures that have been introduced, tend not to have operated in the way they were intended to. For example, the Foundation for Crediting SMEs which was set up in September 1993 (and reorganised in July 1994), has offered loans at market rates although it had been previously agreed that SMEs would benefit from subsidised loans. In Latvia and Lithuania by contrast, some support has been provided for SMEs through tax concessions, as we have seen; and in the case of Lithuania there have also been attempts to promote the sector more actively. In 1994, the Lithuanian Ministry of Economic Affairs announced a new programme for promoting both the establishment of new enterprises and the development of existing firms (Lithuanian Ministry of Economic Affairs, 1994). The programme allows for the establishment of new agencies to support SME development and includes measures to promote exports (such as credit and insurance schemes); an investment promotion package; and training in business skills. Another recognised priority is the development of business education with an associated development of a business support infrastructure of consultants and associated business services. Although this represents a positive step in that it recognises the need to actively support the development of the SME sector in Lithuania, as yet few policies have been put in place and there are no programme initiatives offering specific aid to small firms (Segal *et al.*, 1995).

KEY POLICY ISSUES AFFECTING THE DEVELOPMENT OF THE SME SECTOR

In this final section of the chapter, we summarise the main policy issues that arise from the analysis undertaken of the characteristics of the external environment in the Baltic States. These issues will need to be addressed if the contribution of manufacturing SMEs to the development of competitive market economies in the Baltic States is to be maximised:

The need to develop a strategy for developing the SME sector to guide a more proactive policy approach to SME development

As in other C&EE countries, the first priority in the Baltic States during the transition period has been macro-economic stabilisation, followed by a restructuring of the large state-owned companies and banking reforms. The establishment of small private companies in the transition period has been made possible by the removal of legal and bureaucratic restrictions but government policy has so far tended to be *laissez faire* rather than proactive towards SME development. Although there are some signs of this changing, there is little evidence of strategic thinking on the part of Baltic governments with respect to the development of the SME sector. Whilst such an approach may be understandable (and possibly justified) in the short term, it will need to change if the potential role of SMEs in economic development is to be fulfilled, and the maximum benefit gained from what are at present a set of relatively uncoordinated foreign aid projects. Governments need to recognise the variety of ways in which policy may impact on small firms whilst at the same time taking steps to actively promote SME development for a combination of economic and social reasons.

However, the issue does raise fundamental questions concerning the role for state policy within the context of an emerging market system. Because of the legacy from the recent past, there is a danger that 'support' or 'promotion' by the state (in this case of SMEs) will be rejected because it is seen as a form of intervention in the market which cannot be justified. An additional problem concerns the credibility of the state whose interventions may be viewed with particular scepticism by private business owners (Piasecki, 1995). Perhaps the key point to stress in relation to SME development, is that the state should be viewed as a complement to and not a substitute for, the private sector in relation to aspects such as the supply of finance to SMEs, or developing a business support network. In this respect, the potential roles for the state are those of a catalyst or 'pump-primer'; co-ordinator (although to be effective this does require some strategic vision); and facilitator (e.g. in mobilising international resources) rather than as a direct provider of support services. At the risk of using a term that can sometimes be reduced to little more than a political slogan, the development of a competitive SME sector almost certainly requires an effective partnership between the state and private sector institutions.

The need to address the supply side failure in the market for finance for SMEs

A shortage of domestic capital has undoubtedly constrained the development of the private sector in all three Baltic countries, and the financial needs of smaller companies have been seen as secondary to the financial resources required for restructuring former state owned enterprises. However, the apparent shortage of longer-term finance for SMEs described above is of particular concern in Baltic economies because of the financial resources needed to achieve the modernisation which is essential to the future competitiveness of SMEs in markets that are becoming increasingly internationalised. This is a particular issue in the manufacturing sector, where investment in modern equipment requires longer term loan facilities than are typically available at present. Unless the supply of longer term credit can be improved, it is clear that the ability of manufacturing SMEs to invest in modern production technology will remain severely constrained.

The need to establish and implement an appropriate legal framework and tax environment within which a culture of legitimate private business can evolve

Although in principle a minimalist approach to government regulation of the private sector is most likely to create the conditions in which enterprise can thrive, there clearly is a need to establish appropriate ground rules for private sector activity in order to give it credibility. Establishing and implementing a legal framework that will facilitate the development of a sustainable and competitive small business sector has many dimensions to it. In terms of the minimum requirements for business registration, it is not easy to strike a balance between avoiding unnecessary barriers to the establishment of enterprises on the one hand, and encouraging the development of the 'phantom company' phenomenon on the other, which, if it continues, risks discrediting the concept of private business. However, legal issues are not confined to business registration. A more fundamental issue concerns property rights and a reduction of uncertainties over land ownership to enable property to be more easily used to secure business loans.

It is also important to aim for greater continuity and stability in the regulatory regime since continual changes in legal requirements produces uncertainty as well as being time-consuming for managers seeking to understand the changes. In Latvia, for example, more than 40 changes have been made to the system of taxation for enterprises since its introduction. This is a particular problem for smaller companies where management time is very scarce and compliance costs proportionately higher than in the case of larger firms. At the same time, it must be recognised that establishing a private business culture involves more than changing laws; it also requires a change in attitudes. In this respect, it is not surprising that it is taking time to change attitudes from a culture in which it was illegal to re-sell an item without adding value to it, to a market-based, trading culture. However, if the state were to develop a clear strategy to set out the role of SMEs in the transformation process as a guide to policy development, such a change in cultural attitudes should take place more quickly.

The need to prioritise the improvement of business education and training

Although at the formation stage new businesses may depend more on initiative and enterprise than the level of education or training of the individual entrepreneur, a deeper knowledge of how businesses operate and an acquisition of management competencies become more important if new firms are to develop and evolve into established enterprises. To achieve this, requires a commitment to increase the provision of high quality training and business skills for managers in firms at different stages of their development. It also involves increasing the opportunities to study business related courses within the educational system, although in this respect it is not only the content of courses that needs to be considered but also the process or pedagogy involved in communicating that content (Gibb, 1993).

The need to recognise the potential role of SMEs in a programme of regional development

Most of the arguments for encouraging and supporting the development of SMEs at national level also apply at a regional scale where the priority is to reduce spatial disparities in economic development. In the context of the Baltic States, there are two particular aspects of spatial imbalance to which SMEs could make a positive contribution. One issue concerns the future development of rural areas, where employment in agriculture is decreasing and is likely to continue to decrease as agriculture is modernised. Already, regions with the highest rates of unemployment tend to be those where there no large towns. In rural areas where relatively low densities of population limit the scope for large-scale development projects, SMEs would seem to have a particularly important role to play in economic development if future pressures for population to migrate to urban areas are to be limited. Unfortunately, the experience so far is that rates of new business formation tend to be lower in the countryside than in the large urban areas. Another issue concerns 'core–periphery' differences which although they exist in most western countries, appear to have been widened in Baltic countries (e.g. Estonia) as a result of international interaction so far being heavily concentrated in core regions. As a consequence, the development of SMEs in Baltic countries has tended to reinforce existing spatial disparities rather than compensating for them, which suggests that some policy intervention may be required to stimulate new firm formation in the more disadvantaged regions, if the trend is to be altered.

CONCLUSIONS

Although the changes that have taken place since 1987 in the Baltic States have enabled a private business sector to become established, the rapid pace of change together with the difficult economic conditions of the transition period and the evolving legal framework, have created many problems for enterprise development. In all three Baltic States, the contribution of government to the development of the SME sector has been passive rather than proactive although, as we have seen, it is possible to detect some change in emphasis over time. So far there has been little direct support for SMEs from government in any of these countries which may be explained by a number of factors. One reason is that the development of a SME sector has been a lower order priority compared with issues such as the privatisation of state owned industries. A second reason may be that having established a legal framework to allow private enterprises to be formed, governments have viewed the explosion of entrepreneurship that occurred as an indication that the market could create a small business sector without a need for government intervention. A third factor is that where direct support measures have been attempted, they have not always been fully implemented because of a lack of financial resources. However, it must also be questioned whether the political will has existed to support the development of small firms. If not, then as Gibb (1993) has argued, an opportunity may be missed to create economic systems in the emerging economies that learn from both the positive and negative experiences of western countries (in the First and Third Worlds), with the aim of laying the basis of competitive national economies and stable societies.

Notes

1.   This paper has been produced as part of a research project – 'The Survival,
      Growth and Support Needs of Manufacturing SMEs in Poland and the
      Baltic States: Developing a Policy Agenda' – funded under the Phare (ACE)
      Programme (ref. 94 743R). The authors gratefully acknowledge the con-
      structive comments made by Professor Niels Mygind of the Copenhagen
      Business School who acted as discussant when the paper was presented at
      the conference 'Micro-Level Studies of the Transition in the Baltic States',
      Riga, August 1995.
2.   Drawing on economic base theory, economic base is used here to refer to
      activities which sell outside the domestic economy.
3.   Date of Business Registers.
4.   Although still high by western standards, price inflation does appear to be
      stabilising: 42 per cent in Estonia, 26 per cent in Latvia and 45 per cent in
      Lithuania in 1994 (Venesaar and Hachey, 1995).

REFERENCES

Central Statistical Bureau of Latvia (1995) *Statistical Yearbook of Latvia* (Riga:
    Central Statistical Bureau).
Dominiak P. and Blawat D. (eds) (1993), *Small and Medium-Sized Enterprises
    and the Role of Private Industry in Poland* (Technical University of Gdansk:
    Faculty of Management and Economics).
EIM (1994) *The European Observatory for SMEs: Second Annual Report.*
EIM (1995) *The European Observatory for SMEs: Third Annual Report.*
Eesti Bank (1995) *Bulletin No 4* (Tallinn).
Estonian Statistical Office (1994) *Estonian Statistics: Month 8* (Tallinn).
Estonian Statistical Office (1995) *Estonian Statistics: Month 5* (Tallinn).
Gibb, A. (1993) 'Small Business Development in Central and Eastern Europe:
    Opportunity for a Rethink?' *Journal of Business Venturing*, 8, 461–86.
Gudgin, G. (1982) *Unequal Growth: Urban and Regional Employment Change in
    the UK* (London: Heinemann).
HLT Gesellschaft fur Forschung Planung Entwicklung MBH (1995), *Regional and
    SME Development in Estonia, a working paper*, presented to First Workshop on
    Regional and SME Development, Tallinn, May 16–19.
Keeble D., Walker S. and Robson M. (1993) *New Firm Formation and Small
    Business Growth in the UK: Spatial and Temporal Variations and
    Determinants*, UK Employment Department Research Series No 15.
Klaamann, V. (1994) *The Environment of Entrepreneurship and its Greatest
    Problems in 1994* (Tallinn: Estonian Small Business Association).
Latvijas Valsts Statistikas Komitejas Galvenair Snaitlosanas Centrs (1995)
    'Latvijas Republikas rupniecibas darba galvenie ra ditaji (minesa parsnatu dati)
    Januari- Decembri 1994' [Main work indicators of industry of Latvian Republic
    data of monthly reports in January–December 1994]' Riga, 3–11
Lithuanian Department of Statistics (1995a) *Statistical Yearbook of Lithuania
    1994–95*, (Vilnius).

Lithuanian Department of Statistics (1995b) *Main Economic Indicators of Lithuania* (Vilnius).

Lithuanian Ministry of Economic Affairs (1994) *The Programme for SME Development* (Vilnius).

Lumiste, R. (1993) 'Prospects for Estonian SMEs: Understanding of a Financial Situation and Perspectives for Success', in M. Virtanen (ed.), *Proceedings of the Conference on the Development and Strategies of SMEs the 1990s* (Mikkeli, Finland).

Mason, C. (1991) 'Spatial Variations in Enterprise: The Geography of New Firm Formation', in R. Burrows (ed.) *Deciphering the Enterprise Culture: Entrepreneurship, Petty Capitalism and the Restructuring of Britain* (London: Routledge).

Naujafif kapitalas (1995), 3 (Vilnius).

Piasecki, B. (1995) 'Dilemmas of SME Sector Promotion Policy during the Transformation Period', in D. Fogel and B. Piasecki (eds), *Regional Determinants of SME Development in Central and Eastern Europe* (Lodz: University of Lodz).

Piasecki, B. and Rogut, A. (1993) 'Self-Regulation of SME Sector Development at a More Advanced Stage of Transformation', paper presented to the 20th Annual Conference of EARIE, Tel Aviv, September.

Reynolds, P., Storey, D. and Westhead, P. (1994) 'Cross-National Comparison of the Variations in New Firm Formation Rates', *Regional Studies* 28, (4), 443–56.

Segal *et al.* (1995), *Small and Medium Enterprise in Lithuania: The Results of a Business Survey'*, Ecofin Baltic Consulting Ltd, Vilnius.

Smallbone, D. (1995) 'SMEs and Regional Economic Development: Developing a Policy Agenda', in B. Piasecki and D. Fogel (eds), *Regional Determinants of SME Development in Central and Eastern Europe* (Lodz: University of Lodz).

Smallbone, D., Venesaar, U., Budreikate, D. and Rumpis, L. (1996) 'The Development of Manufacturing SMEs in the Baltic States: Employment and Labour Market Issues', paper presented at the 41st ICSB World Congress, Stockholm, 16–19 June.

Stanworth, J. and Gray, C. (1991) *Bolton 20 Years On: The Small Firm in the 1990s* (London: Paul Chapman).

Storey, D. (1994) *Understanding the Small Business Sector* (London and New York: Routledge).

Venesaar, U. (1995) 'The External Environment for SMEs in Estonia', paper presented to a conference 'Industrial Organisation and Entrepreneurship in Transition', Varna, Bulgaria, June.

Venesaar, U. and Hachey, G. (1995) *Economic and Social Changes in the Baltic States in 1992–94* (Tallinn: Institute of Economics, Estonian Academy of Sciences).

Venesaar, U. and Vitsur, E. (1995), 'Development of Entrepreneurship,' in O. Logus and G. Hachey (eds), *Transforming the Estonian Economy* (Tallinn: Institute of Economics, Estonian Academy of Sciences).

13 The Investment Behaviour of Individual Private Farmers in Latvia

Hans-Joachim Zilcken

INTRODUCTION

This chapter reports on a survey of private farmers in Latvia and was prepared under the auspices of the World Bank office for the Baltic States in Riga. The main task was to identify the current behaviour of individual private landholders/owners with a view to determining their needs for liquid assets and capital goods, and their likely future investment behaviour. Since interviews could not be conducted with all the private farmers in Latvia, a sample had to be taken. The results presented are based on 120 personal interviews.[1]

The scope of this study is rather narrow, representing roughly one third of Latvian agriculture. In contrast to many other republics of the former Soviet Union, restitution due to heritage is possible in the Baltic States. For the well-known historical reasons which did not give the opportunity for self-determination in Latvia over a lengthy time period, long-lasting traditions of privately-owned small-scale farming were not established in the country. For this reason any advice on agricultural policy coming from the West has therefore to be given with caution and in full understanding of the context (Abele and Veilands, 1994; World Bank, 1994; King and McNabb, 1994).

Project definition

The purpose of the study was to review the present state of small-scale privatised agriculture in Latvia and to investigate its future market potential for World Bank activities. Large-scale farms of the Soviet type are not included in this survey. For the purposes of the research, agriculture is defined in the traditional way, consisting of both crop and livestock production. In line with this definition, the substantial forestry sector in Latvia has been excluded. Investment behaviour is also to be understood in its widest sense, examining the long-term horizon, the medium-term needs and also the short-term requirements for working capital.

Survey focus

This survey has to be viewed in the context of declining agricultural output in Latvia, as shown in Table 13.1.

The investment behaviour of the Latvian private farmers should be seen in relation to two issues. From the interaction of these, different outcomes can be hypothesised.

Transition: There is an ongoing transition from the previous large-scale farms of the Soviet type to a system of individual private farmers.

Capacity: The demand for investment arising from the above transition should, however, also be correlated with the general experience of declining output in agriculture since 1991.

These two elements constitute development trends moving in opposite directions. The first would indicate increasing investment needs due to the existence of bottlenecks in production, whereas the second would point to decreasing investment needs due to the presence of surplus capacity.

Roughly 80 per cent of the Soviet Sovkhozes and Kolkhozes in Latvia have now been privatised and nearly half of the farmland is in individual private farms.[2] Ninety-five state-owned agricultural enterprises remain, these being mostly sort-testing stations.

Table 13.1 Agricultural output indices by type of farm – at constant prices

Year	All types of farms	State and collective farms, and statutory companies	Peasant farms, household plots, and private auxiliary farms
1990	100	100	100
1991	96	88	116
1992	81	55	148
1993	63	30	145
1994	50	19	129

Source: Latvijas Republikas Valsts stastistikas komiteja (1995), *Latvija Skaitlos 1995*, p. 74.

Table 13.2   Number of rural enterprises as of 1 January 1995

State farms	95.0
Privatised large-scale farms	656.0
Private farms ('000s)	64.3
Household plots ('000s)	118.7
Private subsidiary farms ('000s)	124.7

Source: Latvijas Republikas Valsts stastistikas komiteja (1995), *Lauksaimnieciba Latvija, 1990–1994: Statistiko Datu Krajums*, p. 7.

The overall pattern of rural enterprises is shown in Table 13.1. The progress of ownership transition in agriculture is ahead of that in industrial sectors, where only some 30 per cent of the enterprises had been privatised by early 1995.[3]

In this survey a distinction was made between the two main reasons for private ownership, namely whether it was due to heritage or to the agricultural reforms after Perestroika. It has been suggested that the first case should be labelled restitution or *Reprivatisation*,[4] whereas privatisation as such is represented by the latter case.

Figure 13.1 provides an overall impression of the transition. The dismantling of the large-scale Soviet farms into smaller plots, and their return to their legal owners in the interests of justice, is an issue which is not called into question here. However, the economics of such small-scale privatisation in the Latvian agricultural sector remain to be settled. While there has been considerable discussion about the mechanisms of privatisation, there is surprisingly little information on how the reforms have impacted on the economic behaviour and choices of firms.[5] Neither is there much known about the behaviour of the emerging private farms and their owners. Hopefully this study provides a few preliminary answers to at least one of the critical questions, namely, what would be appropriate investment behaviour in order to achieve the successful development of agriculture following the splitting up of the Soviet large-scale farms into small-scale privatised units?

One indication of the early demand for funds is given in Table 13.3, which shows the customer portfolio achieved by the World Bank in Latvia from its launch in Spring 1994 until June 1995.

The funds to support private farmers are channelled via one of the local credit institutions ('Laukkredits' or Agricultural Finance Company) and the EU-Phare programme assists the World Bank in this task. However,

Figure 13.1   Latvian agriculture in transition

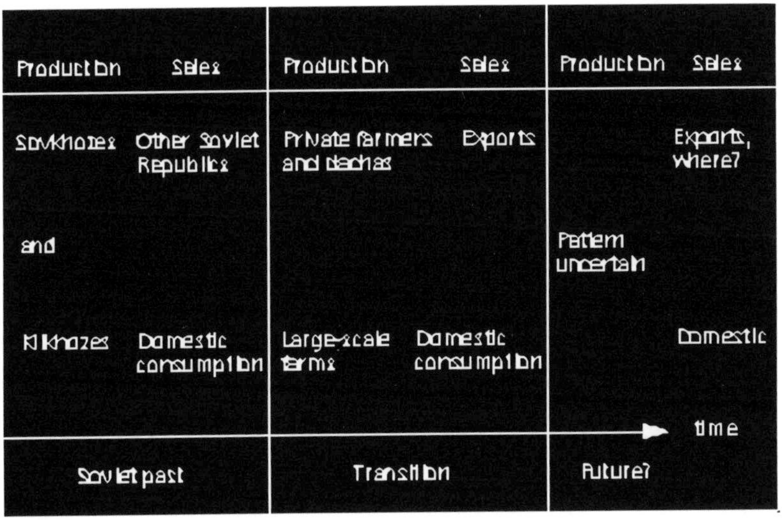

Production	Sales	Production	Sales	Production	Sales
Sovkhozes	Other Soviet Republics	Private farmers and dachas	Exports		Exports, where?
and				Pattern uncertain	
Kolkhozes	Domestic consumption	Large-scale farms	Domestic consumption		Domestic
					time
Soviet past		Transition		Future?	

Table 13.3   The customer portfolio of the World Bank in Latvia

Private farmers	New clients	Rejected
Applications 1994	160	340
Applications 1995	320	56
Total 1994 + 1995	480	396

detailed information on the recipients of the World Bank credit lines and their investment behaviour, is rather scarce, though their overall repayment performance appears to be good.

RESEARCH METHODOLOGY

The three main sources of information for the study consisted of the following primary and secondary data:

- 120 empirical interviews with private farmers by the research team, based on standardised questionnaires

- various meetings with the World Bank, Laukkredits and the Latvian Agricultural Advisory Centre
- previous studies and statistical reports.

The willingness of the individual farmers to answer questions was very high. Other contact routes were not available. For example, private farmers' associations have not yet been established in Latvia, but it seems that they are beginning to emerge. Such associations could be useful as an identification entrance and afterwards as a network for support activities to the individual farmer.

Sample procedure

It would have been meaningless to choose just one sample randomly from the total population of claimants on a private farm, or even just a land plot. Such an approach would probably have missed most or all of the actual, as well as the potential, World Bank clients. It would have included approaches to many hobby farmers who simply prefer life on their dacha in the countryside. Instead, the sampling was designed according to purpose and the survey covers the following three homogeneous sub-samples of private farmers, namely, private farmers who are clients of Laukkredits; those who applied for credits without success; and, finally, those who had not applied at the time of the study. The subsamples of Laukkredits' clients and of rejected applicants were both further split up in half, one half covering 1994 applications and the other covering those for 1995. Here, however, there had to be a compromise in some cases, when the sample sizes were too small.

To achieve an appropriate geographical spread, we chose our three subsamples from the following eight districts: Aluksne, Bauska, Cesis, Daugavpils, Jekabpils, Liepaja, Saldus and Tukums. These eight districts are at the same time evenly spread among the better performing (the upper row for each region), and the lesser performing (the lower row, accordingly). They are also evenly spread among the four main regions of Latvia, that is, Zemgale, Vidzeme, Kurzeme and Latgale. The final respondents were chosen by Laukkredits, each cell randomly from its files. The geographical districts were then weighed accordingly to their number of private farmers. The final sample is shown in Table 13.4.

Data preparation

The analysis of the questionnaires was done by the use of a statistical package. The reason why the investigated sample does not exactly corre-

Table 13.4   Study sample

Regions	Districts	World Bank clients	Rejected	Other private farmers	n (weighed)
Zemgale	Bauska	7	5	6	18
	Tukums	5	6	4	15
Vidzeme	Cesis	6	5	7	18
	Aluksne	4	4	4	12
Kurzeme	Ljepaja	7	7	7	21
	Saldus	2	6	4	12
Latgale	Jekabpils	5	3	4	12
	Daugavpils	2	5	5	12
	n	38	41	41	120

spond to the outlined design is that a few respondents changed position during the interview period. For example, rejected applicants reapplied and became clients, while some respondents belonging to the group of 'Other Private Farmers' approached Laukkredits in the meantime, and so on.

FINDINGS

The selected findings presented in this section are mainly counts of frequencies and cross-tabulations from the questionnaires. Some further analytical conclusions on the initial hypotheses are presented later.

Identification

More than half of the respondents became private farmers in 1991 or earlier, either due to heritage or to Perestroika. Based on comparative national data, it appears that these respondents have been farmers for longer than the average in Latvia. Those who own their farms due to the agricultural reforms after Perestroika often have a relevant education. They were typically agronomists, mechanical engineers, and so on. However, the number of operating units of commercial size remains much lower than expected.

It should be noted, however, that the formal process of official registration is still pending in many cases. Out of the eight districts included in the study, Bauska seems to be the most advanced when it comes to the transition from collective to individual private farming.

Ownership

More than half of the respondents became farmers due to the agricultural reforms of 1989, after Perestroika. Most of the others received their farm due to heritage. But it must be stressed, however, that this sample is not representative of the individual private landowners in general, given its origins and connections to funding applications.

Procurement and marketing

Since the sample was chosen as outlined, and for a particular purpose, it is not representative of the economic development of Latvian agriculture in general. For example, contrary to expectation, the majority of the farmers we spoke to reported unchanged, or even increasing, production volumes during the previous five years. This must, however, be seen against the background that only active farmers were included and that growth in their agricultural production was from a low starting point. Since two-thirds of the respondents had to answer similar questions while preparing their business plans and subsequent credit applications to Laukkredits, the findings in this survey on performance and profitability should be fairly reliable. Some of the farmers even referred directly to their book-keeping records during the interviews in order to check their responses.

There were a number of interesting findings. For example, the positive impact of farmers engaging in their own food processing on profitability seems to be lower than expected. The high share of meat sold in the private markets would imply farm slaughtering, but the respondents obviously did not really consider this a processing activity. In any event, these marketing channels are sometimes organised by private wholesale traders. The poor payment record of some of the meat co-operatives and dairies might have caused the farmers to search for alternative marketing outlets. It would appear that a high share of cereals is still sold via state organisations. However, in interpreting this finding, it should be noted that a shareholders' company can be state-owned, whereas a co-operative would be considered a privatised business. The majority of the respondents reported that the prices for their agricultural products are partly set by the food processing industry and partly set in the market place. Price controls established by the state now hardly exist.

Profitability and financing

The economic performance results of the private farmers appeared to be similar, whether their ownership was due to heritage or due to Perestroika. Equally, on the basis of the survey data, it was difficult to conclude whether the regional location had any evident influence on farm profitability.

The great majority of the private farmers were of the opinion that additional financing would be required for their farming activities. There was a reasonable congruence between the responses identifying the need for short/medium/long-term credits and those identifying possible investment needs for machinery and equipment, livestock, buildings and so on. It was interesting to note that only half of the respondents knew that the previous handling fee of 1 per cent per credit application has been abolished by Laukkredits. The high interest rate levels were the main reason for farmers' reluctance to take additional loans. The survey showed that the main alternative sources for short and medium term finance were, in decreasing order, commercial banks, equipment dealers and suppliers of agrochemicals. Access to long-term sources of finance seems to be particularly difficult.

Production and investment needs

In 1994, perennial grasses and barley were the most widely grown agricultural crops.[6] This reflects the structure of Latvian farming, in that most of the crop harvest is for fodder consumption by the farmers' own livestock. The reason behind the frequent counts of potato-growing in the records seems to be the farmers' own consumption, since they do not represent significant production volumes.

Whereas the majority of the private land plots in Latvia had a farm area of 10 to 20 ha, the size range of the farms investigated by this survey was 25 to 50 ha. Ninety per cent of the sample farms had over 25 ha, with 20 per cent having over 100 ha. The declared obstacles to agricultural production were evenly spread across the range, including working capital, machinery and equipment, and buildings. In general, livestock and the further purchase of land looked to be less critical needs at this stage. The desire to grow agricultural production was the main stated reason for future investment needs. The replacement of worn-out buildings and equipment was also considered to be important. Table 13.4 summarises the context in which the farmers in the survey saw their future investment needs. As is evident, replacement and growth of production were regarded as of more importance than the starting of a normal farm business after privatisation. The latter may have effectively already happened in these larger farms.

Concluding comments

Unfortunately, most of the private farmers interviewed stated that they are disappointed by the privatisation of Latvian agriculture as carried out to date. Among the former Soviet republics, only the Baltic States have a reasonable chance of joining the EU within a relatively short period, but most of the private farmers did not expect that EU membership would improve their conditions.

These two sets of responses have to be seen in context, in that the private farmers have not lost their spirit. Most of them consider committing their future to agriculture only, and this willingness remains, even in spite of marginally decreasing standards of living. It must, however, be mentioned that many farmers consider this necessary in order to channel some share of their earnings into investment in their farms. As regards market outlets, most of the private farmers agreed that the former Soviet Union should be their most important export market.

CONCLUSIONS AND IMPLICATIONS

At the outset of this study, it was recognised that there were two development trends moving in opposite directions. Latvian agricultural output had been declining in aggregate since 1991. Within this the transition to private farms from the former large-scale Soviet farms might be expected to create production bottlenecks and thereby reduce output. On the other hand, output from the privatised small scale production units might be expected to increase as efficiency gains emerged.

Table 13.5   Future investment needs

Count	To begin normal operation	Replacement	Growth of agricultural production	Others
Yes	18	79	88	7
No	102	41	32	113
Total	120	120	120	120

Although the survey data were partial, the results suggested that bottle-necks were not a major issue restricting the output of this group of farmers and were not generally cited as reasons restricting their capacity utilisation. In contrast, there did appear to be considerable efficiency gains emerging from the privatisation process. However, it would seem that the future investment needs of the private farmers will much depend on further market development and possible new product opportunities. The latter might include the substitution of niche products, presently imported into Latvia. Some confirmation that these developments were occurring emerged in the study. For example, profitability and increasing production volumes were closely linked. In specific terms, farmers producing growing volumes of cash crops such as wheat and sugar beet seemed to be among those with growing profitability.

In spite of the many difficulties faced by Latvian farmers, the survey revealed a reasonably optimistic environment for this particular group of active farmers, with larger holdings, who were among those applying for credits for the development of their business. This sample is reasonably close to the present target group of the World Bank. The general decline in Latvian agriculture output has impacted severely on the state and collective farm section and the smaller scale end of the privatised sector. This evidence suggests, however, that it may have created new opportunities for an enlivened and properly financed private farm sector to emerge. It is, of course, early days and market development remains the key to its future prosperity.

As regards policy implications, long-term loans to finance privatisation activities should perhaps be best channelled via the Latvian Privatisation Fund, whereas other long-term loans for the ordinary purchase of a private farm or land, as well as for land improving measures, should be channelled via Laukkredits. The latter set of demands will most probably be of increasing importance, in order to pay off other inherited family members, or to enable the merging of several smaller plots into one viable business. By definition, there should not be any need for long-term finance in the case of restitution. To meet competition from abroad, the further development of attractive marketing channels remains one of the main challenges for Latvian agriculture, together with the emergence of up-to-date food processing industries.

Notes

1. The questionnaire employed is available on request from the author.
2. According to the official statistics from the Ministry of Agriculture (1994), p. 3.

3.   *Baltic Times* (1995), 3, p. 12.
4.   Frydman *et al.* (1993), pp. 227–9.
5.   Estrin, Gelb and Singh (1993), p. 1.
6.   According to official statistics from The Latvian Agricultural Advisory Centre (1995), p. 8.

REFERENCES

Abele, D. and Veilands, U. (1994) 'The Latvian Agricultural Crisis and Ways of Overcoming It', in University of Latvia: *Latvian National Economy from Crisis to Stabilisation*, Humanities and Social Sciences, 4, No. 5.

Estrin, S., Gelb, A. and Singh, I. (1993) 'Restructuring, Viability and Privatisation: A Comparative Study of Enterprise Adjustment in Transition', EE-RPS 31 (Washington, World Bank).

Frydman, R., Rapaczynski, A. and Earle, J.S. (1993) *The Privatisation Process in Russia, Ukraine and the Baltic States* (London: Central European University Press).

King, G.J. and McNabb, D.E. (1994) 'Marketing in Latvia: Uneven Progress,' in *Latvian National Economy from Crisis to Stabilisation* (University of Latvia, Humanities and Social Sciences), *Latvia*, 4(5).

Lapukins, N. (1995) Privatiseringen har nu kommit i gång på allvar, *Baltic Times*, 3 (Stockholm).

Latvijas Lauksaimniecibas konsultaciju centrs (1995) *Latvijas zemnieku saimniecibu ekonomiskas analises raditaji 1994*, gada [The Latvian Agricultural Advisory Centre, Economic analysis of Latvian farms for 1994] (Ozolnieki).

Latvijas Republikas Valsts statistikas komiteja (1991) 'Latvijas tautas saimnieciba', *Statistikas gadagramata 1990* [State Committee for Statistics of the Republic of Latvia, 'National Economy of Latvia', *Statistical Yearbook of Latvia 1990*] (Riga).

Latvijas Republikas Valsts statistikas komiteja (1995) *Latvija Skaitlos 1995 Iss Statistiko Datu Krajums* [Central Statistical Bureau of Latvia, *Latvia in Figures 1995, Collection of Statistical Data*] (Riga).

Latvijas Republikas Valsts statistikas komiteja (1995) *Lauksaimnieciba Latvija 1990–1994, g. Statistiko Datu Krajums* [Central Statistical Bureau of Latvia, *Agriculture in Latvia, 1990–1994, A Collection of Statistical Data*] (Riga).

Latvijas Republikas Zemkopibas Ministrijas Razosanas Prognozasanas un Informacijas Nodala (1994), *Lauksaimniecibas Razosanas Raditaji* [The Ministry of Agriculture, Planning and Information Department, *Figures on Agricultural Production*] (Riga).

World Bank (1994) *Latvia, Agricultural Sector Review*, Report No. 12401-LV (Washington: World Bank).

SECTION FOUR

CONCEPTUAL CONSIDERATIONS

14 Values of the Latvian Road to the Market[1]

Gundar J. King

AN INTRODUCTORY ANALOGY

This chapter is about values and related aspects of managerial behaviour and capabilities in Latvia. Together with the other two Baltic nations, it claims a commitment to a membership to the European Union. All three are in a difficult transition to a market economy. The following analogy illustrates several aspects in this change.

Latvians, as well as the Estonians and Lithuanians, desire the benefits of the high plateau of the market economy. As they leave the arid and unappealing desert plains of the Soviet society, they need more than wishful thoughts to climb up the mountain. They need to plan and to prepare for the rigours of this venture with the full realisation that not everyone will get to the top at the same time. Some will never get there.

Exploration and experiments by smaller, select and best prepared groups should take to the mountain first. Only such teams will succeed. For every team there is knowledge to be acquired, equipment and funds gathered, training to be done and routes to be mapped out. There is a need for constant review to identify new bottlenecks and problems. While some of the obstacles can be taken in stride in the foothills, inadequate preparation and limited resources may make the task to go higher up impossible for many. Thus, what begins as an easy walk, turns out to be hard and dangerous. Every next step up is harder. Any reckless move calls for expensive rescue and a waste of scarce resources and valuable time. Assistance by experienced international partners is very helpful.

The climbing tasks are for teams. This essentially is thoughtful shock therapy for entrepreneurial managers and their organisations. It is these teams that build skills with such values as mutual trust, careful risk taking and reliance on each other. Others, such as economic planners and policy makers can clear some paths and make the tasks easier. Fundamentally, however, every team is unique, with their own strategic goals and choices, and with their own strengths and weaknesses. They also have their own

261

different rates of progress. In this chapter, attention is drawn to the changing values in the Latvian environment, the need for well-prepared managers for new organisations, and the institutional means to help make the transition more quickly and effectively.

Following the destruction of the entrepreneurial class and most market institutions under the Soviet rule, the Baltics now also have to deal with a net depletion of their capital resources in the broadest sense of the word. The physical capital assets are increasingly obsolete; working capital is very short; housing is not maintained, and much of the transportation infrastructure is crumbling. The labour force is ageing. Educational and research institutions are falling behind and the knowledge needs for a market economy are not widely understood. Social capital or the culture to support the creation of prosperity, to use the terminology of Rand Corporation's Francis Fukuyama (1995) is weak.

This contribution draws heavily on observations made in Latvia. Compared to managers in Latvia, Estonian managers tend to be more pragmatic and not as bureaucratic. They have already done a better job in linking Estonian values with those of the West. Compared to Latvians, Lithuanians treasure their communal values. The Latvian situation is, in some ways, more complex than in the other two states. An important factor in Latvia is the greater ethnic diversity. This diversity tends to reinforce restricted ethnic roles in the economy and has significant value differences. Thus, traders of urban Russian Old Believer families hold to religious values important to them. Latvians consider trust relatively more important than others in the area. There are also significant regional differences within the country. For example, the city of Riga, an internationally oriented metropolitan centre, has a development dynamic leading other Latvian towns and cities.

VALUES AND ECONOMIC PERFORMANCE

For purposes of this discussion, values are preferential orientations about what is practical or unrealistic, what is right or wrong, and what is pleasant or unpleasant. As conceived by Connor and Becker (1994), England (1975) and Hofstede (1980), values are part of a business culture, values form attitudes and they shape actions. As part of the social capital at work, they are important in making economic and business performance harmonious. This performance depends on interrelated values and a work environment that fit the tasks. Indeed, a market economy cannot function well without this engaged social capital. Although some values are known to change very slowly and gradually, others are more readily influenced by tangible and intangible factors operational in a personal and managerial environment. More than others, some individuals are predisposed to adapt to new demands and to modify their values in the process.

In Latvia, there is an underdeveloped business culture. Values as choices of preference represent a wide range. Individuals within this range do not have a strong consensus on economic issues and policies. Leaning one way or another, managers are often confused and passive. Relatively few are entrepreneurial and many are bureaucratic. Most are not active change agents in the slowly emerging market economy.

There are several value layers acquired and modified over time. The values commonly held by Nordic farmers are typical of Latvian decision-makers at the turn of the century. These values reflect an ethic of honesty and hard work and an acceptance of an autocratic management. There is a strong preference for small units where work and play are integrated. Production is valued. There is also an almost xenophobic distrust of marketing and finance. Joint ventures are not favoured because economic relationships are frequently seen as a zero-sum game.

Prevailing values may or may not advance, delay, or block economic changes. In this regard, it is illuminating to compare Latvian economic performance in recent history. Latvia's economic reconstruction of a devastated economy after World War I is an unusual success story. It is marked by traditional values, expansion of the family farm sector, use of familiar skills and institutions, quiet capital formation in a more intensive agriculture and keeping faith in a highly paternalistic government. Education is treasured as a source of knowledge and improved skills. Altogether there is a good fit of values, resources and economic realities.

During World War II and under the Soviet rule there is, at least initially, a strong resistance to Soviet institutions. The best managers and individual farmers are removed. With private sector finance and marketing functions gone, profit becomes a bad word. Central planning substitutes for much of the risk taking and making of choices by individual managers and workers. Personal responsibility becomes collective irresponsibility. The Latvian economy is now part of a large Soviet system of farms and factories. Quality of products and services is shabby. Productivity is low and it rises slowly. Although production is not withheld, attitudes and actions become more passive. Modest direct and indirect rewards centre on basic necessities. High social costs and ecological disasters are a major public concern. As the fit of values to the tasks is tilted heavily by Soviet demands, it no longer conforms with many traditional values. Some values are reinforced, others weakened, and still others are gradually accepted.

Economic gains are modest and generally disappointing. Values are torn between the preservation of the traditional and the adoption of new philosophies.

The emergent Latvian values under the Soviet rule favour rewards and entitlements for production. Other business functions, such as finance and marketing, are perceived and treated as not important. With an increased dependence on large organisations, new values appear. Security, entitlements and bureaucratic controls become important. Managerial risk-taking and commitments are avoided. Theft and corruption are tolerated. Autocratic and often arbitrary management is not effectively checked by confused and confusing legal systems. Education is seen as the acquisition of simplistic, often uniformly used knowledge, and as tickets to be punched to gain bureaucratic positions of power.

Today, without the old cover for lies, and no obvious benefits for telling the truth, value modification is again in disarray. As Gulens (1995) reports, many individuals in the Latvian society suffer from serious stresses and personality distortions. The value mix present does not serve the collapsed Soviet system and it is not good for a market economy. There is no firm value foundation for a good performance in the market economy. Superficial and limited skills give rise to the most opportunistic short-term grab-and-run business activities at best. Successful performance is hard to find and mistakes made discourage further change. Under these circumstances, the important inter-relationships between values and managerial performance are far from optimal. Performance of the Latvian economy is not strong enough to stimulate changes in managerial values. Growth elements do not push changes fast enough to accelerate economic transition.

VALUES FOR THE FUTURE

Latvian enterprises are of necessity driven to form international alliances in a global, or at least European, market economy. This direction is mandated by the shortage of various capital resources and the very limited Latvian domestic markets. For best results, leading Latvian companies will have to be flexible enough to grasp emerging opportunities as they appear. Values for the future will have to support this strategic posture. In other words, the current state of Latvian development suggests an increasingly less traditional approach to economics. The Latvian economy is not Marshallian. There are no well-informed companies actively competing with each other. Latvian market forces lack the entrepreneurial ingredients for aggressive moves to exploit new imbalances and new equilibria. There are no Schumpeterian gales of destructive innovation. They are yet to come.

For the future, however, it is important to look at the moving forces in the market and opportunities they present. World-wide, fortunes are made and are lost in using new information in processes that are described by Michael Rothschild in his stimulating book on Bionomics (Rothschild, 1992). He suggests that fast acquisition of knowledge and quick use of modern technology are mandatory for survival in the new economy. These processes call for technically and managerially competent leaders. Thus, Latvian development is currently limited not only by confused values, but also by the lack of managers skilled enough to work with, and to compete within, the rapidly changing world economy.

VALUES FOR MANAGEMENT

Optimally, values supporting the transition to a market economy should extend to the whole Latvian society. In practice, priorities should include the education of managers. They have the first responsibility to make the transition work. They will also be among the first to benefit in a market economy.

The uneven progress of managers in Latvia suggests that the most rewarding targets for change are found in companies most compatible with change. *Ceteris paribus*, the choice should often fall on smaller, family-owned enterprises. The dominant reason for it is that they may well build on the trust that exists in a family or any other smaller group that has worked together over time. They also have simpler goals to reach. They may build on the remains of a family corporate memory to form value clusters which are fundamental to the culture desired in an emerging enterprise. Last, but not least, they do not have to resolve value conflicts evident in a government enterprise attempting the transition. There are other factors favouring a more gradual and cautious, yet still rapid, value modification in smaller companies. This approach, compared to a pure sink-or-swim shock therapy, may also help minimise failure. Failure, given the fragile state of Latvian economic and managerial development, can be very damaging to the progress desired.

There is a good argument for building organisations which evolve from a relatively simple set of operations to the performance of increasingly complex functions. For example, some public policy-makers advocate the use of Latvian forest resources to make valuable end products such as fine furniture. Elsewhere in the world, however, foresters are not doing well in marketing consumer products. Others suggest building large and capital-intensive pulp mills which would use Latvian forest resources together with large foreign investments, leaving Latvian human resources relatively undeveloped. In practice, a chipping operation for export may be a simpler and safer option to combine rapid learning with the generation of cash. Generically, this is still close to the traditional producer ethic of Latvians. Success factors in this case combine a strong materials base with the potential management team. It is likely to share business functions in joint venture with partners from the West. In a similar fashion, it may be better to start making medium-quality apparel on contract for a firm from the West than to plunge into producing for the high fashion industry. Again, it may be easier to learn productivity improvement than to undertake truly novel tasks without experience or other preparation.

Some of the future developments are hard to see. Even though Latvia is known as the Soviet Silicon Valley, the electronics industry is slow to adapt to a different environment. It is precisely this adaptability to the market economy, effectively using new market information to integrate it with other resources at hand which handicaps much of Latvian industry at the present and promises information technology related service growth in many fields. Others, perhaps those with developed professional expertise may follow the paths suggested by the technology advocate Beck (1995) more directly. They may build on their previous successes in the medical and pharmaceutical industry, computer programming for export, or even the development of composite materials. In such cases, many functions can be effectively related to each other in a smaller organisation. Smaller niches can be found in the market for them.

More importantly, a smaller organisation can facilitate and accelerate value changes with simpler assignments of responsibilities and the monitoring of performance. Managers cannot readily hid from the responsibilities to make individual, or help in group, decisions and to be responsible for the implementation of change. There is no one else. Thus, management in smaller groups provides better settings for vertical and horizontal problem solving, improving communications, absorption of new technology and building new relationships. It can easily be at variance with the traditional authority structure of the Soviet factory and be more effective in changing the Master of the House management style on a traditional family farm. Lastly, to lead with smaller companies or smaller groups of larger organisations simply requires less time. The smaller organisation can learn more quickly what it needs to accomplish today and it may see more readily what it has to do in the future.

From a larger perspective, effective management provides the whole national economy with important integrated experience and credible models. In such situations, emerging values strengthen emerging patterns of practice. Good performance reinforces value change.

CRITICALLY IMPORTANT VALUES AND SKILLS

The preceding observations suggest the need for an almost comprehensive change of economic values in Latvia. In practice, however, desirable supporting values can be identified beyond the economic sphere, for example in law. Realistically, value adjustments are most likely to come with new learning and new experience to managers and others seeking new skills. New, hopefully better, value bases for the youth are families, schools and churches. In any case, value acquisition usually takes place together with skill formation. The major difference from the traditional Latvian experience is that formal education at college and university level replaces what was apprenticeship on the family farm.

Perhaps the most promising values of managers in Latvia today are expressed in a strong orientation to personal achievement. This is the value that urges many of them to go back to school to acquire new knowledge and skills. This value should encourage them to experiment with new concepts and ideas to improve their performance.

Effective work in teams should be fundamental to the building of strong organisations. The sweeping changes in the modern market economy do not permit reliance on slow learning in a command system. Moreover, knowledge of teams can be changed more readily than that of individuals.

According to field studies (Barnowe and King, 1992; King, Barnowe and Banmkovskaya, 1994), managers in Latvia, be they Latvian or Russophone, should become more pragmatic in their orientation to business and economic issues. This is especially the case in the large factories inherited from the Soviets. At this time, almost one third of Latvian managers can be characterised as moralists. Moralist managers in the private and in the public sectors can be generally identified as bureaucratic. They appear to be guardians of established relationships, norms and entitlements. Worse yet, the moralist managers may insist on the use of their own personal criteria for organisational performance. They are more likely to value compliance to authority.

Other managers, again many ethnic Latvians, do not seem to treasure any particular value commitments, or they hold to preferences that are very complex and confused. Together with those who seek a comfortable work environment, these managers have difficult adjustments to make. Above all, they should seek values of purposeful and organised management. They should appreciate careful planning which goes with appropriately careful risk taking (as compared to gambling) in market economies. They should have more 'laissez faire' entrepreneurship and less 'lazy fair' management of the old style bureaucracy. Even the commonly observed expensive socialising at work should become goal oriented.

Parallel to these desirable shifts in values and attitudes, much has to be done about change itself as a desirable value. Today, rapid change is a low value in Latvia. It requires much encouragement and nurturing. Strengthening goal oriented change as a value should counteract much of the attitudes of victimisation among most managers in Latvia. Continuing learning and training programmes are increasingly important sources of new values and skills. They should become very regular parts of economic life in Latvia.

THE ROLE OF BUSINESS SCHOOLS

In terms of desired knowledge, economic development calls for more than well-educated business managers. A developed economy is built by a whole society. Indeed, this function cannot succeed without major academic reforms.

The role of business schools are unusually important in Latvia. Essentially new institutions for Latvia, they themselves are part of the academic reform processes. Ideally, business schools are sources of values which help develop a new business culture and shape more constructive attitudes towards institutions of a market economy. More than just a provider of academic degree programmes, business schools are sources of business research for both improved course materials and assistance to commerce and industry. Business schools, or schools of economics with a broad interdisciplinary programme content, are models for academic reforms in other disciplines. Riga, of course, is the logical location for changing values and acquiring new skills.

In a more mundane context, business schools are destined to be the major source of business managers. This is evident in the very strong demand for business education by new students and by older graduates seeking new knowledge. They fit the traditional professional orientation in Latvia where education and skill formation are combined. The risk is mostly related to the residual Soviet orientation to value vocational training. To minimise this risk, business schools must develop and maintain programmes which are more substantial than what is normally observed in the United States. While these business schools offer strong professional programmes, these programmes follow broad studies which help link up values and institutional knowledge gained earlier. Business schools in the United States are weak in providing internships and other linkages to the work environment in particular companies.

This education cannot be made uniform, business schools in Latvia cannot simply import any good western model of business education. In practice, some schools may include very substantial information systems components in their curricula. Others may elect to serve particular business institutions. Hopefully, competition from private schools, and among state universities, will be useful in generating what is needed. In any case, current American and European business school models do not fit the emerging Latvian situations well. It can be expected that most new business schools will be providers of comprehensive services, including research and consulting, academic programmes and executive training. They will serve a multitude of domestic and international students and clients. They will share many features of the institutions envisaged by Hague (1991).

Working managers are most likely to select graduate programmes of business. A master's degree usually takes the equivalent of about two years of full time study of business functions. Even though such graduate students may have desirable work values and attitudes, they may also neglect the study of values in favour of what is considered practical knowledge. Therefore, graduate programme design should carefully provide substantial value dimensions for all studies, from basic economics and account to business policy formulation. As values incompatible with a market economy are considered, it is clear that an important programme content has to be the study of societies in market economies rather than just the concepts and techniques applied to business decisions.

Undergraduate programmes, running from three to four years of full time study provide greater opportunities for the study of values. Again, value dimensions must be included in such traditional courses as management principles, finance, marketing, and especially human relations. Indeed, even the acquisition of computer skills may be designed to let students learn a great deal about decision choices and the work of teams in smaller and larger groups. This learning can be further enhanced in programmes of residential (campus) character. Programmes where students study and live together, especially if they include a significant number of international students from the West, are in the long run the better investment in the education of future managers.

This absorption of western values, concepts and applications is a much larger task than is commonly perceived. It requires not only an understanding of economic policy alternatives, but also their fit to relationship abroad and in Latvia. Tax systems may be an example of this complexity. It is relatively simple to include tax system information from international agencies in the curricula. In practice, however, any workable tax system in Latvia must be integrated with Latvian values on what is fair and with practices of collection which are feasible. Any tax system which is perceived as unfair by the population is going to fail, and fail miserably.

There are many other topics of special interest and application. Special situations to be addressed across the board, that is, across the company policy manual and across the curriculum. They may include group reviews of decision ethics, discussions of prudent choices on security, and team assignments on human relations issues in company situations.

There is more. Beyond the core knowledge and desirable attitudes, there is the particular weight to be given in company training and supervision to various issues. On the other hand, there is no single approach that will fit all individuals and all organisations equally well. It is predictable that learning in a transition situation will always be inadequate in some ways. This learning will always require new fine tuning and programme redesign as the Latvian economy moves to the market. Education will have to be reinforced by examples from new experience in the field. These changes can be enhanced further by building close relationships with companies in Latvia and abroad.

CONCLUSIONS

Fundamentally, Latvian successes will be based on work well done by individuals and teams. To link the potentially excellent performance to the market requires far more than more modern machinery, more money, or modern methods. This linkage requires a close fit of values and attitudes to the company and the customers it serves. They can be integrated with the professional study of business and economic subjects in business schools. Even with the help of business schools, values compatible with the market are likely to emerge gradually and slowly.

It is fortunate that in Latvia there is very strong demand for education in business and economics. Students and practising managers, drawn voluntarily to study management in market economies, are likely to change their values and acquire new skills more quickly than others.

To put in another way, the tasks to accomplish range from knowledge transfer to the shaping of values and adopting attitudes. Behaviour can be changed by new attitudes. Any behaviour learned, however, is likely to need further work as the world turns. In effect, the task of integrating values with the work and market environment never ends. To return to the mountain climbing analogy, Latvians will also find that there are competing climbers. The mountains will be higher than expected.

Note

1. This is a revised version of the remarks originally made on 17 August 1995. The collegial suggestions of Professor Pavel Pelikan of the Industrial Institute of Economics and Social Research in Stockholm are much appreciated.

REFERENCES

Barnowe, J.T., King, G.J. and Berniker, E. (1992) 'Personal Values and Economic Transition on the Baltic States', *Journal of Baltic Studies*, 23(2), 179–90.
Beck, N. (revised 1995), *Shifting Gears: Thriving in the New Economy* (New York: Harper Collins).
Connor, P.E. and Becker, B.W. (1994) 'Personal Values and Management: What We Know and Why Don't We Know More?' *Journal of Management Inquiry*, 3(1), 67–73.
England, G.W. (1975) *The Manager and His Values* (Cambridge: Ballinger).
Fukuyama, F. (1995) *Trust: The Social Virtues and the Creation of Prosperity* (New York: Free Press).
Gulens, V. (1995) 'Distortions in Personality Development in Individuals Emerging from a Long-term Totalitarian Regime', *Journal of Baltic Studies*, 26(3), 267–84.
Hague, D. (1991) *Beyond Universities: A New Republic of the Intellect* (London: Institute of Economic Affairs).
Hofstede, G. (1980) *Culture's Consequences* (Beverly Hills, CA: Sage).
King, G.J., Barnowe, J.T. and Bankovskaya, S. (1994) 'Complementary and Conflicting Personal Values of Russophone Managers in Latvia', *Journal of Baltic Studies*, 25(3), 249–72.
Rothschild, M.L. (1992) Bionomics: Economy as Ecosystem (New York: H. Holt).

15 The Intangibles of Transition: Attitudinal Obstacles to Change
George Schöpflin

INTRODUCTION

This chapter explores some of the underlying patterns that have so far shown considerable resilience in the post-communist world and which frequently impact on official reform by generating unintended consequences for change, which impede or distort adopted policies. Essentially, the problematic in this connection concerns unquantifiable and intangible factors, the tacit assumptions by which all societies are governed, but which are often enough excluded from identification by the actors because they are regarded as 'natural' or 'normal' (Kertzer, 1988).

THE NATURE OF POST-COMMUNISM

Precisely because these factors and patterns are unexamined and difficult to examine, they can constitute serious difficulties for policy-makers. To clarify the author's position, a number of personal methodological assumptions are set out about the nature of post-communism. In the first place, it is assumed that post-communism does, in fact, exist in the sense that all the countries under communist rule underwent broadly comparable experiences and, therefore, carry roughly similar baggage from the communist past. Although there are, indeed, major variations to be observed as between the practice of one post-communist state and another – this is a perfectly viable approach to the study of these systems – the analytical emphasis in this chapter is placed on the shared patterns in order to offer clarification as to where the efforts of policy-makers can make a real difference.

Second, it is assumed that actual communist experience was similar enough to make valid comparisons. To this end, the various divergent parts of the communist experiment are subsumed with the presumption that the similarity was sufficient for the purposes at hand. In particular, the communist system was marked by a near identical form of legitimation (the Leninist utopia), a near identical very uneven distribution of power, a commitment to the use of the state as the dominant, indeed monopolistic political actor (to the exclusion of unsanctioned political activity) and it relied on high levels of explicit or implicit coercion (Tismaneanu, 1993).

Further, the strategic goals of the communist system were again comparable in all the states under communist party rule – the construction of a rather static industrial base, with rapid, possibly over-rapid urbanisation; formal commitment to social equality counterpointed by a fairly rigid hierarchy; and the provision of a low-level welfare net, which was not open to questioning by the individual but which did offer a degree of existential security. Parallel to this monopolisation of power, the language of politics was firmly controlled by the party through its alliance with convergent intellectuals. The outcome was that the language of politics was subterranean, allusive, Aesopian and marked by high contextuality. To understand a statement one had to understand the context in which it was made. Finally, communist systems adopted a contradictory attitude to nationhood. In both its civic and the ethnic dimension, nationhood was formally marginalised and the desired identity to be adopted was a class-based one; however, in real terms there was constant offstage reference to nationhood, overwhelmingly to the ethnic dimension of the nation, which as a result acquired far-reaching symbolic resonance (Szporluk, 1988).

The communist system never acquired legitimacy. Indeed, while it might have had the support of a significant minority after the take-over, gradually as idealism waned it used new and less effective measures to pacify public opinion. This meant that the values of the system were internalised only by a small minority and the bulk of the population rejected it and refused to give it its loyalty. Crucially, there was little or no identification with it at the symbolic and affective levels. It was perceived as alien and contrasted with a mythopoeic alternatives of 'Europe', prosperity, neutrality and freedom.

BUILDING NEW SYSTEMS

The challenge facing the elites who took over from the communists was how to construct democracy on this foundation. With hindsight, it is evident that the size and complexity of the challenge was gravely underestimated. This is an issue with many implications, but the concentration here is on two of them – elite–popular relations and the impact of upheaval. The problem of elite–popular relations is that the role models bequeathed by communism, as well as those dimly remembered or reconstructed from the pre-communist period, are not particularly democratic in the sense that democracy is based on participation. The institutional channels for regulating popular inputs were not well understood and tended to be seen in a formal rather than a substantive sense. The proposition that public opinion should play an active role in the shaping of policy was frequently interpreted as something akin to direct democracy, for example, in the idea that legislatures, possessed of popular sovereignty, should govern rather than governments. The reaction to this was to emphasise technocratic solutions, based on the concept of the rational state, the essential underpinning of communism (this concept is at the heart of the functioning of the modern state everywhere but is offset by popular inputs, so that the analytical point made here should be understood relatively, as a matter of nuance) (McNeill, 1983).

Secondly, the new elites were inclined to underestimate the impact of the upheaval that the end of communism signified. Although communism was not sanctioned by popular consent, it did operate as a real system and this had consequences for the way in which large numbers of people depended on it (even when in an antagonistic way), derived status and meaning from the system and structured their lives by reference to the communist system. Understandably the end of communism brought with it a massive disorientation, that the new elites were not well placed to ease. There was a simultaneous collapse of the structures that provided meanings and a very different set of political conditions in which meanings were sought (Siklova, 1992). Furthermore, the upheaval was exacerbated by the redistribution of power, status, identities and benefits, bringing into being new winners and new losers, by no agreed criteria.

The creation of a new system, therefore, was bound to give rise to major conflicts without any very clear way of resolving them. Indeed, the very concept of conflict was perceived as deeply unsettling and the central feature of democracy, an ongoing legitimation and delegitimation of interests, was alien and troubling for the majority. This built the prospect of new conflicts into the system and made the culture of compromise, essential for the effective functioning of democracy, that much harder to establish. The inexperience of populations as well as of elites with politics (the distribution and regulation of power), the unrealistically high expectations of rapid and painless access to prosperity, stability and an absence of conflict, similarly contributed to the difficulties (European Commission, 1995).

The loss of certainties and the perception of rapid change also had the result of creating a confusion of identities. In this context, the communist system was in any case damaging, because it had been highly reductionist, imposing a synchronised, homogenised identity on social structures that were, in reality, far more complex, so that these complexities could not be articulated politically (or for that matter in other spheres like the economy, law, and so on). Thus the simplified identity structures and the absence of civil social institutions made it highly problematical for political relationships to be expressed in a regulated, ordered way, thereby accentuating conflicts and making them appear intractable. Intractability of this kind tends to promote polarisation, which is by definition inimical to democracy (Jowitt, 1992).

Given this confusion and the paucity of materials from which identities could be constructed, it was unavoidable that rather than material interests gaining the greatest emphasis, non-material interests should have acquired the saliency that they have in the working of post-communist systems. The contrast here is that whereas material interests are relatively easy to make the subject of a bargain, non-material ones – morality, status, ethnicity, religion – are not.

The role of ethnicity under post-communism demands greater scrutiny than is possible in this chapter, but some discussion of it is essential. In politics, ethnicity provides very clear boundaries around a community and gives information about who are fellow members of the community as well as who are not. On the other hand, ethnicity has very little to say about the distribution of power, the institutional framework, the resolution of conflicts or the routinisation of politics. Indeed, if anything, reference to ethnicity tends to promote irrational – rationality here being defined as a pattern based on the prior assumptions of the process in question – answers, because it appeals so strongly to the emotions (Schöpflin, 1995).

Under post-communism, partly for reasons to do with the legacy of the interrelationship between ethnic definitions of nationhood and communism and partly because of the epistemological void that followed the end of communism, ethnicity is required to do the work that civic identities should do. In less abstract terms, this means that all sorts of activities that should be assessed by non-ethnic criteria are, in fact, judged from whether it has an ethnic content or not, e.g. Does this particular initiative help the ethnic group in question or not? In (largely) mono-ethnic states this does not matter so much, but in multi-ethnic contexts, it can seriously affect attitudes in a variety of situations. For example, as regards investment, labour market relations, education and so on, where the ethnic issue should be secondary, it cannot be so treated because both (all) ethnic groups concerned tend to see decisions through ethnic spectacles. Multi-ethnicity does not inherently vitiate the functioning of a democracy, but it does make it more difficult, especially in that it demands patience and tolerance on the part of all the ethnic actors concerned (McGarry and O'Leary, 1992).

In the light of what has been sketched in the foregoing – inexperience, loss of meaning, confusion of identities, the existence of ethnicity as a possible political tool – it was hardly surprising that post-communist politics should have become so far-reachingly politicised. Quite apart from the factors noted above, overarching politicisation was in any case a part of the communist legacy – indeed, a key roadblock on the road to democracy. The difficulty with over-politicisation is that it infuses all sorts of situations which *prima facie* have nothing to do with politics with political implications and meanings. The outcome is that the emergence of a rounded civil society is repeatedly blocked.

Civil society is understood here as a process – the increase in the number of political, economic, social and so on actors; the growing complexity of interactions; and the fact that activities obviously need a different kind of regulation from the one used by the communists (ideology, coercion) (Hall, 1995). Blockage of this kind tends to produce frustration and that, in turn, will encourage the sections of society affected to use non-institutional measures and to rely on the state to validate their interests. The outcome is that the state, which is notionally and ideal-typically even-handed in its treatment of all citizens, is used to enhance the power of some groups at the expense of others. The opportunities are endless. Post-communist states inherited a massively over-regulated system; the abuse of the state machinery through the differential application of rules is wide open to temptation.

A further set of macro-political problems concerns the nature of democracy as compared with current post-communist practice. The first level definition of democracy, the one most frequently used in popular language, restricts it to free elections and the separation of powers. This is clearly insufficient. Democracy, to operate in such a way as to provide reasonable access to power to most of society, must be structured more subtly and must include mechanisms and the willingness to make those mechanisms function according to a set of values that help to bring formal provision into line with the realities of power. Underlying this proposition is the need to recognise that power is one of these realities, that it cannot be made to disappear, that myths of social harmony are utopian and harmful and that logically this requires political actors to accept compromise. Centrally, groups and individuals must accept that they cannot achieve all their goals. Furthermore, the requirements of democracy are that both institutional arrangements and the values by which they operate will change over time, as expectations rise or are transformed by, for example, the impact of new technologies.

As far as the post-communist states are concerned, the institutional mechanisms are largely in place, though some of the legislative tidying up is still proceeding. It is noteworthy that while in West, presidential systems are the exception (United States, France), the post-communist states, even the ones which have adopted parliament systems, find that presidents play a strong or indeed preponderant role. One of the enduring themes of post-communist politics is conflict between presidents and parliament (for example, Poland, Bulgaria). This is not in itself a weakness as long as the machinery for resolving disputes is in place and is accepted, which is something else again (Dunleavy and O'Leary, 1987).

All states formally accept the doctrine popular sovereignty, the rule of law, the separation of powers and constitutional government. Practice may be different. In particular, the widespread distrust of institutions as they are, a propensity to ignore formal provision and to use personal connections are very characteristic of these systems, resulting in a personalisation of politics, which thereby continues to undermine respect for institutions, reproducing the cycle of weakness.

Two values, however, are essential for a system to be genuinely democratic – openness and self-limitation. There are problems in both these areas, but equally some impressive advances. As far as governments and politicians are concerned, both the communist legacy of obfuscation and rejection of criticism are unlikely to make for a readiness to accept that the role of a free press – in practice as opposed to theory, when press investigation really does begin to bite – is essential for the proper functioning of democracy. The way in which the electronic media have tended to remain under state control exemplifies this state of affairs. But the particular tradition of the way in which the media operate and the evolution of the journalistic ethos of post-communism, are likewise unhelpful.

This ethos tends to emphasise comment rather than reportage (admittedly the dividing line between can be blurred in certain circumstances) and to prefer polemics to reasoned argument. The outcome is to enhance polarisation, overreaction and a rejection of criticism as something akin to hostile propaganda or conspiracy. On the other hand, new entrants of the media, especially the print media, are by and large not impeded and the pressure of public opinion as reflected in the media is accepted by governments as relevant to the way in which policies are pursued.

Self-limitation is likewise vital. Unless those with access to power recognise that the pursuit of that power to the utmost is counter-productive because it creates resentment among the losers and long term resentment can promote a readiness to use violence, democracy will not operate. There are countless examples of this, notably where ethnic issues are involved, for example, as regards education or administration in minority languages. But at the same time note should be taken of two crucial areas where self-limitation appears to have become accepted.

Since the collapse of communism in Central and Eastern Europe, every change of government has taken place as the outcome of an election and no government has sought to extend its power by suspending elections. However bitter political conflicts may be, this limitation has been integrated. This is a major change. The second remarkable feature of post-communist self-limitation has been the role of constitutional courts as legal-political actors. This form of regulation appears to be more widely used under post-communism than in the West, although the United States and Germany have both built it into their systems. Constitutional courts can and increasingly do act as regulators of the rules of the political game and significantly are used by opposition parties as a way of offsetting the power of governments. Examples of this trend can be cited from Hungary, Poland, Bulgaria and elsewhere.

Party systems, however, have tended to evolve in a direction different from the West. Rather than serving as instruments for the transmission and articulation of interests, political parties have assumed some of the features of the communist parties. They are often closed institutions which act as much to protect the interest of their leaderships and which seek to control as much of the public sphere as is feasible, not least through the construction of new nomenklaturas. This inevitably weakens or undermines any sense of a broader public interest and prolongs popular suspicion of politics and the view that politics as such is an elite game from which society is excluded. True, this phenomenon is not unknown in the West – partitocrazia in Italy and Proporz in Austria have many of these features.

Finally, the question should be raised as to whether democracy is a single, seamless whole or whether there are various different models of democracy in the context of which a Central European model can be conceptualised. British and American analysts of post-communism have tended to operate with a set of tacit assumptions about the nature of democracy which unconsciously reflect their own experiences. A more nuanced definition of democracy is proposed here and a somewhat crude taxonomy suggested. In the first place, there is the Anglo-Saxon model which is formally adversarial though in practice it is increasingly etatist (for example, the United Kingdom, Canada). The question then is to determine how effective popular control over the state is.

The French model may be described as technocratic, with important popular inputs into the working of the system. The German model emphasises consensus and efficient bureaucracy. The Netherlands and the Scandinavian states are pluralistic and consensual, though there too the state plays a key role in redistribution. The Italian model has already been mentioned and it is fair to add that it is still in a state of flux. Greece is far closer to post-communism than most people would like to admit.

CONCLUSIONS

This brief chapter should demonstrate that the palette of choice in democratic practices is far wider than is frequently realised. The implication of this is that a Central European model or possibly several Central European models could emerge over time. The suggestion is that given both pre-communist and communist traditions, this model or models are likely to place greater stress on collective action than individual – these are relatives rather than absolutes – and that the state will retain a pre-eminence as the dominant political and economic actor, at any rate in the foreseeable future. No doubt as social, economic and technological conditions change, political systems and political cultures will change with them.

REFERENCES

Dunleavy, P. and O'Leary, B. (1987) *Theories of the State: The Politics of Liberal Democracy* (London: Macmillan).

European Commission (1995) *Central and East European Eurobarometer*, 5.

Hall, J.A. (ed.) (1995) *Civil Society: Theory, History, Comparison* (Oxford: Polity).

Jowitt, K. (1992) *New World Disorder: the Leninist Extinction* (Berkeley, CA: University of California Press).

Kertzer, D.I. (1988) *Ritual, Politics and Power* (New Haven, CT: Yale University Press).

McGarry, J. and O'Leary, B. (eds) (1992) *The Politics of Ethnic Conflict Regulation* (London: Routledge).

McNeill, W.H. (1983) *The Pursuit of Power* (Oxford: Blackwell).

Schöpflin, G. (1995) 'Nationalism and Ethnicity in Europe, East and West', in C.A. Kupchan (ed.), *Nationalism and Nationalities in the New Europe* (Ithaca: Cornell University Press).

Siklova, J. (1992), 'Nacionalizmus Kozep- es Kelet-Europaban', *Valosag*, 35(1), 114–16.
Szporluk, R. (1988) *Communism and Nationalism: Karl Marx versus Friedrich List* (Oxford: Oxford University Press).
Tismaneanu, V. (1993) *Reinventing Politics: Eastern Europe from Stalin to Havel* (New York: The Free Press).

16 Concluding Remarks
Neil Hood, Jan-Erik Vahlne and Robert Kilis

INTRODUCTION

Any attempt to make some concluding comments on, and extract policy implications from, such a rich and diverse collection of papers has to be undertaken tentatively and with humility. This is the case for several reasons. Firstly, the book is about the Baltics in transition – a transition which is recent and still underway. Inevitably, some of the phenomena under scrutiny have as yet only been subject to a limited amount of analysis in the Baltic context. Secondly, this book represents only a relatively small cross-section of the academic and policy-related activity directed towards these countries in recent years. It is, however, based on a thorough attempt to identify a wide range of contributors who have been actively involved in studying aspects of the transition in these countries. Thirdly, the mix of chapters reflects the type of on-going work in the mid-1990s. Although it is diverse and offers a wide range of different insights, there are a number of important areas where relatively little academic work at the micro level has yet emerged. These include, for example, the detailed study of sectors, enterprises and entrepreneurs; the design, implementation and evaluation of policies directed to promote economic development; the exploration of areas of economic and social life within which government initiative would be best directed to aid the transition and so on.

For all of the above reasons, this chapter does not attempt a synthesis of the findings, observations and analysis offered throughout the book. The variety of underlying disciplines, methodologies and subject areas makes that an impossible task. Moreover, any attempt to force the individual contributions into a rigid taxonomy would tend to diminish them as valid in their own right. What this chapter attempts, as Chapter 1 indicated it would, is a brief set of comments on selected recurring themes, with the focus being on informing both managers and policy-makers as to the priority areas for the implementation of the transition in the Baltic States.

SELECTED THEMES

While examining micro aspects of the transition from different perspectives, the authors have regularly converged on a number of themes
which have profound implications for the prosperity of the Baltic States.
These are considered in this section, without attributing frequency to their
being mentioned or implying any order of priority by the sequence in
which they are set out.

Micro–macro-level interactions

The interpretation of micro variables under scrutiny, whether individuals,
groups, enterprises or aspects of attitudes and political behaviour, are
shown to require a considerable understanding of the macro context in
which they have developed. In some instances, for example, micro-level
changes in attitudes have been shown to outstrip the macro environment
which could support and sustain them, as individuals have shown greater
adaptability than systems. This is well illustrated in Mygind (Chapter 7),
where the determining conditions behind the development of employee
ownership in the privatisation process in the Baltics are shown to be differentiated by the existence of four different subsystems of values, social
framework, institutions and production. Equally, on a different theme,
Radosevic (Chapter 2) argues that the development of organisational
capabilities in post-socialist enterprises lies at the heart of the regeneration of the economics. He shows that micro, mezzo (sector, market, technology and privatisation context) and macro variables all shape the
prospects for the development of organisational capability and enterprise
growth.

There are distinctive challenges for policy-makers arising from the
complexity of some of the micro–macro interactions highlighted throughout the book. Some of these relate to the need for the synchronisation of
changes in both dimensions to facilitate the transition, some to the relative
pace of change at the individual and governmental level. These issues
emerge for example in considerations about the hidden economy
(Raagmaa, Chapter 8) where micro change at the family level has been
driven by survival instincts, but has outstripped the institutional capacity
to encourage conventional business development. Another illustration is
provided in the Rainys paper (Chapter 11) where, at the micro level, managerial preferences are to avoid enterprise bankruptcy, while from a macro
policy perspective the resources involved in such enterprises would probably be more efficiently deployed elsewhere.

Tensions between systems and values

Most of the chapters provide interesting and distinctive insights into the different levels at which there are tensions between the previous and present systems and values pervading in the Baltic countries. Their individual distinctiveness as countries also emerges, and the relevance of these differentials is explored from several different perspectives.

At the more philosophical and reflective level, these issues are carefully explored in the contributions by King (Chapter 14) and Schopflin (Chapter 15). King concludes that values compatible with the market are likely to emerge gradually and slowly, a view to which many chapters of the book give ready evidence. For example, he emphasises the way tensions between values impact on economic performance in areas such as the low value attached to marketing and finance functions and to managerial risk-taking. Schopflin calls for a deeper exploration of the nature of the attitudinal foundations in these societies, stressing that the end of communism brought such massive disorientation that the new elites which have emerged have not been well placed to solve many of the emerging problems.

There is little doubt that these types of observation point to a substantial need for relevant education and training over the long term, recognising that there are many layers of events and experiences which have shaped thinking in the Baltics. However, several cautionary notes are sounded in the chapters about the danger of transposing Western or other Central European solutions without appropriate adaptation. Consistent with the relative scale of the resources available and the need to focus these on parts of the societies, there is a consistent call for business education and for more attention to be paid to the training of government officials to be able to handle the complexities of mixed economies.

The tensions between systems and values are amply illustrated throughout the book. For example, Liuhto (Chapter 3) shows that the transition in Estonian management culture has mostly been caused by the emergence of new organisations, but that the organisational and management culture of the latter was largely constructed from the old components. Reference is made in several of the chapters to a new and distinctive form of 'capitalism' emerging in this region. Whether or not it is effective, or whether it constitutes a workable harmonisation of these tensions, remains to be seen.

The role of elites

This is another theme which underlies several of the chapters and is clearly a crucial micro-level issue in the transition. It is explicitly explored in the contribution from Vadi and Buono (Chapter 4), which brings out the way in which individual psychological processes are influenced by the various socio-cultural contexts in which the individual is embedded. The empirical work presented shows that the Estonians who are likely to play a critical role in the transformation of the business sector are more individualistic than their more traditional counterparts. The issue of individualism versus collectivism again arises in several of the chapters. Vadi and Buono draw an important conclusion, which is echoed elsewhere, namely that while it is possible to identify the elites who will have the most critical roles to play, they will require managerial and organisational training and many other developmental efforts directed towards them if they are to facilitate the continued transition in these economies.

The particular question of these (new) elites requiring recognition and support, emerges in another context in Jerschina and Gorniak's paper (Chapter 5). Viewing the Baltic States and other neighbouring countries in transition from the perspective of leftism and achievement orientation, they identify three clusters of countries. The liberal-democracy group includes Estonia, as countries less oriented towards leftism, nationalism and authoritarianism, and more towards activism and achievement in both their economy and politics. Lithuania and Latvia are both shown to be in a group between the liberal-democratic and the national-socialist, and to be societies where there are tensions between the conductors of change and active citizens. They conclude that the Baltics show themselves to be subject to the pull of Central Europe, it will be a considerable task for their elites to be able to maintain this position and break free from some of the tendencies associated with nationalism and socialism.

These two illustrations draw attention to the key role of these elites in ensuring the transition proceeds, both at the enterprise and political levels. The role of the new exemplars is evident throughout the book. However, Vadi and Buono note that while younger managers appear to be moving away from collectivist beliefs, they lack the experience, skill and training to carry weight in many business situations. But some positive role models are evident in aspects of Latvian agriculture (Zilcken, Chapter 13) and in some aspects of small business (Smallbone *et al.*, Chapter 12). Raagma, on the other hand, makes a plea for the promotion of honest entrepreneurship and for the appropriate infrastructure to support it in areas such as customs, revenue offices, property rights, preferential access to training and credits.

It is evident that, in the round, the nature, quality and support of the elites in the Baltics is an issue of general concern to many of the contributors. The fostering of international linkages towards the West, the careful and considered input of appropriate advice and training, and the accelerated membership of the EU, are among the many policy proposals which emerge in the preceeding chapters.

Comparisons and lessons learned

About half of the chapters specifically present comparisons within the Baltics (Radosevic, Mygind, Smallbone *et al.*) or between the three Baltic countries and other parts of Central Europe and the former Soviet Union (Jerschina and Gorniak, Rose, Schopflin). In the former group, Mygind is able to chart and compare the detailed development of privatisation and employee ownership in the three countries and test it against a model (Figure 7.1). For others this approach is more difficult and fine-grained cross-comparisons between the countries at the enterprise or sectoral level are not readily made at this stage. Yet the papers often refer implicitly to the alternative routes which may be chosen by these countries and there is evidently a strong interest in ensuring that lessons are transferred one to another.

On the broader international front, Rose (Chapter 6) deploys the New Baltic Barometer to measure micro-economic differences. He highlights the resilience of the populations of these states to changing economic conditions and addresses the important question (and sometimes the source of another tension) of ethnic differences within the Baltics. Relatively speaking, his comparisons give some grounds for optimism about the adaptability of the Baltic citizens, even although the conventional indicators show that Latvians and Lithuanians are less well-off than Estonians.

Observations have already been made on the important signals to emerge from the Jerschina and Gorniak chapter of the relative stability of the political environment in the Baltics when compared to its near neighbours. There are salutary lessons in this chapter which, if confirmed by other evidence, would stress the importance of both internal and external resources being more specifically directed to sustain the more open and liberal directions to which these economies in transition initially aspired. The presence of powerful and persistent internal and external push and pull factors should guide policy makers in Western capitals and the EU as a whole.

Policy priorities

There is much evidence from the studies undertaken within the book, that government is still expected to have a crucial role in shaping the microlevel aspects of the transition. The various different perspectives of the authors inevitably show through as to where their expectations lie in that direction. The more fundamental question of what the appropriate role of government might be in the transition is not examined in any depth.

At the more technical level, and specifically in two aspects of finance, the papers by Ludborys (Chapter 9) and Jedrzejczak and Fleming (Chapter 10) are indicative of the policy detail which has to be addressed. Ludborys gives further evidence of the tensions between the old and the new, and of the balance between external advice and internal reform, in his examination of accounting transitional issues in Latvia. While progress is recorded, and has been achieved by a combination of passing the appropriate laws and the development of professional associations, deficiencies remain in the lack of accepted accounting principles, the lack of knowledge of finance among practising accountants and in the absence of self-regulation. This example is a microcosm of the many new dimensions of public–private sector interaction which are a critical part of the transition process.

Jedrzejczak and Fleming's chapter is a detailed, insightful and technical policy piece on capital markets, directed specifically to the Latvian situation. They show, for example, how the method of case-by-case privatisation adopted in that country, whether for large or small enterprises, has created a serious risk that the supply side of privatisation has become one of the bottlenecks of the transition. By implication, a policy priority would be to free up this mechanism, whereas in fact Latvia appears to be moving towards a bank-led, control-oriented financial system. In this model the commercial banks could become major controllers of enterprises and of other financial institutions. As they point out, this will result in capital markets having a much smaller role in the essential process of restructuring large inefficient enterprises whose radical transformation under privatisation is a crucial element of the transition. This process holds the key to stopping unprofitable production and enabling better design, production and marketing of Latvian products.

These two papers are an important part of the balance of this book. They remind the reader that there are many detailed policy changes which underlie the transition process, and counter any tendency to think that there are broad-brush solutions to these problems. They also act as a reminder of the need to link government priorities with the aspects of enterprise development which are the genuine triggers of change. The corollary to this, as several of the contributors point out, is that government officials require to have a knowledge of the operation of the market economy and an ability to co-operate with trade and professional groups, as much of the transition can only be achieved by such new forms of alliance between the public and the private sectors.

Many contributors focus on the role of government and others in fostering different types of training as a matter of priority. For example, Smallbone *et al.* (Chapter 12) express the view that governments in the Baltics have tended to assume that a healthy small firms sector will simply emerge if the legal framework is adjusted. Among other things, they call for the need to prioritise the improvement of business education and training and recognise the potential role of small firms in a programme of regional development – such a programme being essential to address the new problems of the transition associated with rural areas, differences between the core and the periphery in Baltic countries, as well as the range of unemployment between city and other locations. Radosevic (Chapter 2) and King (Chapter 14) are among the others to take up this theme of training for business.

EPILOGUE

'There is a certain relief in change, even though it be from bad to worse: as I have found in travelling in a stage-coach, that it is often a comfort to shift one's position and be bruised in a new place.'[1]

There is merit in ending this volume with the above quotation. The early 'relief in change' has passed for many people in the Baltics, the serious business of shifting positions without further and damaging bruising is well underway. This volume and others like it suggest that it has not been, and will not be, painless. The early transition vision has sometimes dimmed and, for some, aspects of the past are appealing. This volume is produced in both hope and realism. It is also undertaken in the spirit of encouragement to the people of the Baltic States and all who would seek to support them in the transition process.

Note

1.   Washington Irving (1783–1859), as quoted in the *Oxford Dictionary of Quotations* (Oxford: Oxford University Press, 1983), p. 270.

Index

Note: 'n.' after a page reference indicates the number of a note on that page.

289